REVOLUTION PRINCIPLES

Cambridge Studies in the History and Theory of Politics

THE FORD LECTURES 1975-6

REVOLUTION PRINCIPLES
The Politics of Party
1689-1720

J. P. KENYON

CAMBRIDGE UNIVERSITY PRESS
CAMBRIDGE
LONDON · NEW YORK · MELBOURNE

Published by the Syndics of the Cambridge University Press
The Pitt Building, Trumpington Street, Cambridge CB2 1RP
Bentley House, 200 Euston Road, London NW1 2DB
32 East 57th Street, New York, NY 10022, USA
296 Beaconsfield Parade, Middle Park, Melbourne 3206, Australia

© Cambridge University Press 1977

First published 1977

Printed in Great Britain
at the University Press, Cambridge

Library of Congress Cataloguing in Publication Data
Kenyon, John Philipps, 1927–
Revolution principles.
(The Ford lectures; 1975–6) (Cambridge studies in
the history and theory of politics)
Includes bibliographies and index.
1. Political parties – Great Britain – History.
2. Great Britain – Politics and government – 1689–1702.
3. Great Britain – Politics and government – 1702–1714.
4. Great Britain – Politics and government – 1714–1727.
I. Title. II. Series: Oxford. University. Ford
lectures; 1975–6.
JN1118.K45   329.9'41   76-53518
ISBN 0 521 21542 0

CONTENTS

PREFACE

This book is an extended and revised version of the Ford
Lectures in English History which I delivered at Oxford
in the Hilary Term of 1976. I am grateful to the Ford's
Electors and the University for conferring this distinction
upon me, and to many Oxford colleagues, notably Professor H. R. Trevor-Roper, for their hospitality during my
visits.

These lectures had their origin in a paper I contributed
to a *Festschrift* for J. H. Plumb five years ago, and this
constitutes not the least of the debts I owe this extraordinary man; though in this case his assistance was quite
unwitting, and I want to stress that neither he nor anyone
else mentioned here is responsible for the outcome. Subsequently I expanded this paper into three lectures (com-
prising parts of what are now chapters 2, 4, 5 and 8) which
I delivered at the University of Chicago in 1972 on the
invitation of the Committee on Social Thought, funded by
the John U. Nef Foundation. I am grateful to the members
of the committee, particularly Saul Bellow and David
Grene, for making my stay in Chicago such a pleasant one,
and to John M. Wallace and John Pocock for their helpful
and constructive comments on the lectures. Later I had the
benefit of advice and information from Dr G. V. Bennett,
Dr R. A. Beddard, Professor Geoffrey Holmes, Professor
Maurice Goldsmith, Miss Betty Kemp and Dr Blair
Worden, as well as much general encouragement from
Professors G. R. Elton and J. H. Plumb, previous Ford's
Lecturers. Dr Bennett kindly allowed me to read his new

life of Francis Atterbury (since published) in page proofs, Professor Holmes lent me a transcript of the account of Sacheverell's trial from the Osborn MSS. at Yale, and Miss Kemp lent me her transcript of Sir Richard Cocks's parliamentary diary. Dr Martyn P. Thompson was also generous enough to allow me to use parts of his unpublished dissertation on contract theory in the late seventeenth century, and Mr Mark Goldie showed me the first draft of his dissertation on 'Conservative Political Thought in England 1688–1714', as well as an unpublished article on Edmund Bohun. Some of these debts are also recorded in the notes, of course.

I owe a further debt to the staffs of the various libraries in which I have worked over the past five years: the British Library (formerly the British Museum), Cambridge University Library, the Bodleian Library, Oxford, the Houghton and Weidener libraries at Harvard and the Muger Library at Boston University, the Newberry and Regenstein libraries at Chicago, York Minster Library and, not least, the Brynmor Jones Library at Hull. The Deputy Keeper of the House of Lords Record Office patiently answered several queries by correspondence, and sent me photocopies with remarkable promptitude. I am also grateful to the University of Hull for giving me six months' leave to complete this work, and making generous research funds available. I would also like to express my gratitude to the staff of the Cambridge University Press, and especially to the subeditor.

My wife bore very patiently with a husband who was more distrait even than usual.

J.P.K.

July 1976

NOTE

The punctuation, spelling and capitalisation in all quotations have been modernised, except in a few cases where to do so would weaken the sense.

I

INTRODUCTION

In the past twenty years much important work has been published on the identity, the formation and the tactics of the two major political parties under William III and Anne,[1] but very little on their political ideas. The political thought of the age has been explained largely in relation to the writings of John Locke, supplemented occasionally by those of Hobbes, Harrington and Algernon Sidney.[2] The political leaders of Whiggism after 1689 are assumed to have embraced a fully developed 'Lockean' ideology, giving the nation the right to depose kings under the terms of the Original Contract. This sophisticated and up-to-date weapon, it is assumed, gave them the initiative in a power struggle which ended only with the accession of George I. The Tories, on the other hand, were saddled with such outdated concepts as divine right and hereditary succession, which by implication denied the validity of the very Settlement under which they operated. This numbing internal contradiction in their philosophy ensured their eventual defeat.

In this case, it is difficult to see why Locke's theories of government should have been mentioned so rarely in the early stages of the Revolution, up to 1692, and even less thereafter, unless it was to heap abuse on them. It is also hard to understand why Whig politicians who are supposed to have been his deferential disciples should have been so reluctant to use his name. His closest friend and patron amongst the Junto leaders was John Somers, but in all the various political pamphlets attributed to Somers Locke's name is invoked only once, and then to clinch a technical point.[3] As for the managers at Sacheverell's trial in 1710, that grand set-piece of Whig theory, they never mentioned him at all, though they were free enough with the names of Grotius, Puffendorf and 'the judicious Hooker'. A Whig of the mid-eighteenth century like Speaker Onslow was astounded to notice that Locke did not appear at all in Burnet's *History of My Own Time*, though lesser thinkers like Filmer and Hoadly did.[4]

The truth is, the constitutional theories put forward by defenders of the Revolution were not really 'Lockean' at all, except for their use of the term 'contract', which in any case was part of the common vocabulary of politics long before Locke appeared on the scene.[5] Nor is it likely that this surprised Locke himself. Shortly before his death in 1705, discussing the reading appropriate to a gentleman, he wrote: 'Politics contains two parts, very different the one from the other; the one containing the original of societies and the rise and extent of political power, the other, the art of governing men in society.' To master the first required a study of political philosophy, and apart from his own works he recommended those of Hooker, Sidney and Puffendorf; but the second was 'best learned by experience and history, especially that of a man's own country', and here he mentioned James Tyrrell's recent *General History of England* (1696–1704) and the two volumes of *State Tracts* published in 1689 and 1692.[6]

'Experience and history' were in fact to be the keynotes of the Whigs' political philosophy after the Revolution. The problem was not whether they could establish a new, abstract model of the constitution, but whether they could offset the entrenched theories of Toryism, and at the same time live down their damaging association with political radicalism under Charles II. As late as 1714 their success in both these modest endeavours remained in doubt.

Because the establishment of British parliamentary monarchy is held to date from the Revolution of 1688, and because this kind of government is regarded by the great

majority of people as 'right', in general terms; because the
ideas behind the Revolution are seen as Whig, or at least
'whiggish', and because for most of the eighteenth century
Britain was governed by a series of ministers calling themselves Whigs – because of all this it is easy to assume that
Whig political ideas enjoyed general support from the
beginning, and that apart from a few setbacks engineered
by the malice and prejudice of their opponents their success
from 1689 onwards was continuous, their ultimate victory
in 1714 and 1715 assured.

But this is not borne out by the record. Modern research
has confirmed that the Tories enjoyed an inbuilt majority
which their opponents found it very difficult to overcome.[7]
The overall results of general elections in this period are
notoriously difficult to assess, but it is significant that prior
to 1715 there is no parliament which can unhesitatingly be
described as Whig; apart from the Convention of 1689, the
nearest candidate is the parliament of 1708. On the other
hand, the Tories, with their 'Country' allies, clearly domi-
nated at least five parliaments (in 1698, 1700–1, 1702, 1710
and 1713), with the rest doubtful. True, neither William III
nor Anne trusted the Whigs, so that the full weight of royal
patronage was never behind them; but neither was it ever
clearly behind the Tories, except perhaps in the election
of 1702. On the other hand, in a period of continual
warfare it was to the Whigs' advantage that they were the
'war party' or the 'patriotic party', and it is noticeable how
their fortunes slipped during times of peace or impending
peace, from 1696 to 1702, and again after 1710. Moreover,
their organisation was unparalleled. As Geoffrey Holmes
remarks, 'The Whigs of the Age of Anne achieved not only
an unbroken unity of front but an underlying solidity of
purpose which was not to be approached again by any
political party in Great Britain until well into the eighteenth
century.'[8]

But organisation alone was not sufficient. To justify the
use of party at all – something this generation was never
entirely willing to allow – both sides needed a working

ideology. This was not easy for either to formulate when all previous political assumptions had been reversed by the flight of James II in 1688 and the installation of William III in his place, and when the previous political mechanism had been subtly but profoundly altered by the institution after 1689 of annual sessions of parliament and after 1695 of triennial general elections.

Moreover, the Revolution of 1688 was a traumatic shock to the English political conscience, coming so soon, as it did, after the Great Rebellion and the Interregnum. Tory thinking on the matter was confused. The traditional role of the Anglican Church as the principal adversary of popery (a role particularly stressed after 1660) made it difficult for it to mourn the removal of James II, however it was accomplished; but it was unable to accept the Revolution without setting at nought the basic doctrines of passive obedience and non-resistance which had been central to its doctrine for the greater part of its comparatively short life. An English Protestant succession in perpetuity might be held to justify the sacrifice, but this concept perished with the young Duke of Gloucester in 1700.

But the Whigs' thinking was similarly confused and contradictory. Their whole-hearted approval of the Revolution was tempered by the knowledge that this was distinctly a minority view. Moreover, it was increasingly difficult to give whole-hearted approval, or whole-hearted anything, to an event whose nature was in serious dispute. The confusion of politics between 1689 and 1714 was partly structural and partly ideological, and this confusion began with the Revolution itself.

2

BY FORCE OR BY MIRACLE
The immediate debate on the Revolution

In the next generation it was generally assumed that the Revolution of 1688 had been an act of resistance, even rebellion. Many Whigs gloried in it; most Tories condemned it. This was so axiomatic that Robert Walpole, opening the case against Sacheverell in 1710, told the Lords: 'It cannot now be necessary to prove resistance at the Revolution; I should as well expect that your lordships would desire me to prove, for form's sake, the sun shines at noon day.'[1]

Modern opinion would, I suppose, incline towards Walpole's view. But there is in fact little evidence for it, and what there is comes mostly from James II. In two proclamations, on 28 September and 6 November 1688, James accused the Prince of Orange of mounting an unprovoked invasion, and he gave his own physical danger as the sole reason for his flight in December. This continued to be Jacobite orthodoxy right down to 1715 and beyond. William himself, in his declaration of 30 September, denied any intention even of coercing James, let alone conquering him, and swore that his army was merely intended to protect his own person against the king's 'evil counsellors'. When he read James's proclamation of 28 September, which accused him of 'purposing an absolute conquest of these kingdoms', he published an additional declaration, protesting that his forces were 'utterly disproportioned to that wicked design...[even] if we were capable of intending it'.[2] In the brief military campaign that followed his landing the two armies never came within a hundred miles of each other, and only a handful of casualties were sustained, in cavalry scuffles and civil commotions. As for the English magnates who rose against the king, they announced that they did so to secure the assembly of a free parliament under the terms of the prince's declaration, almost unanimously sheltering behind such unexceptionable abstractions as 'the Protestant religion, our laws and liberties, and the ancient constitution of England'.[3] This included those who signed the Association at Exeter, under William's immediate eye. Only the extremist Lord Delamere, whose father had led a premature revolt against the Protectorate in 1659, ignored such constitutional proprieties and announced: 'I am of opinion, that when the nation is delivered, it must be by force or by miracle. It would be too great a presumption to expect the latter, and therefore our deliverance must be by force.'[4]

But apart from this, the only attempt to justify the use of force against King James was made by 'The Nobility, Gentry and Commonalty at the Rendezvous at Nottingham' on 22 November 1688. Delamere was there again, but he was supported now by the Earl of Devonshire, the Earl of Scarsdale and an impressive turn-out of Midlands gentry. Their published declaration roundly stated:

> We assure ourselves that no rational and unbiassed person will judge it rebellion to defend our laws and religion, which all our princes have sworn [to do] at their coronations... *We own it rebellion to resist a king that governs by law, but he was always accounted a tyrant that made his will his law; and to resist such an one we justly esteem no rebellion, but a necessary defence.*[5]

This could stand as a succinct exposition of Whig principles under Queen Anne – what later came to be known as 'Revolution Principles' – and it is not surprising to find it given considerable prominence in the pamphlet warfare of that reign. It gained in piquancy from the fact that the then Princess Anne, with Henry Compton, Bishop of London, later a prominent High Churchman, joined this group at Nottingham a few days later, and could therefore be supposed to have accepted the terms of the declaration by implication – a fact neither was allowed to forget. Yet the very prominence given to the Nottingham declaration in later polemics only exposes its isolation; it was supported at the time only by the assertions of a few anonymous pamphleteers.

Yet if the nation had not rebelled, if it had not fought against James II, could he be said to have been deposed? And if he had not been deposed, then it was difficult to argue that contract theories of government applied to this case, since such theories assume the outright deposition of a ruler who has broken some previous agreement or other.

True, the waters of the Revolution, never very limpid, were muddied by a number of extraneous factors. In the interregnum between James's flight and the installation of William as king the breakdown of press censorship let in a flood of pamphlets which asserted in crude terms that the deposition of an unjust or tyrannical ruler was eminently permissible. Secondly, in the Convention the Commons discussed the Original Contract, and it featured prominently in their resolution on the state of the nation, which was accepted with some demur by the Lords. Moreover, late in 1689 Locke published his *Two Treatises of Government*, the second of which was a detailed exposition of the theory of an Original Contract, and he avowed in his preface that his purpose was to justify the Revolution just accomplished. In view of this pronouncement by the great philosopher it was natural to suppose that the Revolution hinged on contract.

Natural, but not true. Certainly, in the famous debate on the state of the nation held on 28 January 1689 several Whig MPs warmly embraced contract theory. Sir Robert Howard boldly claimed, 'The constitution of our government is actually grounded upon pact and covenant with the people', and he was supported by John Somers, and by the veteran lawyer John Maynard, who said, ''Tis no new project; our government is mixed, not monarchical and tyrannous, but has had its beginning from the people. There may be such a transgression in the prince that the people will be no more governed by him.'[6] Sir William Pulteney added, '[The] crown descends not from heaven; then [it] must come from the people.' They dismissed with contempt the idea that they should look for justification in the institutions of a free Anglo-Saxon society. Maynard remarked, 'It has been said, we must go beyond the Conquest. [I am] puzzled to find what was law in the Saxon times; [it is] a tedious and fruitless search.'[7]

But the general sense of the House was much more conservative, and was probably better expressed by backwoods spokesmen like Sir Christopher Musgrave, who warned MPs, 'Have a care of deposing.'[8] Meanwhile the former prerogative lawyer Sir Robert Sawyer told them that they were not representative of the people anyway, and if the people's consent was required the only proper method was a referendum, or the election of a constituent convention on a broader franchise.[9] Outside the House at least one anonymous pamphleteer with a similar attitude had proposed a drastic reform of the franchise and the distribution of seats; he also wanted most officials now appointed by the crown – Privy Councillors, bishops, judges, sheriffs, even army officers – to be elected, and he justified this wholesale assault on privilege and patronage with these fell words: 'If the departure of the king amounts to such a desertion as dissolves the government, then the power must necessarily revert and vest in the people, who may erect a new one, either according to the old model, if they like it so well, or any other that they like or approve of better.'[10] He then compounded his blasphemy by urging that William be made sole monarch, 'absolute and arbitrary', on grounds of efficiency and common sense, and for reasons of gratitude. He was perhaps not entirely serious, but another pamphleteer certainly was when he put the radical view that to instal William alone, without his wife, would be 'a clear asserting of the people's right, firm evidence of a contract broken, and a sure precedent to all ages'.[11] Other authors even advocated the establishment of a republic.[12]

Remote as such a prospect might be, the Commons' hysterical reaction to the news that the notorious republican and regicide Edmund Ludlow had suddenly returned to London from abroad is significant.[13] It is easy to forget that in 1689 the deeds of men like Algernon Sidney and the Duke of Monmouth came fresh to mind. Sidney's conviction for high treason was quashed in 1689, but only on a technicality; few regarded him as anything but a dangerous incendiary, his *Discourses concerning Government* remained unpublished, and the Whigs were ill-served by pamphleteers who hastened to recall his theories and beliefs in the hope of making a martyr of him. Monmouth's attainder was never reversed, and his Taunton declaration of 1685, with its violently radical reform programme drafted by Robert Ferguson, remained the last public statement of Shaftesbury's Whigs.[14]

Fear that James's deposition, especially if it were made to hinge on the sanction of the people, would open the way to a republic or a radically weakened monarchy obviously dictated the nature of the compromise which eventually emerged from the Convention. But the sense of the Commons is difficult to assess in the absence of a vote. Considering its great constitutional significance, the debate in a Committee of the Whole House was brief:

> They were by nine o'clock got upon such a large subject, about the nature of government, and of our constitution in particular, and about the nature of the crimes of a king that warrant a deposition, etc., that many thought they would never have disentangled themselves, nor have got to a question, but might have pursued these debates weeks or months; but these apprehensions were soon over, for not long after two o'clock the Committee came to resolve.

The whole business was over by three.[15]

The accounts we have of the debate are remarkably restrained, though of course they are not complete, and the stern warnings of Musgrave and Heneage Finch against deposition suggest that they must have had some provocation. On the other hand, according to Roger Morrice, 'None did plead for calling back the king, nor did [they]

affirm we had a king in being',[16] and if the Tories were able
to admit the possibility of an interregnum, a hiatus in the
even flow of kingship, then it was a short step to agreeing
that James had relinquished the crown in some way.

John Maynard suggested a compromise when he said, 'It
is not the question whether subjects can depose their king,
but whether the king can depose himself.' This point was
taken up by Sir Thomas Clarges, Hugh Boscawen, Sir
George Treby and John Somers, the two last carrying the
greatest weight. Treby quoted with approval a phrase used
by his Tory opposite number, Dolben, that the king had
'fallen from the crown', and declared that the question
posed by many anxious Members, whether or not they
could depose a king, was fortunately irrelevant. 'We have
found the throne vacant', he assured them, 'and are to
supply the defect; we found it so, we have not made it so.'
Sawyer was clear on this point, too. 'To refuse to govern
according to the constitution', he said, 'is absolutely to
disclaim the government, and he who withdraws on such
account abdicates.' A third lawyer, Sir William Williams,
testily agreed. 'Should you go into the beginning of
government', he said, 'we should be much in the dark;
every man in town and country can agree in fact on the
state of things.'[17]

So the Convention saddled itself and its successors with
the unreal fiction of an abdication. The supporters of
contract were strong enough to insert it into the final
resolution of the House, but they could not give it teeth.
The resolution ran:

That King James the Second, having endeavoured to subvert the constitution of the kingdom, by breaking the Original Contract between
king and people, and by the advice of Jesuits, and other wicked persons,
having violated the fundamental laws, and having withdrawn himself
out of this kingdom, has abdicated the government, and that the throne
is thereby become vacant.

The key word, of course, is 'abdicated'. At first sight it
might seem that 'breaking the Original Contract' was one
of the three facts from which James's abdication could be

deduced, but it is in fact dependent on the preceding clause; he had subverted the constitution by breaking the Original Contract *and* violating the fundamental laws. It could even be argued that he had abdicated by withdrawing from the country, the preceding part of the resolution being merely illustrative.[18]

It is not any easy piece of prose to construe, but that this was the received interpretation is shown by the tenor of the discussion which followed, in the conferences between the two Houses the following week, and in pamphlets published on both sides right down to 1714. It was assumed that James had abdicated by fleeing abroad, by destroying the writs for parliament (which also involved an infringement of the Triennial Act), and by jettisoning the Great Seal. It was never an easy doctrine to defend. Constitutional law at this level was rarely defined with any closeness, but the familiar examples of Queen Christina of Sweden (1654) and the Emperor Charles V (1555) confirmed the general assumption that abdication could be effected only by a formal deed of renunciation. The Commons' idea of 'implied abdication' was distinctly novel; in fact, it was much more novel than current and well-understood ideas of contract or popular rights.[19]

The Scots Estates, in the Claim of Right, made no bones about declaring that James had 'forfeited' or 'forefaulted' the crown.[20] The Scots had a more highly developed sense of royal obligation than the English, but it is difficult to believe that the House of Commons could not have come to a stronger decision than it did, if only by a majority vote. On 5 February, in face of the Lords, the House affirmed its belief that the throne was vacant by 282 votes to 151 – the first time it had divided on a constitutional question. But on 28 January everything was sacrificed to unanimity; there were only five votes against the resolution in Committee, possibly one in the full House.[21] The point is, the Lords were unlikely to accept any stronger resolution – they had rejected a regency, a plan not even considered by the Commons, by only three votes. It was doubtful if they would accept the resolution even as it stood if it was not unanimous.

As it was, when the resolution came before them, the Lords at once pounced on the words 'Original Contract', and asked their legal advisers for a ruling. The pronouncements of the lawyers were tentative, but on the whole favourable. Sir Robert Atkyns 'Thinks it must refer to the first original of government. Thinks the king never took any government, but there was an agreement between king and people.' He even found implied mention of it in a speech of James I and the preamble to a statute of Henry VIII.[22] After some further debate the House accepted all but the last two clauses of the resolution, but stuck on the words 'abdicated' and 'vacant'. None of the lawyers present would give a ruling, on the grounds that this was 'a question of state rather than law', and it was eventually decided by narrow majorities (55:51 and 54:53) to amend 'abdicated' to 'deserted' and to delete the reference to the vacancy of the throne altogether.[23]

After a formal conference between the Houses the Commons rejected both amendments, and a free conference was called for 5 February. Here the Earl of Clarendon launched an intemperate attack on the Original Contract. But it is interesting that Nottingham, another High Tory who spoke next, did not support him, and Sir George Treby for the Commons, after citing Hooker, and rather daringly suggesting that Charles I had agreed that government was by 'compact or agreement', pointed out that the matter was now settled, since the Lords had in fact accepted this part of the resolution.[24] Before the obstinacy of the Commons the Lords ultimately gave way, but even if they had not, clearly the Lords' word 'deserted' implied a voluntary act on James II's part, just as much as the word 'abdicated', so that legally there was no question of his being deposed, whether he had broken the Original Contract or not. In fact the Declaration of Right submitted to William and Mary on 14 February, and enacted as the Bill of Rights later in the year, contained no mention of contract, compact or agreement at all. It merely listed the more notable of James II's crimes, and concluded that they were all 'utterly and directly contrary to the known laws and statutes of this realm'. But even this was not given as the reason for his removal; indeed, it seemed he had not been removed at all, for without any connecting or consequential word the next paragraph went on to say that he had abdicated the government.[25]

These pragmatic and rather disingenuous manoeuvres were probably in advance of majority opinion, but they fell far short of the recommendations put forward in a number of pamphlets published in December 1688 and January 1689 for the purpose of assisting the Convention in its deliberations.

At first sight it is surprising that these pamphlets, produced in a great hurry in response to a quite unexpected crisis, and after a long period during which political discussion had been actively discouraged, nevertheless featured in one way or another most of the theories which were to be brought forward in defence of the Revolution in the next few years. Obviously this owed something to the public debate on the constitution which had taken place during the Exclusion Crisis.[26]

However, though all these writers were robustly confident that James II could and should be deposed, they tended to eschew abstract theory in favour of an appeal to historical precedent. Indeed, a number of instant histories were published at the same time which dropped very broad hints – *A True Relation of the Manner of the Deposing of Edward II*, for instance, or *The Causes and Manner of Deposing a Popish King in Swedeland*.[27] The pamphleteers in general did not invoke immemorial or abstract contracts of government, but grander and even less precise abstractions like divine law, the law of nature or the inbuilt right of self-preservation. Gilbert Burnet was the most prominent of those who took this line, in *An Enquiry into the Measures of Submission to the Supreme Authority*, a tract he probably wrote in Holland before ever the prince sailed.[28] He did

say that 'the true and original notion of civil society is that
it is a compromise', by which the subjects surrendered
certain rights in return for the ruler's protection; and
'compromise', here meaning 'co-promise', carries the
sense of contract. But he expressly rejected 'general considerations from speculations about sovereign power', and
he went on to say that 'the degrees of all civil authority are
to be taken either by express laws, immemorial customs,
or from particular oaths which the subjects swear to their
princes'.[29] Any contract he had in mind must be recent. In
another, shorter pamphlet, also of December 1688 and
published 'By Authority' (which can only mean William),
his argument was even simpler. 'The clear and natural
method of proceeding' was to declare a Catholic king
'incompatible with' a Protestant kingdom; and in view of
James's flight, he said, 'It is natural to declare the throne
void, and that the king has fallen from all right to it.'[30]

Other writers appealed to some kind of compact or
agreement, but usually a recent one, or at least one that
was within historical memory. For instance, the 'compact'
discussed in *A Brief Justification of the Prince of Orange's
Descent into England* (published early in 1689 and probably
by Robert Ferguson) is clearly intended to be specific and
historical, and renewed from time to time, or even from
prince to prince.[31] *An Essay upon the Original and Design of
Magistracy* (1689) argued that in any political society the
ruler was sworn to abide by the fundamental laws; these
were enacted 'at the first constitution', but they maintained
their force because they were renewed with each successive
reign.[32] In fact, though they do not specifically mention
the coronation oath, both these writers foreshadow the
emphasis soon to be placed on it.

Much more threatening was the emphasis other writers
placed on the power of the people. *A Word to the Wise*
argued that James's flight was tantamount to his death, and
his power could devolve only on his heirs, who were not the
Princess Mary nor the Prince of Wales, but the people.[33]
The author of *Four Questions Debated* was perhaps over-

subtle when he cited Filmer's definition of government as 'the exercise of a moral power', and argued that James's government, being 'contrary to all moral power', had lapsed; but he went on to say that since there was now no evident government 'there must be a sort of reverter to the people, who first chose the king'.[34] It was perhaps unfortunate that it was this kind of writer who laid most stress on the Original Contract, and at the same time argued that the Convention had the authority to make a completely fresh start, even looking towards a republican solution of the present crisis. For instance, *Proposals Humbly Offered* distinguished between 'the supreme power real', which the people had surrendered one to another when they had submitted to government, and 'the supreme power personal', which was the subject of specific agreement between the king and his people. The supreme power personal vested in James II was now forfeit, and by virtue of the supreme power real the people could make what provision they chose for the government, without restraint. The author reminded his readers 'that it was the community of England which first gave birth to both king and parliament, and to all other parts of our constitution', and 'that those kingdoms and republics subsist longest that are often renewed, or brought back to their first beginnings'.[35] *A Discourse concerning the Nature, Power and Proper Effects of the Present Convention* made a similar distinction between the 'rectoral contract', entered into by a chosen magistrate and his people, and the 'popular contract' under which men had united themselves in a community in the first place.[36] Even more radical in tone was *Good Advice before It Be Too Late*, which located authority in the 'original agreement of the people' – a phrase with unfortunate echoes of the Levellers of 1647 – and argued that the people had instituted a corporation of king, lords and commons, any one of which failing, the corporation was forthwith dissolved. In common with other writers of this kind, the author awarded the Convention higher powers than a parliament enjoyed – 'a parliament makes laws for the administration, but the people as a community make laws for the constitution' – and thought it entirely within their power quietly to drop the kingship and vest authority in Lords and Commons alone.[37]

In fact, from the beginning the idea of the Original Contract was associated with popular rights, even republicanism; not unnaturally, since it implied the pre-existence of a commonwealth, or a formed political society, before kingship. It was safer by far to associate the contract with renewable oaths, and shelve the problem of how it originated. In fact, this was evident from the beginning, when the Lords sought the advice of counsel on the Original Contract. As we have seen, Sir Robert Atkyns referred the House to 'the first original of government', when there had been 'an agreement between king and people'. But he was not at all certain that there had in fact been such a contract, and if there had it was certainly not immutable – 'If there were an Original Contract', he said, 'yet it is subject to variations as [to] the times.' He further added, 'The contract is the laws of the kingdom.' Bradbury posed the rhetorical question, 'What is the original agreement?' and answered, 'In England there are steps, as king, lords and commons. The body of the Common Law must be taken to be that Original Contract.' Cresswell Levinz pointed to the mutual oaths taken by king and people: 'You may call it an Original Contract', he said, 'though you know not when it began, because there are oaths on both sides, king and people, one to govern, the other to obey.'[38]

When the Lords came to confer with the Commons on the matter, the Commons managers did their best to evade the question, but the Earl of Clarendon would not be denied: 'This breaking the Original Contract', he said, 'is a language that hath not been long used in this place; nor known in any of our law books, or public records. It is sprung up, but as taken from some late authors, and those none the best received.'[39] He was obviously glancing at Thomas Hobbes, and the close association of Hobbes with contract was in itself sufficient to damn the idea in most men's minds. Hobbes had, after all, divorced political obligation from the supernatural altogether, and posited a purely mechanistic, even animal view of human behaviour, which contemporaries found deeply distasteful as well as reprehensible. The constant need to dissociate themselves from Hobbes restricted his successors' freedom of manoeuvre.

Moreover, Hobbes had assumed that in entering upon the Original Contract men surrendered their civil rights, except those of physical self-protection. Nor did one need to be a Hobbist to put forward this argument. It was used by the Earl of Pembroke and the Bishop of Ely, in the Lords' debates of February 1689, to support their argument that the oath of allegiance and the law of succession were immutable, being part of the Original Contract.[40] This is perhaps why Whigs like Sir Robert Atkyns preferred not to regard the contract as unchanging, and why even some radical pamphleteers had reservations on the matter. For instance, the author of *Some Remarks upon Government* wrote, 'Our general and original rights cannot totally be swallowed up by a compact that can be made to settle liberty and property, neither is all that is natural now made civil.'[41]

On the other hand, some earnest Whigs were pained at the general scepticism with which a literal-minded and legalistic age greeted the concept of a contract which did not survive in documentary form. 'Some...have expressed themselves in a flouting way', it was said, 'that the House of Commons would have done well to have sent the Lords a copy of this Original Contract drawn from their registers, wherein they ought to have preserved it, if any such were.'[42]

All this explains why the contract theories of John Locke, though they were to achieve almost universal acceptance by the mid-eighteenth century, were not pressed into service by the first-generation supporters of the Revolution of 1688. The impact of the *Two Treatises* was blunted by their anonymity, and their austerely unhistorical approach made them seem irrelevant to the problems of current politics. John Dunn reminds us that they 'at no time secured the sort of unquestioned acceptance and esteem which it is customary to assert for them today'.[43] Martyn Thompson points out that in fact they fell remarkably flat, and when they did begin to be taken up in the late 1690s it was with reference to the first treatise – Locke's refutation of patriarchalism – rather than the second, which embodies his exposition of contract theory.[44]

Indeed, as an avowed justification of 1688, contemporaries found the second treatise a puzzle, and its lack of any but the most perfunctory religious sense and of any historical frame of reference at all was distinctly unsettling. It is even now uncertain whether Locke viewed the Original Contract as something which *had* happened in some remote and undiscoverable antiquity, or as just a philosophical construct, which had to be imagined if modern politics were to be made explicable. The conclusion is irresistible that Locke himself did not care, and it is this indifference which caused his contemporaries most disquiet.

For instance, his views on abdication – the precise circumstances of the Revolution, according to orthodox dogma – were profoundly radical. According to him, unless the ruler in abdicating makes express provision for his successor, 'the government visibly ceases, and the people become a confused multitude, without order or connection'; yet even in these anarchic circumstance the people are 'at liberty to provide for themselves, by erecting a new legislature, differing from the other by the change of persons, or form'.[45] This is precisely the possibility many of the parliamentary classes found most alarming in 1689, and which the myth of James's abdication had been designed to prevent. William Atwood, one of Locke's few public supporters, took him to task for this, and argued that parliament was the organ of continuity, to which authority automatically reverted on the king's abdication.[46]

Atwood recommended 'those who are not able to think of themselves' to 'take every morning some pages of the

Two Treatises of Government, for an effective catholicon against nonsense and absurdities',[47] but Locke's other disciples were few in number. James Tyrrell was a personal friend, so it is conventional to regard his *Bibliotheca Politica* as 'Lockean'. In fact, it was firmly historicist in its approach, and no more Lockean than the Bill of Rights; it contains only five citations of Locke (in a volume of nearly a thousand pages), and three of these refer to patriarchalism.[48] The only other author to invoke his aid was William Molyneux, in an attempt to prove the independence of the Irish parliament; Locke disowned him, and his book was ordered to be burnt by the common hangman in 1698.[49] Under Queen Anne Locke fell into positive disfavour, and was the subject of a full-scale assault by the Jacobite polemicist Charles Leslie, in his influential weekly *The Rehearsal* – by no means an unsuccessful attack, either.[50] As we have seen, the Whig politicians of Anne's reign were exceedingly wary of citing him, and his supposed influence on men like Somers and Halifax is mainly conjectural; their patronage was probably extended to the author of the *Essay concerning Human Understanding*, not the author of the *Two Treatises*. Walter Moyle cited the second treatise admiringly, it is true, but only as the best introduction to Sidney's *Discourses*; and it is easy to see why Sidney, with his firm historical approach, his identification of parliament with the people's will, and his superior literary style, should have had the greater appeal.[51] Even those, like Tutchin and Hoadly, who most furiously opposed Leslie's views, did not appeal to Locke in their defence. Hoadly's ponderous work on civil government, published in 1709, was in the idiom of Locke, and even copied the arrangement of the *Two Treatises*, yet his only reference to Locke was on a detailed point regarding patriarchalism.[52]

At first sight the failure of Locke to offer any assistance to those Whigs who were trying to justify the Revolution in contract terms seems of little importance; by definition Whigs were committed to the Revolution anyway. But thousands of other Englishmen were not, particularly

Anglican Englishmen. The Revolution was an abrupt reversal of every trend in Anglican thinking since 1660, or even 1584, and if it could not be accommodated or explained the church was in danger of internal schism. This was a problem as immediate to Whig churchmen as it was to their Tory colleagues.

3

THE MEASURES OF SUBMISSION
The triumph of *de facto* theory

On the face of it, by the end of 1690 acceptance of the Revolution was almost universal. Only a tiny minority of prominent laymen held out, and the clergy, who had naturally been expected to exhibit greater scruples, had taken the oaths to the new regime in overwhelming numbers. So little was this expected in February 1689 that the Lords had proposed that the clergy be exempted from the oaths altogether.

Yet the non-jurors, headed by Archbishop Sancroft and some of his most respected bishops, made up in distinction for what they lacked in numbers, and polemically they were highly active. The success of Abednego Seller's *History of Passive Obedience* (1689) was ominous, and in John Kettlewell and Charles Leslie they possessed two of the ablest theological controversialists of the day. Their contention that the oath of allegiance was quasi-sacramental, and could not be abrogated in King James's lifetime, was difficult to counter in a generation which assumed as a matter of course that political forms had been established by Almighty God and were constantly monitored, if not controlled, by Him. Moreover, the oaths to the new rulers had been stripped of any reference to their right or title, and it was well known that many Tory leaders – Nottingham and Rochester, even Danby and Halifax – had only accepted the Revolution as a *fait accompli*, and had given their allegiance to William and Mary as *de facto* rulers, without prejudice to James II's continued existence as king *de jure*.[1] This was an attitude which was not calculated to

withstand acute political shock – a French invasion, or a
Jacobite rising – and it left the ultimate succession to the
throne wide open, especially if the Princess Anne's baby son
should not survive. This uncertainty in the kingly title
caused the Whigs the greatest concern, especially up to the
time of Queen Mary's death in December 1694,[2] and the
efforts of conformist churchmen to counteract it were
unceasing.

The issue was confused by the fact that some of the most
prominent advocates of the Revolution employed a
blunderbuss technique, throwing in every argument they
thought would serve. In *An Enquiry into the Measures of
Submission to the Supreme Authority*, published at the end of
1688, Burnet appealed to the law of nature, the law of God,
the continuity of English history, and some sort of contract.
A few months later, in a famous pastoral letter to the
clergy of Salisbury, he appealed vigorously to conquest
as conferring a *de facto* right. Edward Stillingfleet, in
The Unreasonableness of a New Separation (1689), firmly
eschewed conquest or contract, but appealed instead to
Providence and the laws of God as evinced in human
law.[3]

Both Stillingfleet and Burnet expressed the standard
Whig–Anglican view of the origins of political society: that
the concept of government originated with God, but its
operation depended on the sanction of human laws. In
earlier writings Stillingfleet had shown an unusual sense of
the development of government over the centuries in
response to increasing population, outward expansion, and
the growing sophistication of man's temporal concerns,
and he had striven to reconcile this with the biblical
accounts;[4] but he continued to believe in 'indirect intervention'. That is, princes were appointed by God for the
public good, and their rule was only justified so long as
they worked for that good – a theme later to be resumed
by Hoadly. The touchstone of the common good was the
law of the land, which expressed this concept independ-
ently of the will of the legislators, and was therefore

(we are left to infer) in some sense divine.[5] Pierre Allix, the exiled Huguenot theologian, adopted much the same stance.[6]

Burnet's view of the matter was rather more secular and direct. The English constitution, whose continuing survival down the centuries left little doubt of its providential sanction, depended on a mutual understanding between ruler and ruled which was defined and confirmed from generation to generation by mutual oaths, and the history of the nation showed innumerable instances of kings being deposed for misconduct towards their people, and the hereditary line of succession being broken, without subsequent evidence of divine disfavour – except in the case of Charles I, whose death was acknowledged not to be covered by these rules. Burnet's ideas continued to develop, stimulated no doubt by further reading of English history, and may be said to have reached their climax in his speech at Sacheverell's trial in 1710,[7] but as early as 1689 and 1690 they were shared by other Whig clergy. In *A Resolution of Certain Queries* Thomas Long, prebendary of Exeter, argued that 'the ordinance of government is from God and nature, but the species of it, whether by one or more, is from men, and the rule for administration is by mutual agreement of the governor, and those that are governed'.[8] In *A Dialogue between Two Friends* (1689) White Kennett followed Long most of the way, while also stressing an overriding concern for self-preservation.[9]

All these writers placed great emphasis on the coronation oath, as living evidence of a compact or agreement between a king and his people,[10] and it is obvious why this should be so; apart from anything else, it counterbalanced the oath of allegiance. This argument was strengthened by the example of the Scots, who gave as their principal reason for dethroning James the fact that he had not taken the coronation oath, and who obliged his successors to do so before they could assume the executive powers of government.[11] The answer to those who dismissed such things as 'matters of formality and ornament' was

All those ceremonies are certainly significant of something; and as it cannot be doubted but they were at first instituted upon just and grave reasons, so long custom has made them essential to the solemnity of the coronation itself; otherwise it is easy to believe that these things, which look so like making the regality dependent on popular consent, had been before this time laid aside by some dark and jealous princes.[12]

But even more popular in Anglican circles was the theory which has been christened 'the divine right of Providence'. This was not so much a theory as an assumption that the Revolution could never have succeeded, against all the odds, and against all expectations, without the potent assistance of Almighty God; and His intervention in so marked and decisive a manner abrogated all existing obligations and overturned all previous theories, including those of passive obedience and non-resistance. Burnet's excited, almost hysterical thanksgiving sermon to the House of Commons on 31 January 1689 set the theme:

Who can look back on those black clouds that were hanging over our heads, and that seemed charged with storms and thunders, and observe the present calm, and consider the steps of Providence, I had almost said the prodigies and miracles of Providence, that have attended our deliverance, without letting his heart run out into all the joyful expectation possible?

And it was a theme to which he returned in old age, to salute the advent of George I.[13] In the intervening years it was developed in countless sermons, sometimes to the point of absurdity, as when Bishop William Nicholson of Carlisle remarked in 1703, 'The all-wise Providence of God has frequently of late (and, as some of us always thought, very graciously) exchanged our governors.'[14]

But it is worth noticing that the most prominent supporters of Providence all had other theories at their disposal. Burnet had several, as we have seen, and so had Thomas Long, who in A Resolution of Certain Queries called not only on Providence, but on the coronation oath, natural rights, English history, legal arguments and the de facto theory. Stillingfleet used it, albeit rather tentatively, in The Unreasonableness of a New Separation, and it even appealed to the republican author of Proposals Humbly Offered to the

Lords and Commons in the Present Convention (1689).[15] In fact,
this so-called theory was little more than the expression of
a devotional platitude; it did not change men's minds, it
only confirmed them in decisions they had already reached
for other reasons. Even Professor Gerald Straka, who may
be said to have discovered the concept and made it his own,
cautions us: 'It must be remembered that Providence was
not the whole of the Anglican revolution theory, but a
necessary supplement to its legal position.'[16] This was neatly
expressed by Sir George Treby, Recorder of London, who
greeted the Prince of Orange on 20 December 1688 with
the words 'Your Highness, led by the hand of heaven, and
called by the voice of the people, has preserved our dearest
interests.'[17]

True, Providence had firm official backing; it was used
in the proclamation of William and Mary as king and queen
in February 1689, and it was enshrined in the new prayers
for the thanksgiving service held on 5 November: 'We
adore the wisdom and justice of the Providence which so
timely interposed in our extreme danger, and disappointed
all the designs of our enemies.' It was even used abroad:
by James Johnston, for instance, at Berlin, when he invested the Elector of Brandenburg with the Garter in 1690.[18]
But its presence in such uncontroversial settings is sus-
picious in itself; it was very much the small change of
polemical or intercessory vocabulary.

As a formal theory of political obligation it was open to
many objections, the main one being that it existed merely
to stamp worldly success with the brand of divine approval,
an easy and tempting doctrine for which the Puritans had
been sharply criticised in the past. The Reverend Samuel
Johnson caustically remarked,

[The clergy] have departed from the standing rules of right and wrong,
and the standing revelations upon that subject, and have betaken themselves to the intimations of Providence, and the outgoings of the
morning and evening, which were their scoff the other day, when those
expressions were used in the parliament army. The Revolution is
supposed to be right, because at Torbay the wind chopped about;

and even some of its firmest advocates felt obliged to hedge a little. Wrote one: 'I am not one of those who rashly judge the goodness or badness of an attempt by its success, or conclude God's love or hatred from a frowning or favourable Providence, which is not the rule of our duty.'[19] Indeed, the heroic sufferings and the eventual triumph of the church in the Interregnum were a graphic demonstration, fresh in the mind, of the fact that immediate failure, short-term disaster, was no proof of God's ultimate disapproval.

Finally, some theorists were acute enough to see that if God's Providence were allowed absolute sway, it might be wayward enough to endorse divine right. Pierre Allix felt it necessary to state:

God is said to overturn thrones, in like manner as He is said to erect them; He is said to settle tyrants, as well as the most lawful kings, all which expressions relating to His Providence, which does or permits things by the intervening ministry of second causes, can have no influence upon the judgments we are to make concerning the authority of princes, with regard to their divine institution.[20]

But William Sherlock took up and enlarged on this very point, and in so doing finally discredited Providence theory.

Sherlock, Master of the Temple and one of the most celebrated clergymen of his generation, at first refused the oaths, and even published a pamphlet explaining his views. But in 1690 he took the oaths and accepted promotion to the Deanery of St Paul's, making little attempt to disguise the fact that his decision was associated with William's victory at the Boyne. He published a long apologia in 1691, *The Case of Allegiance Due to Sovereign Powers Stated and Resolved according to Scripture and Reason and the Principles of the Church of England.*

Ironically enough, Sherlock attributed his 'conversion' to a book published by Sancroft in 1689 to strengthen the non-juring case. This was a set of canons defining church doctrine drawn up in 1606 by John Overall, Bishop of Norwich, and passed by Convocation but prudently vetoed by James I. What caught King James's eye, as well as

Sherlock's, was Canon XXVIII, which averred, no doubt with Henry VII in mind, that Christians could give allegiance to governments founded on usurpation or rebellion once they were 'thoroughly settled'.[21] Braced by this, Sherlock proceeded to extend the theory of Providence to its utmost limits, abolishing on the way any distinction between a *de facto* and a *de jure* ruler. A successful usurpation, resulting in a settled government, was an act of God alone; God conferred the right to rule, and He could also transfer it; the power to govern was overt evidence of this transfer, and the recipient then enjoyed all the advantages of divine right, and was even entitled to the passive obedience of his new subjects.

The resultant furore was unprecedented.[22] *The Case of Allegiance* was a bestseller for more than a year, and attracted a host of critics; it even came to the august attention of Locke and Leibniz.[23] Sherlock made the mistake of trying to answer his critics, in another long pamphlet with the revealing title *Their Majesties Government Proved to Be Thoroughly Settled and That We May Submit to It without Asserting the Principles of Mr Hobbs, Shewing Also That Allegiance Was Not Due to the Usurpers after the Late Civil War* (1691), and he even had the nerve to reiterate these arguments on the occasion of a 30 January sermon to the House of Commons in 1692.

Sherlock was a tactless and thick-skinned man, who contrived to give the maximum offence even to those who found no fault at all with his conclusions. The more extreme Whigs, for instance, could not help but take exception to his argument that the people's rights were irrelevant to the Revolution, and that it had not involved resistance. (He coined the term 'non-assistance' instead.)[24] Whig churchmen were incensed that he should publicise the fact that a learned, experienced and respected clergyman like him was in such a state of confusion that his mind could be made up for him only by the fortuitous publication of an obscure and forgotten text.[25] Indeed, critics of the church fastened upon this point with understandable glee. Wrote one:

It may be there are more manuscript canons still at Lambeth; if there be, the Doctor would do well to use his influence with Dr Sharp for publishing them, for the laity have great reason to be offended and take scandal at this dealing of the clergy with them, to keep them ignorant of the doctrine of the Church of England for fourscore years together.[26]

John Locke, typically, was repelled by Sherlock's intellectual flabbiness, and particularly by his failure to explain precisely when it became lawful to transfer allegiance from one ruler to another. In his private notes he pointed out that Sherlock's answer, when the government was 'settled', was no answer at all: 'How long?' he irritably scribbled, 'a month, a year, or an hundred; and by what rule, what law of God?'[27] But most people objected to Sherlock's moral flabbiness, which he exposed quite ingenuously. Introducing his new theory, he wrote:

This scheme of government may startle some men at first, before they have well considered it. But everyone at first sight must acknowledge, that it is so much for the ease and safety of subjects in all revolutions (which very frequently happen), [and so much] what the generality of mankind from an inward principle of preservation have always done, and will always do, that they have reason to wish it to be true, and to be glad to see it well proved.[28]

It was also virtually impossible – though Sherlock tried hard enough – to explain why, according to his theory, allegiance should not have been given to the prosperous wickedness of Oliver Cromwell, and how his theory differed from that of Thomas Hobbes. Hobbes had argued that power confers right, and that right is therefore an attribute of power; Sherlock insisted that power was still an attribute of right, and right was still conferred only by God, but in the end the only way of assessing this was by reference to the stability of the regime; and stability depended on power. John Kettlewell, the non-juror, made out a case in reply with which conformist Anglicans could only agree, because it was spiritual, whereas Sherlock's was resolutely aspiritual. Essentially, he argued that right was moral, power was carnal; therefore the latter could only be an attribute of the former, not vice versa.[29]

When the dust cleared, the doctrine of Providence was irretrievably damaged, together with Sherlock's reputation. He was a celebrated preacher, in the forefront of the battle against Deism and Socinianism, and his *A Practical Discourse concerning Death* (1689) was a bestseller down the eighteenth century, but when he died in 1707 he was still Dean of St Paul's.

Meanwhile another theory which came to no good end was the theory of conquest. It was easy and natural to suppose that the Revolution was a conquest, and that such conquests effected a transfer of legal right, and thus of allegiance. Burnet argued this in his pastoral letter of 15 May 1689, and so did many others at this time.[30] But in fact, when opinions hardened out it became clear that conquest, still regarded as inherently violent and illegal, was rejected by Whigs and Tories alike. The author of *Political Aphorisms* (1690) stated flatly, 'Conquest may restore a right, forfeiture may lose a right, but 'tis consent only that can transact or give a right.' As for Samuel Johnson, he regarded a conqueror as 'one whom no after-treaties or consent can make a king', and he denounced the efforts of clergymen to base right on force as 'prize-office divinity'.[31] Indeed, the chief exponent of conquest theory, William Lloyd, Bishop of St Asaph, had that same mixture of naivety and worldliness as Sherlock.

In *A Discourse of God's Ways of Disposing of Kingdoms* (1691), Lloyd argued from the Old Testament that God had always reserved the power to depose one king and set up another, usually by conquest; in fact, conquest was the most usual means by which God, as it were, passed judicial sentence on a ruler for crimes against his people or the laws of the land.[32] It was God who granted princes the power of the sword, and therefore an appeal to the sword, on either side, was an appeal to God's judgment, and any conquest which resulted was a just conquest in the eyes of God.[33] Like Sherlock, he thought that the sanctity of these proceedings was then confirmed by peaceful possession; unlike Sherlock, he also thought that the people had a part

to play. 'It seems to be plain', he wrote, 'that the right
should go along with the complete possession. So as that
wheresoever this is once settled, whether by length of
time, or even sooner by a general consent of the people,
there it ought to be presumed that there is a right.'[34]
He was uneasily aware that not all would agree with him,
and that he was putting a high moral premium on success,
but he argued (essentially) that the end justified the means:
'It is the cause that makes a war either just or unjust;
and though the events of both these may be the same, for
either of them may end in a conquest...yet whether this
be justly obtained or unjustly, it makes a great difference.'[35]

Not only was this the rankest casuistry, it also undermined the conventional and accepted explanation of the
Revolution, abdication. (Sherlock, in fact, had specifically
thrown over the doctrine of abdication.)[36] Moreover, the
researches of scholars like Brady and Spelman into medieval history only served to underline the danger of conquest theory. The Conquest of 1066 was the stumbling
block.[37] If William III had conquered England, then so had
William I; but conquest was an absolute, not subject to
qualification. Tory scholars could argue that William I had
acquired by conquest an absolute right over his people
which he had transmitted to his successors down to James
II, and that any 'rights' conferred on the people by intervening rulers were of grace. It could even be argued that
William III's 'conquest' had given him a renewed authority
as extensive as William I's. As early as 1689, in *A Dialogue
between Two Friends*, White Kennett argued with some spirit
that 1066 was a conquest of the most explicit kind, and cited
William's 'hostile and unnatural proceedings, and his
barbarous actions in wading through torrents of blood,
riding in triumph over heaps of slaughtered innocents, to
ascend a throne, and grasp a sceptre, to which he had no
more right than the Great Mogul'. After this, the Conqueror's submission to coronation was an anti-climax, and
the best Kennett could do was to say that he 'compounded

for the crown', though it was not clear, from what had gone before, why he should.[38]

The difficulty was to prove that conquest effected a transfer of right from the old to the new monarch, and therefore safeguarded rights. One means of so doing was to employ an argument of Hugo Grotius, the renowned international jurist, whose *De Jure Belli ac Pacis* had been published in England in 1654, and had enjoyed a wide influence there ever since. Though in general an upholder of monarchical right, Grotius acknowledged the concept of a 'just war', which allowed one sovereign prince to dethrone another to enforce the cause of the people, the *jus gentium*. The events of the Revolution could only be made to fit Grotius's strict rules with some difficulty, but the task was undertaken by the Tory journalist Edmund Bohun, in his *History of the Desertion*, published in 1689.[39] It was a theory which found favour with a wide audience, including Burnet and Lloyd; it opened the way for the Tories to give complete and unfeigned acceptance to the regime, and it encouraged those Whigs who argued for the recognition of William's title as 'lawful'.

Unfortunately, the theory met with an unexpected check in January 1693, when Bohun, as Press Licenser for the government, put his imprimatur on a pamphlet called *King William and Queen Mary Conquerors*, by Charles Blount. The title was unfortunate, since it was only a moderate restatement of Bohun's own Grotian views, and it was brought up for discussion in the House of Commons. What happened then is not entirely clear from the evidence, but it seems that the Tories tried to defend Bohun by delating the Whig bishops Burnet and Lloyd for publishing similar arguments. Lloyd's *God's Ways of Disposing of Kingdoms* narrowly escaped, but Burnet's pastoral letter of 1689 was ordered to be suppressed, together with *King William and Queen Mary Conquerers*, the Lords and Commons declaring in a joint resolution that both works were 'inconsistent with the principles on which the government is founded, and tending to the subversion of the rights of the people'.[40]

It would be going too far to say that this at once outlawed
conquest theory – for one thing, the whole episode was a
very obvious, almost schoolboyish, piece of politicking by
party groups in parliament. Edmund Bohun was dismissed,
but a few months later his successor licensed another pamphlet in which the idea of conquest after a just war featured
prominently.[41] If such theories now fell out of fashion, as
it seems they did, it was probably because of growing doubts
about the Norman Conquest, despite the efforts of Whig
historians to allay them.[42]

This left the strict *de facto* theory in possession of the field;
that is, the theory that the Revolution, whatever its motives,
and the conduct of James II, whatever its precise nature,
had resulted in an ineluctable situation in which the king
de jure, without prejudice to his long-term right, had simply
been replaced by a king *de facto*, to whom a qualified and
limited allegiance was owing, but who enjoyed no legal
rights. That this was a very common attitude is shown by
the Whigs' failure in the new parliament of 1690 to secure
a 'legitimist oath', acknowledging William's 'rightful and
lawful' title and abjuring King James. According to Roger
Morrice, the night before the crucial vote,

The ecclesiastical regents met in very many taverns and places with their
friends, and told them the church was undone if they did abjure King
James, for multitudes did look upon him as their lawful sovereign, to
whom they owed obedience, and could not renounce him, though they
could submit to this king while this force was upon them.

Next day Sir Thomas Lee offered a compromise by which
the new oath would not be tendered to the clergy, but the
Whigs were defeated by twelve votes in a House estimated
at 360.[43] It was on this occasion that Sir Henry Goodrick
told the Commons, 'Though some men will swallow abjuration of a branch of the royal family under a[nother]
branch whereof we sit, those of the Church of England will
not do it. The utmost necessity made me break my oath
to King James; it was utmost necessity, and those are
terrible things.'[44] Yet Goodrick was a Privy Councillor,
one of the Marquess of Carmarthen's chief henchmen,

and his second-in-command in the seizure of York in November 1688.[45]

Of course, the most prominent exponent of *de facto* thinking was Daniel Finch, Earl of Nottingham.[46] He had opposed the granting of the crown to William and Mary with the utmost vigour in the House of Lords:

To declare the prince and princess king and queen of England could never be justified by reason or law, but only by the sword. That it entailed a war upon the nation that children yet unborn were never like to see an end of. That it was contrary to all our pretensions, oaths, subscriptions, etc. That it made this hereditary monarchy elective, with as many more mischiefs as wit, fantasy and frowardness could suggest,[47]

and it was remarkable that he found it in him to take the oath of allegiance and even accept a secretaryship of state from William. The Whigs were furious, and made a motion in the Commons in 1692 to remove him, and all others of like mind; they eventually gained their point in November 1693.[48] But another Abjuration Bill was lost in December 1692;[49] and even in 1696, in the midst of a violent public reaction to the Jacobite plot to assassinate William, at least twenty peers and nearly a hundred MPs still declined to acknowledge his title as 'rightful and lawful'.[50]

Nottingham in the Lords, and Sir Edward Seymour and Heneage Finch in the Commons, said that these words 'had been laid aside in the beginning of this reign; that they imported one who was king by descent, and so could not belong to the present king'. All they would admit was 'that the crown and the prerogatives of it were vested in him, and therefore they would obey him, though they could not acknowledge him their rightful and lawful king'.[51] As late as 1701 Nottingham led the protest against the bill to abjure the Pretender in these famous words:

We conceive that no new oath should be imposed upon the subject, forasmuch as those established by an Act made in the first year of the reign of his Majesty and the late Queen Mary were, together with our rights and liberties, ascertained in that Act under the terms of our submission to his Majesty, and upon which his Majesty was pleased to accept the crown; and which were enacted to stand, remain and be the law of this realm for ever; and which, we conceive, do comprehend and necessarily imply all the duty and allegiance of the subject to their lawful king.[52]

Indeed, he told Archbishop Sharp that to him the abjuration oath was 'like swearing against God's Providence and government of the world'.[53]

But Sharp replied, with worldly realism, 'I am of opinion that [princes] hold their crowns by the same legal right that your lordship holds your estate, and that they may forfeit their rights as well as you may do yours, and the legislature is judge of one case as well as another.'[54] This ought to have been no surprise to Nottingham, for Sharp had laid down the same doctrine in a crucial sermon to the Lords on 30 January 1700,[55] and he had made his views even clearer to an anxious questioner in the early 1690s, to whom he replied,

The laws of the land are the only rule of our conscience in this matter, and we are no further bound to pay obedience to governors than the laws enjoin. If William be king in the eye of the law, we must in conscience obey him as such. As the law makes a king, so the same law extends, or limits, or transfers our allegiance; only with this proviso, that it be not contradictory to the laws of God. In that we must obey passively, though we cannot actively; and with this tacit condition I do suppose all oaths of fidelity in the world are given and taken.[56]

Between the agonising of Nottingham and the bland Erastianism of Sharp there is a great divide. Which view was more typical of English Toryism it is difficult to say. But certainly, any examination such as that undertaken in this chapter places undue emphasis on 'doubts', 'queries', 'scruples'. Such doubts, queries and scruples did exist, of course, but they were not paramount. Considering the bent of Anglican teaching prior to 1688, the surprising thing is that the church accepted the Revolution with such little fuss. The reaction against the Revolution was delayed, and when it came it was as much concerned with the nature of the church as with the state, with the reign of Charles I as with the reign of James II.

4

THIS SKEIN OF TANGLED PRINCIPLES
Whig political thought in the 1690s

The Whig view of the Revolution was based firmly on English history. In *The Fundamental Constitution of the English Government* (1690) William Atwood acknowledged that Locke had established government 'upon the only true foundation, the choice of the people, that original and supreme act of society, antecedent to all positive laws in it'.[1] He also agreed that 'upon King James's abdication...the people were restored to that liberty which they had before the settlement of the crown, which was in force till the Original Contract was broken by him'.[2] But, as we have seen,[3] he flinched from Locke's proposition that society then dissolved into 'a confused multitude', arguing instead that the continuity of the community was represented by parliament, even if, as in 1689, it had not been properly summoned,[4] and the central part of the work (chapters 3–8) is devoted to a detailed review of English history, showing that kingly rule had always been by agreement and consent, that monarchy had always been elective, and that plenty of kings had been deposed or restrained for breaking the contract. He appeared to date the first historical appearance of the contract in Edward the Confessor's reign, but he went back as far as Egbert of the West Saxons to demonstrate the people's exercise of their rights.[5] Daniel Whitby, in *An Historical Account of Some Things relating to the Nature of the English Government and the Conceptions Which Our Forefathers Had of It*, also published in 1690,[6] adopted the same historical method, except that he dated his 'Original Contract, or establishment of laws' from

1066, and ignored Locke's theoretical conceptions altogether.

Unfortunately, over the past ten years belief in the immemorial antiquity of parliament had been undermined by the researches of a group of royalist scholars, notably Robert Brady, who were beginning to construct a picture of English medieval history very much akin to our own.[7] After a brisk controversy during the Exclusion Crisis, when such research suddenly became relevant to current political problems, Brady emerged triumphant over his principal rivals, James Tyrrell and William Petyt, assisted by the royalist reaction after 1681 as well as by his superior scholarship. In *An Introduction to the Old English History* (1684) and the first volume of his *Complete History of England* (1685) he argued that parliament had not emerged until the reign of Edward I, and even then it was not 'representative' in any recognisable way. He ruthlessly demolished the idea that parliament was to be traced back through the Curia Regis of the Norman kings to the Witenagemot of the Anglo-Saxons. Worse still, he argued that William I had effected a complete conquest of the nation, and thereby suppressed any original laws or rights then existing; and any subsequent grant of rights, as in Magna Carta, though tactfully disguised as a 'confirmation', was in fact an act of grace, which could be cancelled at will.

With the royalist sun occluded by the Revolution, and Brady in retirement (he took the oaths and retained his mastership of Gonville and Caius College, Cambridge, but published nothing more), the task of straightening out the record was left to James Tyrrell, whose *Bibliotheca Politica, or An Enquiry into the Ancient Constitution of the English Government*, a long series of dialogues between 'Mr Meanwell, a Civilian' and 'Mr Freeman, a Gentleman', was published in thirteen parts in 1692, 1693 and 1694, and then collected in one volume.[8] By any standards it is a remarkable *tour de force*, 968 closely printed pages devoted to a thorough re-examination of English constitutional history and its bearing on current ideological problems, supported by a wealth of learning.[9] Nor was his Jacobite spokesman, Meanwell, a knockabout figure; he put the royalist and Tory case with great vigour and at considerable length.

The fact that the whole of the sixth, seventh and eighth dialogues, nearly 250 printed pages,[10] was devoted to the history of medieval parliaments demonstrates Tyrrell's scale of priorities, and much of the tenth dialogue was taken up with a valiant attempt to prove William the Conqueror a constitutional monarch.[11] Friend though he was of Locke, Tyrrell found little space for the Original Contract; it was not introduced at all until late in the work, and then Freeman simply argued that it was implicit in 'the original constitution of the kingdom', as interpreted by him.[12] Later, when Meanwell put forward the vulgar argument that the contract did not exist in documentary form, Freeman neatly countered by pointing out that neither did the law of hereditary succession, with which the Jacobites made such play.[13] The strong implication was that this was some form of 'historical contract', even if it was not committed to writing.

In 1696 Tyrrell followed up *Bibliotheca Politica* with the first volume of a massive *General History of England*, devoted to the demolition of Brady's thesis. This volume stopped at 1066; the next, published in 1700, took the narrative down to 1272, and in 1704 he reached 1399, where he stopped, though we know from Thomas Hearne that he was still working away in the Bodleian in 1713, and he lived until 1718.[14] The relevance of this kind of research was shown in 1709, when the non-juror William Higden suffered a belated and sensational conversion. True, Higden was disposed to adopt a 'reasonable' attitude towards political obligation, and was probably influenced by Hoadly more than he cared to admit, but as the title of his apologia shows, he drew his main support from the history of royal government in England from the Conquest to 1485.[15]

This incident shows the value of academic history in constructing a Whig mythology, but in the immediate aftermath of 1689 it seemed a mere luxury. When William's second parliament assembled in 1690, Whig MPs were acutely conscious of the fragility of the Settlement; on the proposal for a regency act to cover William's absence in Ireland Sir Thomas Littleton told the Commons, 'Your government is not strong enough to try experiments upon; you have too many already', and John Hampden was of the same mind: 'The government is settled', he said, 'and I desire to continue it so. The breaches we make in it, neither we nor our posterity can ever repair.'[16] By 1693 Hampden was not even sure the government was settled at all, for he is found lamenting, 'We are entirely unsettled as to the government. The king's title, and the legality of it, are as publicly disputed, and with as little fear of punishment, as any point of natural philosophy in the schools at Oxford, or any moot case of law by the students of the Temple.'[17] The Whigs' uneasiness at the *de facto* principle is shown by their repeated attacks on Lord Nottingham, and there was considerable doubt as to whether the official ruling of the Convention on abdication had removed James II so thoroughly as to make *de facto* allegiance to William even feasible. It was difficult not to sympathise with the non-juror Jeremy Collier when he remarked, 'If a man should forfeit his house to those who set it on fire, only because he quitted it without giving some formal directions to the servants, and be obliged to lose his estate for endeavouring to preserve his life, I believe it would be thought an incomprehensible sort of justice'; and the same proposition was put in lighter vein by a doggerel poet who lamented the ill fate of a virgin who had suffered a gang rape:

> Yet the ravishers' honesty she unjustly accused;
> She's made a mere whore by the vow of our state,
> Cause surely her maidenhead did she abdicate.[18]

As late as 1697 it could be argued that if the official version of events was correct, then the Jacobites were justified in denying William their allegiance; and it was so argued in *A Free Discourse*.[19]

In fact, this last pamphlet closed with the sturdy assertion that the Convention made William 'their lawful and rightful king, or they made him nothing', and in 1689, of course, this was a common attitude. The author of *Reflections upon the Occurrences from 5 Nov. 1688 to 5 Nov. 1689* (1689) bitterly regretted the stress laid on James's flight as implying his abdication – 'as if...the other matters charged against [him] were not criminal or punishable'.[20] Another writer referred in passing to 'the deposition of King James (granting it to be so, and waiving the advantages of the abdication)'.[21] Thomas Wharton told the Commons in February 1689, 'I own driving King James out, and I would do it again.'[22] Many thought that there had been too much preoccupation with legal forms, and far too much theorising. In 1693 Samuel Johnson denounced 'these wretched inventions of usurpation, conquest and desertion', and five years later he renewed his attack on all such 'disguising terms and blinds'. He lamented the use of 'desertion and abdication, instead of plain English forfeiture, which the Scotch parliament honestly called forefaulting'. By this textual hypocrisy the people had been robbed of the important achievement of making a king forfeit his crown; just as the use of the term 'Convention Parliament' ('which they might better have called a Vestry or a Wardmoot Parliament, for that had been an English name') had robbed them of the right to assemble without the king's writ. Nor would he allow arguments from Scripture: 'The Bible', he said, 'is a miscellaneous book, where dishonest and time-serving men may ever, in their loose way, find a text for their purpose.' In fact, he sturdily insisted that

The English government falls under no rules, or terms of art. For it was not borrowed from Aristotle or Plato, or any of those platform men; neither was it moulded by our ancestors out of a mixture of absolute monarchy, aristocracy and democracy, as the Answer to the Nineteen Propositions says. But it is wholly built upon the reason of the thing, it is directed to the high honour of God and the common profit of the realm, and consists of downright honesty and deep thought.[23]

John Trenchard was even more dismissive: 'A government', he said, 'is a mere piece of clockwork, and having
such springs and wheels must act after such a manner;
and therefore the art is to constitute it so that it must move
to the public advantage.'[24]

As for the Original Contract, there was an evident reluctance to rely entirely on something that could be proved
only by inference or implication. Instead, 1688 was hailed
as a new beginning, and John Hampden was careful to
distinguish between 'the Original Contract broken by King
James' and 'that new contract made by King William with
this nation'.[25] This was part and parcel of the untenable
Whig myth that William had been granted the crown in
1689 on condition that he accepted the Declaration of
Right.[26] The Earl of Warrington (formerly Lord Delamere)
even told the grand jury of Chester, 'The king and queen
received their crown from the hands of the people upon
such terms as they gave it.'[27] This was an abiding feature
of left-wing Whig thinking; the author of *A Free Discourse*
(1697) likened the transactions of 1689 to the archetypal
situation in which the first Original Contract had been
made, when men came together for the first time to choose
a ruler.[28] Nor was it an exclusively Whig view: it was shared
by many Country MPs. Sir Thomas Clarges said in 1690,
'We sit not here from the last Convention, but by oaths
framed from the Original Contract, by which the king and
queen took the government upon them'; and later in the
same session Lord Digby made a speech which is reported
as follows: 'The foundation of the government is the Bill
of Rights, wherein the king promises his part, etc., and we
swear fealty. This is our Original Contract. If there be any,
I am of opinion this is it.'[29]

However, the Whig–Country element surviving from the
Exclusion Crisis was swept from the government early in
1690, and its numbers were reduced by death and by
electoral defeat. In the 1690–5 parliament the remnant
combined uneasily in opposition with 'New Whigs' like
Robert Harley and Paul Foley, while another wing of the

'party', represented by John Somers, John Trenchard, Charles Montague and Edward Russell, committed themselves wholeheartedly to King William's government, dragging Thomas Wharton with them, and were increasingly obliged to toe the official line.[30]

Unfortunately, none of the future lords of the Junto left any significant archive, and reports of parliamentary debates, which might have revealed their attitudes, are sparse. Their anonymity is baffling; Lord Brougham said of Somers that his name is surrounded 'with a mild but imperishable glory, which, in contrast to our dark ignorance respecting all the particulars and details of his life, gives the figure altogether something of the mysterious and ideal'.[31] But in the debates on various Triennial Bills put forward in 1693 we can sense that this is a period of transition and confusion. After the experience of Charles II's reign any measure to increase the frequency of general elections chimed in with Whig ideas, and in January 1693 we find 'Old Whigs' like Winnington and Granville joining 'New Whigs' like Harley and Foley in support of a bill for annual parliaments. It was opposed by Tories like Lowther and Seymour, but also, quite strongly, by Somers and Montague.[32] Proposals for annual parliaments were also supported, however, by the Earl of Shrewsbury, who was usually regarded as the Junto's 'patron', and in December 1693 he was joined by Wharton, perhaps out of innate radicalism, perhaps because he was alert to the prejudices of the rank and file. But Charles Montague rejected the whole idea, and the medieval precedents put forward in its support: 'That of annual parliaments', he said, 'is as much an antiquated law as any – annual parliaments were never insisted upon – when perhaps it will not be in the king's power to dissolve. You are setting up a Senate of Venice.'[33]

Unfortunately, the circumstances in which a Triennial Bill finally passed into law in January 1695 are obscure, though we do know that this was a turbulent session, made more turbulent by quarrels between Wharton and

Montague and between them and the king's managers.[34] Somers, as Lord Keeper and Speaker of the Lords, was reduced to silence in public; he was always credited with supporting the Triennial Act in general terms, though he later recanted.[35] It is also unfortunate that no debates survive on the Demise of the Crown Act (1696), which by allowing parliament to meet and transact business after the king's death finally registered the legal and constitutional superiority of the one over the other. But it is reasonable to assume that as the Junto Whigs became more closely associated with the establishment, they and their Commons followers increasingly accepted the establishment view of the Revolution.

And the establishment stuck closely to the official line adopted by the Convention, admitting the Original Contract but playing it down, and insisting on the approved interpretation of James's abdication. This is shown by the fact that the government (and it can only have been the government or the House of Lords) approved for publication in 1695 a transcript of the conferences between Lords and Commons in February 1689, under the title *The Debate at Large*.[36] It is shown even more explicitly by two papers drawn up in 1697 in answer to the accusations made by James II, and his call for justice from the princes of Europe and the peace delegates at Ryswick. It was eventually decided that the best policy was simply to ignore James, and these papers were not published until the next reign, and then in pamphlet form, without official sanction. But at least one of them was attributed to Burnet, and both were supposed to have been approved by a government now predominantly Whig, with Somers as Lord Chancellor, Edward Russell, Earl of Orford, as First Lord of the Admiralty, Charles Montague as First Lord of the Treasury and Wharton confident of the next secretaryship of state or the lord lieutenancy of Ireland. Even if they are spurious – and internal evidence does not suggest this – they still represent a point of view which may fairly be described as 'establishment Whig'.

The larger part of one of these pamphlets, *The Revolution Vindicated*,[37] was taken up with the difficult task of defending the Convention's view of abdication, as against the normal view, trenchantly put by James II – 'a word, when applied to sovereign princes, that was never before used to signify anything but a free and voluntary resignation of a crown, as in the case of the Emperor Charles V, and the late Queen [Christina] of Sweden'. The counter-arguments were now growing stale with repetition, and were still not calculated to convince anyone not eager to be convinced. By this time it was apparent that the Lords in 1689 had been sensible in their choice of the word 'deserted'. However, the pamphlet also contained an unusually pithy and lucid exposition of what could be called the general theory of the Revolution and the nature of contract:

By the Original Contract was meant the agreement that had always been between the kings and people of England, that the government should be a legal government. When this agreement was first made, and the particular form and nature of it in its infancy, are things as obscure as the beginning of [all] governments; but vestiges of it are to be found as far back as we can go, and it may be traced down through the whole history of England, and of the many wars and revolutions that have happened, to make it good, and in which kings have suffered expressly for breaking it. Besides, the thing itself is obvious everywhere in the frame of the government, for how came it to be a bounded limited monarchy, but that bounds and limits were agreed on? And whensoever this was first done, the Original Contract had then its rise and birth.

The author then invoked the aid of James I, who had believed in a 'paction made with his people by the laws', and stressed the importance of the coronation, both as a mutual oath-taking and as a vestigial election. 'The coronation oath', he said, 'and the oath of allegiance, are the seals of this contract.'

The constitution [he went on] comprehends the particular form and nature of the legal government in which the king and people are at any time agreed; which was the same with the Original Contract at first, and was expressed in the ancient fundamental laws made about that time, but which have been explained, and enlarged or restricted by the subsequent Magna Carta, and all other laws made since, to clear and fix the bounds of liberty and prerogative.

He admitted that the Commons' resolution of 28 January 1689 could have been more clearly worded, but he insisted that

> To subvert the constitution, to break the Original Contract, to violate the fundamental laws, are expressions that clear and strengthen one another, and not empty repetitions as is pretended... Allowing that the vote abounds in words, and that some men cannot or will not understand this Original Contract, yet the thing meant by the vote is otherwise plain.[38]

The other pamphlet, which purported to be *A Memorial Drawn by King William's Special Direction*,[39] revised and corrected by 'some of the wisest and worthiest ministers that our nation has produced in this age', employed a rather different approach. It said:

> The king does not think it proper or necessary for him to enter into the discussion of the lawfulness of the late Revolution; that has been copiously done already by men of those professions to whom the managing of such questions does belong, both with relation to the principles and rules of the Christian religion, and to the laws and constitution of these kingdoms.

And it simply went on,

> It is acknowledged by all, that the measure of obedience and subjection do vary in all nations, according to the diversity of their constitution; nor is it denied by any that have looked into the history of the laws of England, that the crown and the regal prerogative here are limited by law.

Of the Convention it said:

> The Convention came to a full resolution, and judged, that the late king had broke the Original Contract upon which this government was at first founded, and after that had abandoned it; so that it was necessary for them, being thus forsaken by him, to see to their own security.[40]

It also issued a firm rebuttal of the criticism usually levelled against Whig theory, that the Revolution of 1688 was a precedent for, and an encouragement to, subsequent revolutions. It made a careful distinction between 'the overthrowing the constitution and fundamentals of a government, and some lesser violations', and argued that resistance to the former had always been 'universally justified by the chief asserters of the sacredness of princes'.

It went on to argue that the conduct of King James, not a hostile conspiracy against him, had brought on the Revolution:

Nothing was done in the progress of the whole Revolution, but that which he made inevitable by some act or other of his own. It went not upon false suggestions, nor barely upon the pretence of redressing particular grievances, or some doubtful oppressions...it was the late king's throwing off the restraint of law, and his setting about a total subversion of the constitution, that drove the nation to extreme courses ...A revolution so brought about carries in it no precedent against the security of government, or the peace of mankind. That which an absolute necessity enforced at one time can be no warrant for irregular proceedings at any other time, unless it be where the like necessity shall require the like remedies.

Despite the sting in the tail, there is a clear indication that 1688 had been a once-for-all-time revolution. Indeed, the author took pains to drive this point home:

There is no great reason to think that these nations, which have been in all past times so careful to preserve their laws and liberties, should at any time hereafter come to lose all regard to them so entirely, as not to maintain a revolution which has secured them from imminent ruin, and has given their constitution such a confirmation, and such explanations, as the injustice and violence of the former reign had made necessary.[41]

To sum up, then, at this juncture (and again in 1705 and 1707, when the pamphlets concerned were published) the Whig establishment held that the Original Contract was a strictly historical, regularly renewable phenomenon, that the Revolution was virtually an act of self-defence, provoked by James II, who had saved everyone a great deal of trouble by withdrawing in circumstances which made his action tantamount to an abdication. It was now the permanent basis of the constitution, yet it offered no precedent for the future, unless another king should arise as tyrannical and irresponsible as James. There was no particular stress on popular rights, except as expressed through parliament.

Yet there is no doubt that throughout the 1690s opponents of the Whigs found it easy and plausible to label them as natural successors to the Puritans of the Interregnum, active republican sympathisers, fanatical devotees of the unlimited rights and coercive power of the whole body of the people, and advocates of rebellion against constituted government at the least excuse. Every Whig pamphleteer felt it necessary to rebut such accusations, yet at the end of it Somers had to admit that a Whig was still generally regarded as 'One who hates the power and prerogative of kings, and is perpetually raising factions in the state, in order to subvert monarchy and set up a popular government'.[42]

It is reasonable to suppose that this belief had some reference to the conduct of the Whig radicals in the Convention and after. They were characterised, even by one of their supporters, as being 'jealous of prerogative, affecting popularity, childishly fond of trifles, and tenacious of lawless liberty';[43] and the freedom with which they now criticised King William, whom they themselves had once greeted as England's 'great deliverer', roused understandable suspicions as to their loyalty to monarchy in general. They were also considered to be unduly obsessed with the merits of the Revolution, which the generality of men regarded as an act of necessity, but one of dubious propriety. Lord Halifax, forced out of office in 1690, 'complained most grievously to all his friends, that he found there was no contesting against the merit of rebellion'.[44] In 1695 he was still criticising those he called 'pretenders to exorbitant merit in the late Revolution'. 'The men who only carried mortar to the building', he wrote, 'when it is finished think they are ill dealt with if they are not made master workmen. They presently cry out, "The Original Contract is broken", if their merit is not rewarded at their own rate.'[45] The Tory James Drake recalled that 'For some years no man whose brains were settled was thought sufficiently sensible of the benefits of the Revolution, and the blessings of his Majesty's reign.'[46]

To this we must add a certain freedom of expression, and a looseness of ideas, amongst some pamphleteers.[47] And almost certainly speeches were made in the Commons now unknown to us, and perhaps even pamphlets published which have not survived. What we do know is that as early as 1692 William Sherlock was bemoaning certain 'loose notions of government and obedience' which were going the rounds, such as 'that all power is radically in the people, and therefore but a trust, which a prince must give an account of'. 'Nay,' he went on, 'there are some amongst us, who charge all men who deny this with being enemies to the constitution, and with reproaching the wisdom and justice of the nation in the late happy Revolution.' He assured his audience (the House of Commons) that "The late Revolution has made no alteration at all in the principles of government and obedience. It does not oblige us to own the superior power of the people over the king, which would be a very tottering foundation for monarchy, and could never support it long.'[48]

The very word 'people' had in fact acquired a somewhat sinister ring, and it is interesting to trace the manoeuvres by which James Tyrrell tried to define and limit it. In the third dialogue of the *Bibliotheca Politica* (1692) Meanwell, his Jacobite spokesman, argues that the people, or 'the mobile', will often rebel for insufficient reasons, particularly against taxes which seem to them unjust but which are in fact for the general good of the nation. Rather surprisingly, Tyrrell replies (through his mouthpiece, Freeman) that though the people lack exact and sophisticated political knowledge they have an instinct for the limits of oppression: 'Though this many-headed beast (as you commonly call them) the people cannot argue very subtly of the future consequences of things, yet they have a very nice and tender sense of feeling, and can very well tell, when they are so injured and oppressed that they can bear it no longer.'[49] Then he changes the subject, but Meanwell shortly returns to the attack with the remark that to make the people judges of their own oppression, and at the same time executioners, is a recipe for continual civil war and rebellion. This forces Freeman to shift ground. He argues that popular rebellions in the past, like Wat Tyler's or Jack Cade's, are something

'the rabble' is prone to, but they have never been supported
by the majority of the people. Constitutional resistance is
something backed by 'the whole people, or the major part
of them, and in which I still include the nobility and gentry,
and other landholders, as the most considerable part'.[50] But
the question still worried Tyrrell, for after a long excursus
on English history at the beginning of the tenth dialogue
(1693) he inserted an 'advertisement' to this effect:

I desire the reader to remember that I do not make use of the word
people for the mere vulgar or mobile, but for the whole community,
consisting of clergy, nobility and commons.[51]

In the subsequent dialogue Meanwell is on top form,
arguing that Freeman is worse than Charles I's judges, for
they had presumed to judge their king only on the
authority of parliament, whereas he is claiming a right to
judge all kings by reference to 'the diffusive body of the
people':

And this [he goes on] upon account of I know not what Original
Contract...so that I do not now wonder that the gentlemen of your
principles are so violent for this right of resistance, since it is only in
order to introduce your darling doctrine of the people's power of
deposing or laying aside their kings (as you term it) whenever they shall
judge they turn tyrants, and have thereby forfeited their crowns, which
is a most dangerous doctrine; and if it should take effect, the princes
of the world had need to look about them, since the people may take
up such a pretence (for ought I know) even against the very best of them
that are now regnant in Europe.

In reply Freeman does in fact assert that it is better to put
the responsibility for such things

in the whole or diffusive body of the people, rather than in the parliament, or great council of the nation; for as to your assertion that the
whole people are more fallible, and consequently more dangerous
judges in such a case...I deny it, since all matters of fact must be so
evident and notorious to the senses and feeling of the greater part of
the people that there can be no doubt or denial of it by any reasonable
or indifferent judges; and the greatest part of the people are willing to
live in peace, without making any disturbance or alteration in the
government, if it may be avoided; whereas in any great assembly or
council there are many...who are governed by faction, ambition or
self-interest.[52]

However, by the time Tyrrell came to the eleventh dialogue in 1694 he had arrived at a new definition of the 'people'. When Meanwell argues that it is ridiculous and illogical to make the crown 'forfeitable to the people, who are and ever were subjects', Freeman replies,

I do not suppose this forfeiture to be made to the people as subjects, but to them considered as a community of masters of families and freemen, who as descendants and representatives of those who made the first king upon a certain contract, or condition[al] upon the non-performance of this Original Contract, do thereupon cease to be subjects, as a servant ceases to be so, and becomes again *sui juris* upon his master's non-performance of the bargain made between them; and so, this authority once forfeited returns to the community of masters of families and freemen who once conferred it upon the first king.[53]

And he later elaborates this as follows:

Since civil authority proceeds from the non-resistance of the subjects, and the concession that the supreme power should freely dispose of their bodies and goods for the public safety, it plainly appears, that in each particular master of a family and freemen there lay (though hidden and dispersed) the seeds or rudiments of supreme power, which by mutual compacts did grow into a perfect civil authority.

He protects himself further by admitting that

This resistance is never to be made but when this violent breach of the laws becomes evident and undeniable, not to the rabble alone but to the whole nation, that is, all sorts and degrees of men.[54]

Tyrrell also took care to insert another 'advertisement' at the front of the collected edition of *Bibliotheca Politica*, repeating his new definition:

I desire always to be understood, that when I make use of the word people, I do not mean the vulgar or mixed multitude, but in the state of nature the whole body of free-men and women, especially the fathers and masters of families; and in a civil state all degrees of men, as well the nobility and clergy as the common people.

But when he came to write his *General History of England* he was still plagued by the same problem, and we find him breaking off a learned discussion of the Anglo-Saxon Witanegemot to 'disown the thoughts of introducing any degrees or orders of men less than those of quality and

estates into the great councils of those times'.[55] This
preoccupation with a certain definition of the people has
caused Tyrrell to be labelled 'aristocratic'.[56]

Yet it was impossible to deny that if republican theories
of government and atheistical notions in religion were
associated with any party it was certainly not with the
Tories. Even Burnet said darkly of some of the Commons
Whigs in 1698, 'Many of them had indeed some popular
notions, which they had drank in under a bad government,
and thought they ought to keep them under a good one.'[57]
Moreover, with the approach of the Peace of Ryswick in
1697 there was a notable revival of religious and political
controversy. Inspired by their success in restraining the size
of the standing army in 1698 and 1699, the Country Whigs
took fresh heart, and gloated at the downfall of their more
worldly brethren of the Junto; the High Church revival
began with Atterbury's *Letter to a Convocation Man* in 1697;
even the Roman Catholics enjoyed a brief Indian summer
which provoked parliament into passing the last penal
statute, in 1700.

Unfortunately, the Whig revanche was almost from the
beginning entangled with questions of religion, and associated with the Deism and Unitarianism which were causing
conservative Christians the most excruciating concern at
just this time. In 1695, John Locke, whose authorship of
the *Two Treatises of Government* was now an open secret,
published *The Reasonableness of Christianity*, in which he
tried to whittle down the obligations of faith to a simple
belief in the atonement of Jesus Christ and the omnipo-
tency of God the Father. The resultant storm was exacerbated by John Toland's *Christianity Not Mysterious* (1696),
which argued for a faith almost devoid of spirituality and
hinging on social conscience.[58] A renegade Irish Catholic,
Toland claimed Locke as his mentor – a compliment indig-
nantly rejected – and over the next four years he became
ever more closely associated with political Whiggism. His
Life of Milton (1699) contrived to give the deepest offence
on political as well as religious grounds,[59] but he cheerfully

went on to publish in 1700 a new edition of James Harrington's *The Commonwealth of Oceana* (1656), dedicated to the Whig mayor and aldermen of London. He was a true prophet when he said in the preface to this last,

Some people...will not fail with open mouths to proclaim that this is a seditious attempt against the very being of monarchy, and that there's a pernicious design on foot of speedily introducing a republican form of government into the Britannic islands, in order to which the person (continue they) whom they have for some time distinguished as a zealous promoter of this case, has now published the life and works of Harrington, who was the greatest commonwealthsman in the world.[60]

His only error lay in underestimating the subsequent furore. Yet in 1701 he was chosen to accompany the Earl of Macclesfield to Hanover, to present a copy of the Act of Settlement to the Electress Sophia, who was demonstrably captivated by his wit and learning.

It is also natural (though the case is not proved) to associate Toland with two other publications of 1698: the first edition of Edmund Ludlow's *Memoirs*, ruthlessly edited, which were greeted as a blatant apologia for regicide and republicanism, and Algernon Sidney's *Discourses concerning Government*.[61]

The *Discourses* re-established Sidney's posthumous prestige. He would always be associated in the public mind with extreme republicanism, but he had undoubtedly suffered as a martyr in the cause of liberty, define 'liberty' how you will, and he had been a practising politician of great experience and a scion of the nobility. This lent his words an authority denied to middle-class intellectuals and journalists like Toland and Locke, and for the rest of this period his *Discourses* were certainly much more influential than Locke's *Two Treatises*.[62] They were much less abstract, and drew upon a wide range of historical analysis, and they were couched in a much superior literary style.

Yet they could only serve to confirm the popular association between Whiggism and the people's rights. Sidney was no more willing than Locke to define the 'people' whose authority lay behind parliament's. In one instance he remarked that by 'the people' he meant the 'freemen', but the precise meaning he attached to this term is still in doubt. He could have meant 'freeholders', but his pre-occupation with Roman history makes it not at all impossible that he meant 'free men' as against slaves, which would have implied universal manhood suffrage.[63] He also spoke freely of 'the multitude', denying that it could ever be sedition for this multitude to set up a new commonwealth, for 'till the commonwealth be established, no multitude can be seditious, because they are not subject to any human law'; and in the context it is clear that he was thinking not merely of the original foundation of political society, but of revolutions in established states. Elsewhere he baldly announced, 'The general revolt of a nation cannot be called a rebellion.'[64] Moreover, from a close study of Roman history he came to the conclusion that such periodic revolutions were positively advantageous, and a symptom of political health and well-being. 'All human constitutions', he wrote, 'are subject to corruptions, and must perish, unless they are timely renewed, and reduced to their first principles'; and the heading of this section of the *Discourses* is 'There is no disorder or prejudice in changing the name or number of magistrates while the root and principle of their power continues entire.' Another heading reads 'Good governments admit of changes in the superstructure, whilst the foundations remain unchangeable.'[65]

Of course, this was a theory of the constitution which had had some earlier currency. John Pym outlined it as early as 1628, at Manwaring's impeachment; it was argued by the Marquess of Halifax in 1684, the year of Sidney's execution;[66] and it was one followed by Edmund Burke, though perhaps in a more evolutionary way. However, just as Burke recognised the potential danger of such theories after 1789, similarly after 1689 too many writers, it was thought, were invoking 'the people' in a loose or anarchic way. The author of *Considerations on the Nature of Parliaments* (1698) believed that 'the last Revolution was the work of the people of England', and if succeeding parliaments had not established those rights and liberties 'for which the people drew their swords, it must be concluded those assemblies did not truly represent the people'.[67] True, the author called for 'a free unengaged House of Commons, consisting of the rich, honest and able men of the kingdom', which was reassuring enough; but *The Claims of the People of England Essayed* (1701) harked back to the Nineteen Propositions of 1642, arguing that parliament should elect ministers of state and exercise a veto over appointments to office, and this on the assumption that 'the common people of England' were politically trained by virtue of their long apprenticeship to local government.[68] The egregious Toland, refreshed by a reading of Sidney, came back into print in 1701 with *The Art of Governing by Parties*, a long pamphlet full of internal contradictions. It was dedicated to William III, but it was scathingly critical of Charles II and James II, and accused the Junto of turning William into a monarch of the same type:

Some of those surly Whigs grew by degrees the most pliant gentlemen imaginable; they could think no revenue too great for the king, nor would suffer his prerogative to be lessened, they were on frivolous pretensions for keeping up a standing army to our further peril and charge, they filled all the places in their disposal with their own creatures, combined together for their common immunity, whoever found fault with their conduct they represented him as an enemy to the government, and even opposed the best of laws, lest the Tories, as they said, should partake of the benefit.[69]

He went on to criticise ministerial corruption, and re-marked that Sidney (*Discourses*, sect. II. 25) had shown 'that the senates of free governments are not so subject to venality as the courts of princes'.[70] In fact, the tract grew steadily more anti-monarchical as it went on. In the beginning Toland argued that the term 'commonwealthsman' had been abused; 'commonwealth' was only a synonym for 'government' or 'political society', and therefore a commonwealthsman was only a responsible patriot; but towards the end he forgot himself, and launched upon a peroration which could have only one meaning: 'A commonwealth is never in love, and so cannot be seduced by fine women; a commonwealth is never a minor, nor subject to the doting of old age; a commonwealth has no favourites, and cannot be deceived by ministers to a party; a commonwealth cannot marry a popish queen', and so on.[71] He closed with a specific demand for the thorough reform of the electoral system, a demand echoed by other pamphleteers, who were shocked at the corruption produced by the implementation of the Triennial Act and the intensification of party disputes.[72]

Nor did republicanism have to be overt. John Pocock reminds us that the theory of a balanced constitution, with power shared by king, lords and commons, was essentially republican, and this was a theory which was increasingly canvassed at this time, particularly by reference to Charles I's Answer to the Nineteen Propositions of 1642.[73] The old 'classical republicans', like Walter Moyle, sought it in the history of Greece, Rome or Venice; in 1698 and 1699 Moyle was composing his two 'Essays' in praise of ancient republicanism, 'On the Lacedaemonian Government' and 'On the Constitution of the Roman Government', though neither was published for many years.[74] Country Whigs like Trenchard embraced it under the pressure of the standing army controversy.[75] It even inspired the young Jonathan Swift, who chose as the subject of his first pamphlet in 1701 *The Contests and Dissensions between the Nobles and the Commons in Athens and Rome*. He began:

'Tis agreed that in all government there is an absolute unlimited power, which naturally and originally seems to be placed in the whole body, wherever the executive part of it lies...This unlimited power, placed fundamentally in the body of a people, is what the legislators of all ages have endeavoured in their several schemes or institutions of government to deposit in such hands as would preserve the people from rapine and oppression within, as well as violence from without ...It was a trust too great to be committed to any one man or assembly, and therefore they left the right still in the whole body, but the administration or executive part in the hands of one, the few or the many.[76]

The advantage of ancient history was that one could discuss such alternative schemes with impunity, but in the real world of politics there was still much confusion. When in 1702 the Tories tried to incorporate in the abjuration oath a declaration maintaining the present government by king, lords and commons they did so 'to prevent a common-wealth', but Burnet denounced it as 'a bare-faced republican notion'.[77]

Ideological debate and party discontent were sharpened at this time by a number of extraneous factors. The king's refusal after 1697 to give his further confidence to the Junto or to construct a new ministry created an unsteadiness at the centre of power which communicated itself to the City, which was coping uncertainly with a return to peacetime conditions and was rent by feuds of its own. Broad-spectrum disagreements, over the standing army and Irish forfei-tures, encouraged party fragmentation; one observer listed 'State Whigs and Church Whigs, State Tories and Church Tories, King William's Tories and King James's Tories, Court Whigs and Country Whigs', to which should be added now 'Old Company men and New Company men, Old Ministry men and New Ministry men, and under-spur leathers to both', and even more up to date, 'Addressers and Non-Addressers'.[78] Bishop Burnet, from the stand-point of 1708, lamented the situation with his usual exaggeration:

We were become already more than half a commonwealth, since the government was plainly in the hands of the House of Commons, who must sit once a year, and as long as they thought fit, while the king had only the civil list for life...The Act for triennial parliaments kept up a standing faction in every county and town of England; but though we were falling insensibly into a democracy, we had not learned the virtues that are necessary for that sort of government; luxury, vanity and ambition increased daily, and our animosities were come to a great height, and gave us dismal apprehensions.

(A 'reverie and outcry' for which he was sturdily reproved by Speaker Onslow.)[79]

The death of Anne's son, the Duke of Gloucester, in 1700, and of her father James II in 1701, were climacteric events, which brought to the forefront once more the problem of the succession, and therefore the problem of the Revolution. Nor was the debate closed in 1701, when parliament plumped for the Hanoverian line. The Old Pretender was a more attractive proposition than his father, and untainted by his sins; the Hanoverians were unknown, or, insofar as they were known, unattractive. Their Lutheranism was as repellent to many Anglicans as James Francis Edward's Catholicism, and they were open to the same objections as King William, that they would drag England ever deeper into foreign entanglements, while at home they shamelessly pandered to Low Churchmen and Dissenters.

As for the Junto Whigs, they were already committed to the European policy of King William, so much so that Somers was generally credited with the authorship of *Anguis in Herba*, a famous restatement of the anti-French case published in 1701.[80] Moreover, the years 1700–1 saw a closing of the ranks. The dismissal of Somers in 1700, and the character assassination practised on the members of the Junto in tracts like Charles Davenant's *True Picture of a Modern Whig* (1701) and many more,[81] forced a break with the Country Whigs which had been impending for some years; this was the moment when Harley threw over his Whig–Dissenting heritage and moved across to take office with Godolphin and Rochester in 1701.[82]

Any likelihood of a reconciliation was destroyed by the impeachment of the Junto peers in 1701, which was, in the words of Geoffrey Holmes, 'a watershed of incalculable significance in post-Revolution politics'.[83] The quarrel between Lords and Commons, and the attempt to bring influence to bear on the Commons from outside, forced even the establishment Whigs to invoke popular rights in this heated and hysterical year. In *Jura Populi Anglicani* Somers denounced the parliament of 1701 as 'plainly popular', though MPs might assume 'the name of loyalists, and call others turbulent, seditious republicans'. Somers even embraced the ultra-radical doctrine, reminiscent of the Levellers, that the House of Commons was not representative of the people at all in a direct sense, and therefore was always subject to the popular will:

The House of Commons are not the whole people of England's representatives. It is very evident that the representatives of the people are those to whom, when they entered into society, they resigned up that power which they had in the state of nature, to punish offences against the law of nature, in prosecution of their own private judgment, and authorised to make laws for them, which are the rules to determine all controversies, and redress the injuries that may happen to any member of the commonwealth. Thus the society or, which is all one, the power legislative are the only representatives of the people. The Commons may be said to represent those freeholders, citizens and freemen who chose them, but what are they to the whole body of the people, who are represented in the political state, and are entitled to all the benefits and advantages of it?[84]

The Junto also had at their disposal one of the ablest journalists of the day. Despite the vast amount of work that has been done on Daniel Defoe, there is much in his life and work which is still mysterious. The thesis that he was in the direct employ of William III rests on casual statements made by Defoe himself many years later, and misunderstands the relations which could possibly exist between a reigning monarch and a low-born Dissenting journalist.[85] It is more reasonable to suppose that he was in the employ of the Junto, severally or collectively, and that he moved out with them in 1700; certainly it is difficult to imagine the king countenancing any of Defoe's writings over the next twelve months, or condoning his *Legion Memorial*.

In 1700, in response to the succession problem and the High Church revival, Defoe propounded a theory of the Revolution which was markedly Lockean in tone. What he said was:

The bringing government and obedience to the proper circumstances of mutual compact between king and people seems to me the only method to unravel this skein of tangled principles; the nature of government has made it the necessary consequence of all arguments relating to power; and I could give instances of all the nations in the world, that, some time or other, even the right of succession to government, which must be as sacred as the power, has been interrupted and limited by the people, in case of tyranny and illegal government; and every nation, and this among the rest, has oftentimes deposed their princes for the preservation of the state, when either incapacity for government, tyrannical usurpation, or other maladministration, has been the case.[86]

This theme was carried forward into his long poem *The True-Born Englishman*, in January 1701. This hymn of praise for King William justified revolt not only against King James but against his successors, though this may not have been Defoe's intention:

> But if the Mutual Contract was dissolved,
> The doubt's explained, the difficulty solved:
> That kings, when they descend to tyranny,
> Dissolve the bond, and leave the subject free.
> The government's ungirt when justice dies,
> And constitutions are nonentities.
> The nation's all a mob, there's no such thing
> As Lords or Commons, Parliament or King.
> A great promiscuous crowd the Hydra lies,
> Till laws revive, and mutual contract ties:
> A chaos free to choose for their own share,
> What case of government they choose to wear:
> If to a king they do the reins commit,
> All men are bound in conscience to submit:
> But then that king must by his oath assent
> To postulatas [conditions] of the government;
> Which if he breaks, he cuts off the entail,
> And power retreats to the original.[87]

Under the pressure of events in parliament as they unfolded, his attitude hardened, and his *Legion Memorial*, on 14 May 1701, put the populist case even more violently:

If the House of Commons, in breach of the laws and liberties of the people, do betray the trust reposed in them, and act negligently or arbitrarily or illegally, it is the undoubted right of the people of England to call them to an account for the same, and by convention, assembly, or force may proceed against them, as traitors and betrayers of their country.[88]

Later the same year he returned to the attack with *The Original Power of the Collective Body of the People of England Examined and Asserted*, in which he attributed William's title to the people – 'If *Vox Populi* be, as 'tis generally allowed, *Vox Dei*, your Majesty's right to these kingdoms, *jure divino*, is more plain than any of your predecessors.' He also put it as an axiom that

The good of the people governed is the end of all government, and the reason and original of governors; and upon this foundation it is that it has been the practice of all nations, and of this in particular, that if the maladministration of governors have extended to tyranny and oppression, to destruction of right and justice, overthrowing the constitution, and abusing the people, the people have thought it lawful to reassume the right of government into their own hands, and to reduce their governors to reason.

Developing this argument, he went on to say:

In this universal right of the people consists our general safety, for notwithstanding all the beauty of our constitution, and the exact symmetry of its parts, about which some have been so very elegant...the last resort had been to the people; Vox Dei has been found there, not in the representatives, but in their original, the represented.

And finally, the sovereign people were not to be expected to display the suavity of their so-called rulers; Sidney had called them a 'multitude', Defoe did not shrink from the word 'mob'. Harking back to 1689, he wrote:

The people assembled in an universal mob to take the right of government upon themselves are not to be supposed to give their personal suffrages to every article, but they may agree to a convention of such persons as they think fit to entrust, to constitute de novo, and may delegate their power, or part of it, to such a convention.[89]

So the reign of William closed in an atmosphere of unprecedented party contestation and bitterness. As one writer remarked in November 1701,

Is it not strange that such a wise and mighty nation, who have from time to time so gloriously asserted their liberties against foreign and domestic usurpations...should not yet know the true boundaries betwixt prerogative and property, but that we should be as ready to cut one another's throats, and fall to sides under the foolish names of Whig and Tory, as the Italians were formerly under the like pernicious distinctions of Guelphs and Ghibellines.[90]

Whig scholars like Tyrrell had set out to construct a historical justification for the Revolution of 1688, based upon an aristocratic constitution, but the alternative republican solution certainly enjoyed great publicity in the late 1690s, though what degree of support it enjoyed is uncertain. The establishment, or Junto, Whigs seemed to be drifting leftwards under the pressure of events in 1700 and 1701.

This apparent drift in Whig thinking stimulated still further a Tory revival which was well under way by 1700.

The new Toryism of the High Church movement did not at first question the Revolution itself; rather it questioned the use to which the Revolution had been put, and set out to prevent the encroachment of those associated evils, republicanism and atheism, now firmly identified with Whiggism.

5

KING CHARLES'S HEAD
The cult of divine right monarchy

The strength of the Tory revival in the late 1690s need not surprise us, for in England conservatism was still the natural political philosophy.

It is true that in the history of the West two main strands of political dogma have always been intertwined: government by authority, and government by consent. In fact, this extended back into Judaic history, and the Old Testament provides examples of both; for if David and Solomon were clearly absolute monarchs, the rule of Moses or the Judges was obviously by consultation or consensus. Despite the authoritarianism of the Tudors, the very existence of parliament demonstrated the survival of the idea of consent through English history, and there were, of course, in the Middle Ages many episodes which showed the ability and the willingness of the English to carry the idea to its logical conclusion, by deposing rulers who did not consult them, or were otherwise noxious. Edward II and Richard III were names much bandied about in 1689 and the succeeding years, and it was an inescapable fact that the establishment of the Tudor dynasty, and through it the Stuart, depended on the deposition of Richard III.

But it must be appreciated that such ideas were unnatural in a seventeenth-century context; they ran directly counter to the inbuilt assumptions of an age of deference – deference of wives to husbands, children to parents, servants to masters, tenants to gentry, gentry to nobility. These assumptions were firmly supported by the church, in its homilies and even in its catechism. It was difficult to believe that man was born to govern, not to be governed, that all men were equal, at least in the political sense, and that government was a secular convenience, not basic to human society and coeval with it, and not ordained and constantly monitored by Almighty God. It was not a coincidence, and certainly no contemporary regarded it as such, that the most advanced political thinkers of the period were deists (like John Toland), Dissenters (like Daniel Defoe) or reputed agnostics (like John Locke).

Moreover, if conservatism was the Englishman's natural political philosophy, Anglicanism was his natural religion, be he Whig or Tory; and Anglicanism, in its power structure and its ethos, remained intensely hierarchical.[1] It had retained virtually intact the disciplinary structure of the Roman Church, the king merely assuming to himself the absolute authority of the pope. From 1584 onwards church and monarchy had been united in defence of the Settlement, and the Civil Wars had cemented this alliance; indeed, insofar as it was provoked by religion at all, the Great Rebellion was directed not so much at the teaching of the church but at its command structure. By 1660 the church had made a huge investment in monarchical authority; an investment it was prepared to defend. On the other hand, Whiggism was discredited by its frenetic attempt to exclude James Duke of York from the succession during his brother's reign. Its principles of contract and popular rights had damaging associations with the Levellers and even with the Jesuits, who had used them to justify the deposition of heretic rulers. Even in the 1680s Locke and Sidney found themselves treading a narrow plank indeed between Filmer on the one hand and Cardinal Bellarmine on the other.

Sir Robert Filmer is a case in point. His *Patriarcha: A Defence of the Natural Power of Kings against the Unnatural Power of the People*, written during the Civil Wars, was first published in 1680 to counter the ideas of the Exclusionists. It put forward a theory which today seems patently absurd: that royal authority was based on the natural authority of

fathers over children, which was absolute and unquestioned, and that it had been handed down from Adam,
the first father, through the Patriarchs, the kings of Israel
and the Roman emperors, down to the present day. This
patriarchal theory was apparently demolished by John
Locke and others, and it is easy to assume that only fools
and knaves took Filmer seriously thereafter. But Peter
Laslett, and more recently Gordon Schochet, have shown
us that this simply was not so. More than a century later
Bentham made the celebrated remark: 'Filmer's origin of
government is exemplified everywhere: Locke's scheme of
government has not ever, to the knowledge of anybody,
been exemplified anywhere', and this attitude was, of
course, even stronger in the seventeenth century. Any
unbiassed study of the position shows in fact that it was
Filmer, not Hobbes, Locke or Sidney, who was the most
influential thinker of the age, and this was because he was,
in Laslett's words, 'that extremely rare phenomenon, the
codifier of conscious and unconscious prejudice'.[2] Filmer's
influence can be measured by the fact that both Locke's *Two
Treatises* and Sidney's *Discourses concerning Government* were
not so much independent and positive contributions to
political thought as elaborate refutations of his *Patriarcha*,
written soon after its first publication. Indeed, but for him
it is doubtful whether either book would have been
written, and certainly neither would have been written in
its present form.

In fact, patriarchalism survived the Revolution, and the
assaults of Locke and Sidney, with little apparent damage,
and under Queen Anne Filmer even enjoyed something
of a revival. In 1705 the non-juring polemicist Charles
Leslie devoted twelve successive issues of the weekly *Rehearsal* to an exposition of his doctrines, and subsequently
republished them in one volume, with the title *A Full
Answer to Mr Locke...and All Others Who Assert the Power
of the People: With a Short Account of the Original of Political
Government in the First Division of Nations after the Flood*; and
this was only part of what one historian has called Leslie's

'hysterical and brilliant ten-year polemic' against Locke.[3] As late as 1709, when Benjamin Hoadly published his considered defence of contract theory, *The Original and Institution of Civil Government Discussed*, he still felt it necessary to follow Locke's plan in the *Two Treatises*, and devote half the book to a step-by-step refutation of patriarchalism before proceeding to more positive arguments. At Sacheverell's trial the following year one of the Whig managers still characterised patriarchalism as 'that absurd yet dangerous opinion'.[4]

In these circumstances, the fact that a majority of Anglicans, probably dazed by the speed of events, had accepted the Revolution and taken the new oaths was only a short-term victory, the capture by shock assault of the first line of defence. It might have been consolidated had theorists been able to produce at once a justification of the Revolution acceptable to the Anglican conscience. But as we have seen, the best they could offer was a neo-Hobbesian theory of *de facto* obedience which was singularly lacking in spirituality or moral authority. And though Whig theorists called their attention to the facts of medieval history, Anglicans were drawn to a contemplation of much more recent events.

For the shock wave set up by the Great Rebellion and the execution of Charles I was far from having ebbed by the 1690s. Naturally Charles's death on the scaffold in 1649 had intensified the church's belief in passive obedience, almost to the pitch of hysteria; nor was this hysteria confined to the church. In 1661 parliament imposed on all clergy and office-holders the famous non-resistance oath – 'that it is not lawful upon any pretence whatsoever to take arms against the king' – and in the Act establishing the day of the late king's death, 30 January, as a fast in perpetuity, it committed itself to a singularly sweeping and comprehensive self-denying ordinance:

That by the undoubted and fundamental laws of this kingdom, neither the peers of this realm nor the Commons, nor both together, in parliament or out of parliament, nor the people, collectively or representatively, nor any other persons whatsoever, ever had, hath, have or ought to have any coercive power over the persons of the kings of this realm.[5]

(As a statutory affirmation of parliament, this was difficult indeed to get over, and James Tyrrell devoted much anxious space to the matter in *Bibliotheca Politica*.)[6]

In fact, the effect of the Restoration was to popularise the extreme doctrine of the divine right of kings adopted by a minority of churchmen under Charles I, and enshrined in the notorious Canon 1 of 1640, 'Concerning the Regal Power':

The most high and sacred order of kings is of divine right, being the ordinance of God Himself, founded in the prime laws of nature, and clearly established by express texts both of the Old and New Testaments. A supreme power is given to this most excellent order by God Himself in the Scriptures, which is, that kings should rule and command in their several dominions all persons of what rank or estate soever, whether ecclesiastical or civil, and that they should restrain and punish with the temporal sword all stubborn and wicked doers... For subjects to bear arms against their kings, offensive or defensive, upon any pretence whatsoever, is at least to resist the powers which are ordained of God; and though they do not invade but only resist, St Paul tells them plainly they shall receive to themselves damnation.[7]

As for the political uncertainties of Charles II's reign, they only confirmed and reinforced this attitude. The Exclusion Crisis swung the church decisively behind Charles and his brother James, and added to divine right and passive obedience the dogma of hereditary succession, according to which the crown must descend in the right line by blood, even if this meant, as in this case, the accession of a Roman Catholic. The Rye House Plot of 1683 was another incentive to blind obedience, and in particular it provoked the notorious Oxford decrees of 21 July 1683, 'against certain pernicious books and damnable doctrines, destructive to the sacred persons of princes, their state and government, and of all human society'. These put the premier teaching institution in the country, and the intellectual centre of the church, firmly against all notions of popular resistance or consent, and firmly in favour of passive obedience, an obedience 'clear, absolute, and without exception of any state or order of men', which was declared to be 'the badge and character of the Church of England'.[8] These decrees were neither repealed nor modified after the Revolution, and it was said they were still posted on the notice boards of some Oxford colleges well into Anne's reign. Certainly one earnest soul thought to confute Hoadly in 1710 simply by citing them.[9] In this context it was difficult to explain away the conduct of the bishops in 1688, especially since contemporaries seem to have assumed that Compton was not the only one involved in the deeper intrigues of the Revolution.

But the more we study the controversial literature of this period, the more central does the execution of Charles I appear: this was the hinge on which the century swung. For if this was wrong, it was difficult to resist the conclusion that the nation's treatment of James II was wrong, too; conversely, if the Revolution could be justified, so could Charles's death, and along much the same lines. In fact, the indictment of Charles I in 1649 employed arguments freely used against his son in 1689; that he was 'trusted with a limited power to govern by and according to the laws of the land and not otherwise, and by his trust, oath and office [was]...obliged to use the power committed to him for the good and benefit of the people, and for the preservation of their rights and liberties'. Instead he had conceived 'a wicked design to erect and uphold in himself an unlimited and tyrannical power, to rule according to his will'.[10]

Therefore it was no accident that immediately after the Revolution there broke out a fierce debate on the authenticity of the famous *Eikon Basiliké*, 'The Portraiture of His Sacred Majesty in His Solitude and Sufferings', which was supposed to have been written by the king himself during his imprisonment by the army. Published immediately after his death, it at once established itself as a bestseller, and deservedly so. The rather mawkish and self-pitying effusions under the name of 'prayers', which end each short chapter, have caused it to be dismissed too easily as an exercise in sentimental pietism, but Charles's more mundane reflections on his confrontations with parliament since 1640 constitute a political testament unique in the history of English kingship, and as skilfully composed as his famous scaffold speech in 1649. It avoided the mistake of representing his opponents as wilfully evil; instead they were acknowledged to be sincere, though misguided. Nor did it pretend that his first concern was not for his own authority and pre-eminence. But it portrayed him as a wise and just ruler, deeply concerned for the welfare of his people, whose mistakes – mainly induced by his advisers – had been exaggerated beyond recognition, so that the many concessions he had been willing to make at every stage had been thrown back in his face. The man who emerged was not weak in the usual sense in which we regard Charles I, petulant, obstinate and wilful, but weak in the sense that he had made too many concessions in an attempt to pacify an ungrateful multitude and avert civil war. It was a view which had a profound influence on the next generation; certainly it coloured James II's attitude to his father.[11]

But in 1690 'some rude and undutiful spirits' produced evidence to suggest that the *Eikon Basiliké* had in fact been written by one of the king's chaplains, Francis Gauden, and that Charles II and James II knew this very well. The battle on this one issue raged right through William's reign and on into Anne's, without reaching any significant conclusion. Against the High Church champions, marshalled and presumably subsidised by the second Earl of Clarendon, and led by Thomas Long and Richard Hollingsworth, was ranged a motley company of anonymous and pseudonymous detractors, many of them sheltering under the name of the great regicide Edmund Ludlow, who had died in fact in 1692. Milton was resurrected, too, to play Satan to Charles's God; his *Eikonoklastes* (1649), and other violently regicide tracts of 1649 and 1650, were reprinted and also freely plagiarised. Conversely, on the strength of his Answer to the Nineteen Propositions and other conciliatory statements made in 1642, Charles could be portrayed as an advocate of limited monarchy – an argument used by the Whigs to recruit him to their ranks, and by the Tories to emphasise the injustice of the proceedings against him. Thus, all the issues of the Civil Wars and Interregnum were rehearsed and re-rehearsed with the utmost vigour and intolerance. Indeed, whether the events of the 1640s had been a rebellion or a civil war was still in dispute. In the Convention debates of 1689 the veteran Presbyterian, Philip Lord Wharton, demanded that Lord Clarendon be brought to the bar of the House of Lords 'for calling the Civil War a rebellion'; yet in 1706 the House of Commons, considering a bill sent down from the Lords, amended a phrase in the preamble to read 'the late unhappy Rebellion', instead of 'the late unhappy Civil Wars'.[12]

This controversy has been charted to some extent by Francis Madan and George Sensebaugh.[13] In his bibliography of the *Eikon Basiliké* Madan lists twenty-two separate works published between 1690 and 1703 bearing on the question of its authorship.[14] But this is not a comprehensive listing, for Madan does not claim to deal with books relating to Charles I in general terms, of which there were several; in fact, scarcely a year passed which did not bring forth a book for or against him.[15] Yet nobody on either side doubted for a moment the importance of such labours, or their direct relevance to current issues. As one of Clarendon's correspondents wrote,

The same spirit be very active and vigorous in these men, [whom] that book is wrote for; they are the same, they are worse...They together with their friends murdered one of the best of kings, and therefore I do not wonder that [they] will not allow the *Eikon Basiliké* to be of the king's writing, because of the shame and confusion that would attend them.[16]

In 1698 the memoirs of Edmund Ludlow were published, which created a sufficient storm, but the climax was reached in 1699, with the publication of Toland's new *Life of Milton*, which tried to claim Charles I as a deist. ''Tis most probable', said Toland, 'the opinion which his intimate friends had of him was too true, that he was really of neither church

[Rome or Canterbury], but believed the pretences of both to be credulity or craft; and that the transactions of his last minutes were only the effect of a weak mind in a distempered body.'[17]

Naturally, this impertinent squib set the pulpits gibbering, but in fact the mythic reputation of Charles I could not be substantially dented, even by the later revelations of Clarendon's *History of the Rebellion and Civil Wars in England*. Further reprints of the *Eikon Basiliké* were called for in 1693 and 1706, and any current political dispute was likely to swoop back without notice to the 1640s and 1650s, where the contestants had to fight the Civil Wars all over again. We have seen this happen to William Sherlock,[18] and it happened to James Tyrrell, too. In 1702, eight years after he had apparently abandoned political theory in favour of history, Tyrrell suddenly published an additional dialogue, the fourteenth, of *Bibliotheca Politica*, 'showing', ran the sub-title, 'that the arraigning and murder of King Charles I can by no means be justified by the proceedings of the Convention Parliament against King James II, upon his abdication, the grounds and manner thereof being wholly different'.

This was a proposition easier to state than prove, yet the official doctrine of church and state was that Charles's execution had been a vile and impious murder, his trial not only illegal but blasphemous. The statute of 1661 continued to impose a solemn fast on 30 January each year (or the 31st if the 30th fell on a Sunday). Lords and Commons even observed it in January 1689, at the height of the Revolution crisis, and though the Lords did meet in the afternoon, after a morning service in the Abbey, this bold experiment was not repeated. On this day, every year, all members of the Church of England, headed by king, Lords and Commons, participated in a special service whose language left no doubt of the nation's inexpiable sin:

We thy sinful creatures here assembled before thee, do, in the behalf of all the people of this land, humbly confess, that they were the crying sins of this nation which brought down this heavy judgment upon us.

But thou, O gracious God, when thou makest inquisition for blood, lay not the guilt of this innocent blood (the shedding whereof nothing but the blood of thy Son can expiate), lay it not to the charge of the people of this land, nor let it ever be required of us or our posterity.

Nor was the obvious comparison with Jesus Christ left to the imagination:

We magnify thy name for thine abundant grace bestowed upon our martyred sovereign; by which he was enabled so cheerfully to follow the steps of his blessed Master and Saviour, in a constant meek suffering of all barbarous indignities, and at last resisting unto blood; and even then, according to the same pattern, praying for his enemies.

They then heard the Epistle for the day, which was 1 Peter 2:13, only slightly less famous than Romans 13:1: 'Submit yourself to every ordinance of man for the Lord's sake, whether it be to the king, as supreme, or unto governors, as unto them that are sent by him'; and for the Gospel the parable of the homicidal husbandman (Matt. 21:33). Finally, the officiating clergyman had to read out the first and second parts of the Elizabethan homily 'against disobedience and wilful rebellion', composed in the aftermath of the Northern Rebellion of 1569, whose drift can be imagined; or else he could 'preach a sermon of his own composing upon the same argument'. (Incidentally, the same directions were given to the preacher on 5 November, despite the fact that this festival now commemorated the Revolution of 1688 as well as the frustration of the Gunpowder Plot!)

The opportunity this gave for High Church rant can well be imagined, and the festival was soon known to the Whigs as 'the General Madding Day'. As early as 1694 proposals were being put forward for its abolition,[19] together with the thanksgiving day for the Restoration of 1660, 29 May, but there is no evidence that this was ever seriously debated in parliament, even in May 1702, when the House of Lords severely censured William Binckes for his 30 January sermon before Convocation, as containing 'several expressions that give just scandal and offence to all Christian people'. (He had fallen into the trap of comparing Charles's ordeal with that of Christ at Calvary, rather to Christ's disadvantage, it seems, though his prose is the reverse of lucid.)[20] At the same time the Lords ordered a pamphlet critical of Binckes, *Animadversions on the Two Last 30th January Sermons*, to be burnt as 'a malicious, villainous libel, containing very many reflections on King Charles the First of ever blessed memory, and tending to the subversion of the monarchy'.[21] In fact, this was one of the very few Whig tracts in this period that attempted to justify the actual legality of the king's trial, on the grounds that he had broken his contract with his people, and government had therefore been dissolved: 'In such a case the law of nature takes place, according to which every man may do himself right upon those who do him wrong.'[22] Others were content to argue that Charles had been a mere puppet in the hands of evil advisers, notably the clergy. All the same, these *Animadversions* were boldly reprinted in *State Tracts* in 1707.

We are handicapped in our study of this question by the fact that only a small minority of such sermons, and usually those delivered before parliament or the monarch, or by a noted preacher like White Kennett or Luke Milbourne, found their way into print, and even these may have been doctored.[23] The glimpses we catch of sermons which remained unpublished are often quite hair-raising. For instance, at Deptford in 1694 John Evelyn heard a young clergyman preach an excellent sermon which was pure Filmer, showing 'the excellency of kingly government above all other, deriving it from Adam, the Patriarchs, God Himself', and so on. 'There were also many passages in this sermon, nearly touching the dethroning K[ing] James, not easily to be answered.'[24] Nor was this bold young man alone. In 1697 Evelyn even heard a bishop (unnamed) preach a staunchly patriarchalist sermon on 5 November at Whitehall, in the presence of the Bishop of London and the Archbishop of Canterbury.[25] In 1707 a London grand jury found a true bill against 'Mr Higgins, an Irish prebend' for preaching an Ash Wednesday sermon at Whitehall in which he said that 'such as those that brought the royal martyr to the scaffold and the block are now preferred to the greater places of trust in the kingdom'. Presumably the queen felt committed, for the attorney-general entered a *nolle prosequi*.[26] In the provinces even wilder excesses were committed; on 30 January 1709 an Exeter clergyman was reported as preaching 'that the Dissenters had murdered more persons than the heathens and the papists together', that 'they would kill the queen as they had killed the king, if they could', and 'they deserved to be boiled alive'.[27]

Yet even the Commons had to accustom themselves to strong language on this anniversary, and 'Turkish' ideas on government. For example, in 1697 William Lancaster, vicar of St Martin-in-the-Fields, told them,

I know not but there may be men in the world, thus left to themselves, who instead of repenting of a most horrid murder, and of shedding innocent blood, have themselves and their posterity justified the doing it, and advanced from the blood of one king, to maintain the lawfulness of resisting all kings.

But, he warned them,

Resisting is a comprehensive word, and includes in it reviling and slandering, deposing and putting to death...Any or all of these are lawful to as many as believe it lawful to resist.

And he concluded:

I wish that sort of men would deal fairly, and instead of vending among the people these jesuitical notions and speculations, they would go directly to the prince's chamber, and tell him, and give him timely notice to look to himself; for that they will rebel when they please, and themselves are the proper judges of their own time.[28]

Nor was the theme of guilt, the concept of an Old Testament Jehovah visiting the sins of the fathers on generations yet unborn, ever very far away. Even a Whig cleric like Robert Wynne, cautiously preaching to the Commons on 31 January 1704 on the theme 'Endeavouring to keep the unity of the spirit in the bond of peace', hoped 'that our deserved doom may not still be in reserve, and that the great and fatal blow from heaven for our sins may not be yet to come'.[29]

In fact, although the bishops who preached before the

Lords did so with predictable moderation, and even some statesmanship,[30] the Commons were served by a succession of men who were prepared to toe the High Church line, and this did not vary very much whether the House at any given time was supposedly Whig or Tory. Apart from the scandal of 1710, which is part of the story of Sacheverell's trial,[31] the only untoward incident was in 1700, when a group of radical Members nominated William Stephens, rector of Sutton, Surrey, who was reputed to be a renegade Dissenter. He opened with the statement that he did not intend to discuss Charles I at all, 'for to insist on the dismal effects of this day's tragedy (with which you have been annually acquainted all your lives) would be superfluous labour'. He then preached – successfully, to his own mind at least – 'to take away that scandal which some have endeavoured to fix upon the Church of England, as if she has laid any obligation upon her sons, in opposition to the present constitution', and he deprecated the use to which the anniversary was being put:

God forbid that this day of solemn humiliation should be made use of to flatter princes with notions of arbitrary power, by drawing any conclusions from the ancient government of God's peculiar people which may colour over modern tyranny... To entertain people with the melancholy thoughts of fetters and chains, which when laid upon them by ill princes, yet they must not endeavour to remove under penalty of eternal damnation, tends only to exasperate human nature.[32]

He certainly succeeded in exasperating the Tories, who denounced the performance as one 'which might have fitted the mouth of a Knox, or a Mariana, but ill became one who would be thought a minister of Jesus Christ, and a true son of the Church of England'.[33] The House of Commons agreed. The usual motion to express thanks and desire him to print his sermon was opposed, an occurrence without precedent, and on a division it was defeated. The House further resolved to invite no one to preach before it henceforward who was 'under the dignity of a Dean in the church, or hath not taken his degree of Doctor of Divinity'.[34]

Stephens was unrepentant, and could afford to be. He sold his manuscript to a bookseller for £25, a large sum for one sermon, and he even brought out a revised version in 1703, trying to pass it off as the sermon delivered to the Commons for that year.[35] Yet the difficulty of coping with 30 January was a very real one for any conscientious Whig divine. Benjamin Hoadly could hardly find anything rational to say on that day which would not betray his conscience or his principles; in 1703 he preached on the Christian virtue of moderation, and in 1709 on 'the divine overruling of the actions of men'.[36] John Tyler, Bishop of Llandaff, preaching to the Lords in 1707, merely used the career of Charles I to illustrate the argument that no earthly dignity, however exalted, could protect a mortal man against the ultimate misfortune, and only righteousness offered an assurance of permanent happiness, and then in the next world. In 1708 Charles Trimnell slid over the anniversary by preaching a farewell sermon to his parishioners at St James's, Westminster, on his elevation to the Bishopric of Norwich. When he threw caution to the winds in 1712, and preached to the House of Lords what Swift described as 'a terrible Whig sermon', he was not desired by their lordships to print it, but he had to publish it himself to meet the attacks made upon him, even in his own diocese.[37] Yet all he had done was to argue that resistance to sovereigns was justified in extraordinary crises, though not in Charles I's case. He went on,

What sort of violations of the whole constitution infer such a dissolution of government as will warrant the people to look more to the end than the words of the statutes, and to go out of the common forms of law and obedience, for preventing their otherwise unavoidable ruin, is as needless as it is invidious to determine beforehand, or when that particular question is not before us. Such extraordinary cases, whenever they happen or are brought into dispute, will speak for themselves; as that of the late wonderful Revolution did and always will do. And whoever shall compare that favourable and providential change to the heinous offence of this day, from which it widely differs in the occasion and manner of its being pursued, the persons concerned, and every consequence of it, can neither do it with justice in itself, nor with any good will to our present happy establishment, which cannot but suffer by those who think them equally just, and those who think them equally wicked.[38]

But perhaps the most remarkable case is that of Gilbert Burnet. This redoubtable Whig, ever ready to preach on 29 May, or 5 November, or on the numerous thanksgiving days appointed for success in battle in two major wars, sedulously avoided 30 January; he must, of course, have delivered sermons on that day, but none were ever printed.[39] Undoubtedly he was wise. Other Whig divines, including Kennett and Nicholson, had the mortification of hearing their own past sermons on 'the King's Day' used by Sacheverell's counsel in 1710 to justify non-resistance.[40]

One obvious effect of the cult of Charles I was to lower the reputation of the Dissenters, which was already sinking at this time. None of the preachers before court or parliament dare make the obvious connexion, but in sermon after sermon the point is made that the execution of Charles was made possible only by Puritan deviation from established religion, and that those who derided Charles in this generation, or derided the observation of 30 January, were themselves of the same anti-monarchical taint. What is also noticeable in these sermons is an acute class consciousness. It was not only the King's execution that horrified these preachers, but the consequent inversion of the social order. Peter Birch told the Commons in 1694, 'We beheld servants on horses, and princes walking as servants on the earth.' Robert Moss read out to them in 1707 the words of Jeremiah (Lam. 5: 7), 'Servants have ruled over us; there is none that deliver us out of their hand', adding 'The estates of the realm were made slaves, and (which is the vilest of all servitude) slaves to their own servants.' Next year they were told by Robert Eyre that England under Cromwell had been 'a kingdom quite inverted, a body without a head, with its heels upwards, and the dregs of the people lording it over their betters and superiors'. 'Slaves became our princes', said Henry Brydges in 1709, 'and violence was in our streets.' A Layman's Lamentation on the Thirtieth of January... (1710), 'addressed to Mr

Hoadly, as a confutation of his principles, and written for the conversion of all such fanatical churchmen, as well as other rebellious miscreants, and sinful sons of Belial', elaborated the same theme:

When the nation then had lost its head, and its glory, 'twas turned with its heels upwards, and governed by a mock-monarchy, a thing as infamous in its quality as its name. The dregs of the populace, the creatures of a sectarian army, the worst part of a body, that was bad enough in its best; these were our senators and the saviours of the nation.[41]

Of course, it is difficult to be sure how widely or scrupulously the fast-day was observed. From the early 1690s onwards almost all preachers on 30 January lamented that laymen were increasingly ignoring these solemnities, or even deriding them. Hard evidence is sparse, but Roger Morrice notes that on 30 January 1689 most London shops were in fact open for business, though their windows were shuttered, and he attributes this slender degree of conformity to the action of the House of Commons in announcing beforehand that it would observe the fast itself.[42] This is no more than we would expect in an increasingly materialist age, but it roused the anger of a majority of clergymen who associated the contemporary decline in morals with a decline in religious observance, and equated both with the increase in political radicalism. It was also unfortunate that the Dissenters, though their meetings for worship were now legalised, were not obliged by the statue of 1661 to observe the day, and apparently none of them had the tact to do so. Even worse, there were reputed to be some miscreants so abandoned as to glory in the events commemorated on that day. As Offspring Blackall said, 'There are still some amongst us deeply tainted with those principles of sedition and rebellion which brought about this day's tragedy.'[43] Men reacted in horror to the fabled impieties of the Calves' Head Clubs, which met on 30 January for profane feastings and blasphemous rejoicings. 'O, may our souls never come into the secrets of such men', prayed Luke Milbourne, 'nor our honours be united in their assemblies'; and he gladly consigned them to eternal damnation, along with all 'our Knoxes, Buchanans, Miltons, Baxters, Sidneys, Lockes, and the like Agents of Darkness'.[44]

It is doubtful, in fact, if these Calves' Head Clubs ever existed at all. Charles Trimnell remarked in 1712 that it was 'more than I have yet found ground to affirm', and contemporary diaries, correspondence or newsletters fail to give any specific instances of such meetings. Whig journalists like Tutchin were as eager as their Tory counterparts to track down these reports, but they were always found to be baseless, and it must be assumed that Jacobite writers like Leslie would have been only too willing to give chapter and verse if they knew them. The whole story seems to have originated with an unbalanced Grub Street hack called Edward Ward. (He referred to Charles I's execution as 'the beloved act of decollation'.) He published at least nine successive editions of *The Secret History of the Calves Head Club* between 1703 and 1714,[45] but even he never gave any specific details of membership or meeting place, and the execrable doggerel he prints as typical of the republican hymns used on these occasions could surely never have been sung by anyone, except as a joke in poor taste.

Nevertheless, just as it was a dangerous anomaly that through 'the King's Day' the Church of England continued to be associated with the divine right of kings in its most extreme form, so the mounting backlash against those who criticised it was even more dangerous, because it identified Dissent and Whiggism on the one hand with revolutionary political ideology on the other. One author said as early as 1691,

The atheists, the Hobbists, the commonwealthsmen are all joined in one cry against the innocent doctrine of non-resistance...with equal noise and boldness, and he...that was a Trimmer in the time of Charles the Second, concerned in the Whig Plot, or the Monmouth Invasion, the Act of Exclusion, or the 41 Rebellion, thinks it is a matter of great reputation, or good qualification, to recommend him to the esteem of all sober men.[46]

Even more dangerous was the inevitable comparison made with the Revolution of 1688. The danger was seen even in 1689, when Defoe put forward the standard view of Charles I, and tried to detach him from the Revolution:

Certainly, nobody that can either consider or compare, can think the cases of 1648 and 1688 parallel. For the great (and I had almost said the only) fault of that good king, and true martyr, was his complying too much with his people, and yielding that to their importunity which both law and conscience told him he should not have consented to.[47]

But such mollifying words were of no avail. In 1704, in her reply to White Kennett's *Compassionate Enquiry into the Causes of the Civil War*, Mary Astell said,

A Dr Binks, a Mr Sherlock, a Bishop of St Asaph, and some few more, take occasion to preach upon this day such antiquated truths as might have passed upon the nation in the reign of King Charles II, or in Monmouth's Rebellion, but since that time have been quite out of fashion; since no revolution (except by foreign conquest) can be compassed, though ever so necessary, but upon those principles by which the Martyr lost his head.[48]

The hostile reception accorded the *Compassionate Enquiry*, preached at St Botolph's, Aldgate, on 31 January 1704, is significant.[49] It contained some dubious history, and Kennett's argument, that Charles's fall had its roots in 'French counsels' and a 'French alliance' dating from his disastrous marriage with a French queen, was rather too obviously directed against Louis XIV and intended to serve the present ministry. But his main offence was to argue that Charles's rule was tyrannical – though of course, this was the fault not of the good king himself but of his ministers – and to compare it with James II's:

We of yesterday remember that when an arbitrary executive power was much more effectually set up in a later reign, it broke short that reign; and for the future it shall never be attempted, without bringing down ruin and confusion upon those who shall attempt it.

He now thanked God that

Our rights have been retrieved by a signal Providence, and committed down to posterity, one would think, beyond a capacity of their ever being deprived of them. May we ourselves take heed, and teach our children to take heed, not to break nor to hurt our happy constitution.[50]

When he came to address the House of Commons on 30 January two years later his tone was much more moderate; so much so that the following passage was snapped up by Sacheverell's defending counsel in 1710:

The principles of government and obedience suffered extremely in the fatal causes and consequences of this day. Before the convulsions of those times the authority of princes and the subjection of peoples stood upon their right bottom, a power of governing and a duty of obeying and submitting, according to our legal constitution.

But he went on to remark that, on the other hand, the unrestrained preaching of passive obedience before the Civil Wars was one of the main causes of the conflict:

The tying of a knot too hard is the frequent cause of breaking the band asunder. They are the greatest enemies to sovereign power, who stretch it beyond the extent of legal constitution.[51]

Even today, he said, such preaching, popishly inspired, continued to threaten the Revolution of 1688:

They and others with them would again make the world believe that our late Revolution was but a sort of returning to this day; and they are still insinuating their odious comparisons, and are branding men with hard names for justifying the Providence of God, the wisdom of a nation, and the honour of a prince in our late glorious deliverance. A mercy which some of these very men have the conscience to submit to, and the comfort to enjoy; and yet they cast it in our teeth as a reproach to us...If they really mean that the same principles of asserting and restoring a legal constitution of church and state might as well justify the death of one prince as the abdication of another, it is a wrong argument of their own making; we know there was a vast disparity.[52]

It was, in fact, difficult to demonstrate this disparity; Kennett could only argue, with other Whig clergymen, that Charles's trial had been illegal, and James's deposition had not. The word 'deposition' was not actually used, but, on the other hand, no attempt was made, rather surprisingly, to plead James's 'abdication'. In fact, until it could be admitted that Charles I and James II were much of a muchness, Whig preaching on the Great Rebellion and the Revolution would remain a contradiction in terms, and there was considerable truth in Defoe's forthright remark,

The difference only lies here; the Whigs in 41 and 48 took up arms against their king, and having conquered him, and taken him prisoner cut off his head *because they had him*. The Church of England took up arms against their king in 88 and did not cut off his head *because* they had him not. King Charles lost his life *because he did not run away*, and his son, King James, saved his life, because he *did* run away.[53]

Conversely, the anniversary continued to be meat and drink to High-Flying divines, and an opportunity for the propagation of the most extreme principles. The annual sermons of Luke Milbourne, rector of St Ethelburga's, became something of an institution in Anne's reign, and the titles he chose for them tell their own story. In 1707 his subject was 'The People Not the Original of Civil Power', in 1710 'The Measures of Resistance to the Higher Powers, so far as Becomes a Christian', in 1711 'The Impiety and Folly of Resisting Governors by Force or Arms', in 1712 'The Curse of Regicides', in 1713 'A Guilty Conscience Makes a Rebel: or, Rulers No Terror to the Good Proved', and in 1714 'The Traitors' Reward, or A King's Death Revenged'.[54]

Clarendon's *History of the Rebellion and Civil Wars in England*, published in 1702, 1703 and 1704, might have been expected to redress the balance; it not only contained a reasoned critique of Charles I and his ministers, but it also read into the record an enormous mass of impartial fact about the Civil Wars, as well as a great deal of royalist prejudice. In the long run it certainly had an effect, and from the beginning it proved useful to Whig clergymen faced with the composition of a 30 January sermon.[55] But in the fevered atmosphere of Anne's reign it at once pandered to extreme Tory prejudices, and brought the old issue of the Rebellion right back to the forefront of current politics. As John Oldmixon remembered later,

Great was the consternation the Whigs were thrown into on the for-midable appearance of that History; and the vogue it got for its un-historical qualities, studied periods and florid narration at once took in unwary and unskilful readers to like the faults as well as the style. It had such a torrent of currency at first, that it bore down all before it.[56]

Clarendon had left the manuscript to his two sons, Henry, the second Earl, and Lawrence, now Earl of Rochester, with discretion to publish when they saw fit. They held back until William's death, though the younger Clarendon, we know, circulated it amongst his friends. In 1698 one of them returned it with the comment,

Were it seasonable to publish that admirable performance I am persuaded nothing would contribute more to bring all sorts of people to their senses again, by making them understand [that] the constitution and true interest of England is to stand by the laws and never pretend to be wiser than the laws. Now the great rock upon which our princes and parliaments have always split [is] this, a conceit of necessities, of exigencies, of an extraordinary case in which the laws must be suspended. This ruined King Charles the First, as my Lord Clarendon demonstrates; this embroiled both his sons, and made way for the same pretences to be set on foot by the people of dispensing with themselves for their legal obligations and their oaths.[57]

In the autumn of 1702, with Queen Anne on the throne, and Toryism apparently in the ascendant, the first volume at last appeared, and Lord Rochester could afford to write a temperate introduction, deploring in statesmanlike fashion the ill effects of party strife. Referring to the rebels of 1642, he said,

If at any time it might be hoped this dangerous generation of men should be discountenanced, one might be allowed to look for it in an age when a revolution hath been thought necessary to make a reformation; for where the foundations of the earth were taken to be out of course, more steadiness, a stricter virtue, and a more unblameable administration will be expected to come in in the room of it.[58]

But by the time the second volume appeared a year later, Rochester had been dismissed for opposing Marlborough's war policy, and the other Tory ministers were out of favour. So he dedicated the volume to the queen, his niece, with a stern lecture on her duties as an Anglican monarch. Queen Anne, who was not much given to reading anyway, was decidedly not amused.

Sir Benjamin Bathurst sent me Lord Clarendon's history last week [she wrote], but having not quite made an end of the first part, I did not unpack it. But I shall have the curiosity now to see this extraordinary dedication, which I should never have looked for in the second part of a book, and methinks [it] is very wonderful that people that don't want sense in some things should be so ridiculous.[59]

The dedication to the third and last volume, published in 1704, was an unashamed party manifesto, arguing that the Revolution had severely shaken the body politic – 'Such deliverances have their pangs in the birth, that much weaken the constitution in endeavouring to preserve and amend it' – and that it had made clear the way for the Dissenters, those secret devotees of republicanism and anarchy, who were poisoning the minds of the nation's youth in their schismatic academies, and had now infiltrated the government itself – essentially the same message as Sacheverell was now trumpeting from the pulpit.

But let any impartial person judge [said Rochester] to whom all the libertines of the republican party are like to unite themselves; and whether it is imaginable that the established government, either in church or state, can be strengthened or served by them. They must go to the enemies of both, and pretend there is no such thing as a republican party in England, that they may be the less observed, and go on the more secure in their destructive projects.[60]

So the Whigs were for the moment worsted in the field of recent history; but this was only one weapon at the disposal of the new High Church movement.

6

THE BLOODY FLAG
The High Church revival

The High Church movement had its origins in the deep and understandable concern felt by many clergymen at the rampant growth of Socinianism, Deism and other 'heresies' in the new atmosphere of liberalism after the Revolution. In the persons of men like John Toland there was a direct link between this religious deviationism and political radicalism, but it was an association that would naturally have been made in any case. In the same way, it was natural to blame the Dissenters, if only because the emergence of a problem of Christian belief coincided with the passing of the Toleration Act of 1689, which gave them freedom to worship in their own 'meeting houses'. Since a direct identification was still made between the Dissenters and Cromwell's Puritans, an identification hammered home from the pulpits every 30 January, it was also natural to regard them as tainted by democratic and 'levelling' notions – an idea confirmed, again, by the attitude of prominent Dissenting journalists like Defoe. Also, in a very direct way the Toleration Act had weakened the authority of the clergy and the church courts over the laity, for in a situation in which some Protestants could legally opt out of church services it proved impossible to enforce the attendance of any, so that the Uniformity Act became a dead letter.[1]

Particularly odious was the practice of 'occasional conformity', by which Dissenters qualified themselves for secular office under the terms of the Test Act by taking the Anglican sacrament on one occasion, or at long intervals. The situation was complicated by the fact that many Dissenters had adopted this practice in the past in perfect innocence, as a gesture of solidarity with their Anglican brethren. But now even moderate churchmen felt obliged to denounce occasional conformity as a prostitution of the holiest sacrament of the church, and the Whigs could only retort that it was already prostituted by being made a qualification for secular employment. The problem was highlighted by a spectacular incident in 1697, when the new Lord Mayor of London, Sir Humphrey Edwin, twice attended an afternoon service at a conventicle in full regalia with his sword-bearer, after worshipping as an Anglican in the morning. It was a scandal which reverberated down Anne's reign, and first provoked the call for legislation to punish such practices. At the same time concern was growing at the success of the Dissenting academies, which offered a more liberal and up-to-date curriculum than the existing schools, or for that matter the universities, but which many Anglicans affected to regard as nurseries of republicanism and schism.

This was, in fact, a church under pressure. The Revolution tended to encourage the anti-clericalism which had always been an attribute of the English ruling classes. The clergy were freely blamed for luring James II to his destruction by the irresponsible preaching of divine right, and denounced as entirely unfit for political responsibility. As one writer said in 1690,

The clergymen (the English especially) being for the most part of mean birth, unimproved by travel, are the worst politicians in the world, yet no men have had greater shares in public counsels and changes. The histories of all ages are filled with their miscarriages, yet they have seldom drawn a greater load of contempt upon themselves, than by their late violences, while the court and they were well with one another; and nothing but the insolence of some of them could abate that pity, which was natural to the observation how they were carried hoodwinked to destruction, and were made tools to subvert their own religion, and the civil rights of the people.[2]

Their agonies of conscience over the oaths were treated with derision, and one of Sherlock's critics in 1691 was aghast at the respect still paid to their opinions in some quarters. 'These are the men', he said, 'that must be cutting us out schemes of politics, prescribing to government, and determining the rights of princes. What a hotchpotch have they made, with their kings *de facto*, their *jure divino*, their passivity and non-resistance!'[3] Another sneered at their pretensions to greatness under the new regime:

I confess that I cannot but laugh at the insupportable folly of these unthinking creatures, that could imagine the Prince of Orange, who made so great a figure in Europe, and whose presence was of so great necessity on the Continent, could be imposed upon to come over to England in the heart of winter, amidst a thousand dangers, and at a vast charge, and that merely to fasten, forsooth, a tottering pillar or two in the Cathedral of Canterbury or the Chapel of Lambeth...These poor monkish statesmen are not able to fathom the genius of a hero.[4]

To more radical minds they were not only fools but hypocrites. Defoe declared that

The members of the Church of England are all apostates from the very fundamental doctrine of their church, perjured in the sight of God and man, notorious hypocrites and deceivers, who having sworn obedience without reserve to their prince are become traitors, rebels and murderers of the Lord's Anointed and their lawful sovereign; and not having the fear of God before their eyes, have deposed and traitorously dethroned their rightful king.[5]

It was particularly exasperating that the Whigs, having previously tried to appropriate the credit for the Revolution, should now try to unload any discredit on their opponents. As James Drake said, replying to Defoe,

The great and only instance of the Church of England's pretended disloyalty, and neglect of principles, is the deposing (for so this author will have it be) of King James. I ask, who did that? While it was a recommendation at court, the Dissenters or Whigs (which are synonymous terms with him) laid sole claim to it, as a meritorious work, and were bountifully rewarded for it. Now the great advantage is thought to be over, the church is to be entitled to the odium.

Indeed, the church was impaled on a kind of Morton's fork, for

Those of it that did concur with others in promoting that Revolution are reviled and vilified, as men of no faith or principles, and therefore not fit to be trusted, countenanced or protected; and those that did not, as men of pernicious principles, inconsistent with, and destructive of, the civil rights and liberties of the people.[6]

But, irrespective of the rights or wrongs of the Revolution, it was the position of the church in the state, and the social ascendency of the clergy, which were at stake. Even a Low Churchman like Burnet was alarmed at the trend: 'It became a common topic of discourse', he said, 'to treat all mysteries in religion as the contrivances of priests to bring the world into a blind submission to them, priestcraft grew to be another word in fashion, and the enemies of religion vented all their impieties under the cover of these words.'[7] One important aspect of High Church propaganda was a passionate reaffirmation of the concept that the church was the state, and the state the church, that politics were religious, and religion political. The Whigs, on the other hand, were committed to the view that politics were a secular matter; God had ordained government in a general sense, but He had not defined the precise way in which it was to be administered. This was a purely lay concern, and the function of the priesthood was strictly pastoral and confessional. Some remarks by Joseph Jekyll at Sacheverell's trial in 1710 epitomise this attitude:

Of later times patriarchal and other fantastical schemes have been framed to rest the authority of the law upon, and so questions of divinity have been blended with questions of law, when it is plain that religion hath nothing to do to extend the authority of the prince, or the submission of the subject, but only to secure the legal authority of the one, and enforce the due submission of the other, from the consideration of higher rewards and heavier punishments.[8]

The re-emergence of Harringtonian republicanism towards the end of the 1690s, coupled as it was with Deism, provoked the hysterical wrath of the Tory pamphleteers.

We are fallen [said one] into those dregs of time wherein atheism and irreligion, sedition and debauchery, seem to divide the world between them; wherein true and unaffected piety is out of countenance, wherein all the sacred ties to our sovereign are as loose as our manners, and in which that generous honesty and religious loyalty which was once the glory and character of our nation is vanished into disobedience and contempt of our superiors. For among all the vicious and impertinent humours of our age, as none are more common, so none are more equally lamentable, dangerous and ridiculous than aspersing things venerable and sacred, and speaking evil of illustrious persons; and yet that is now improved to such a wicked height that he is accounted the wittiest man and staunchest member of his party that dares calumniate loudest.[9]

William Baron denounced such 'politick novels' as Edmund Ludlow's *Memoirs* (1698),

wherein a strange force is put upon all those natural obligations and regular dependencies which were formerly thought the main support of all human societies; such uncouth states of war, and nature, such origins of political societies and subordination of commonwealth powers, as make parents their children's servants, and magistrates their people's slaves, and all this with very little regard to the doctrine of the creation.

True, the Whigs did acknowledge God's existence and His creation of the world, 'but they allow this Almighty Power very little share in the governing part, man being somehow or other placed here, is supposed solely to act upon a principle of self-interest and self-preservation, without any regard to those divine impresses of good and evil, right and wrong'. Yet, said Baron, 'I dare conclude this as an infallible truth, [that] there can be no lasting and happy establishment without some moral assurance of the Almighty's approbation and blessing.'[10]

This reaction against Whiggism, republicanism and materialism[11] found a focus in the demand, first voiced by Atterbury in 1697, for the sitting of Convocation.[12] The Convocation controversy is in some respects a sterile thing; the force and authority of Convocation too easily ran aground in pettifogging disputes over forms and precedents; when it did settle down to work it was not to tackle major problems of church–state relations, but such matters as the growth of marital infidelity and profaneness in speech, proceedings in excommunication, the visitation of prisoners and the establishment of rural deans.[13] But it had as its basis the demand that the clergy, though banned from the House of Commons, yet had a right to be summoned with parliament and to meet as a sovereign legislative authority for the church, and a great victory was won when the Earl of Rochester persuaded William that a Convocation be elected with the new parliament early in 1701.

But these initiatives met with no support from the leaders of the church. John Sharp, Archbishop of York, chose the occasion of his sermon to the House of Lords on 30 January 1700 to issue a stern warning, the more remarkable in that Sharp was already one of the churchmen nearest the throne, and was to move even nearer in the next reign.

He took as his text Paul's words to Titus, 'Put them in mind to be subject to principalities and powers, to obey magistrates' (Titus 3: 1), and he argued from this that it was the clergy's plain duty to preach obedience and submission to the existing government. 'This is no state affair', he added, 'but an affair of the Gospel.' On the other hand, for a clergyman 'to presume to give his judgment about the management of public affairs, or to lay down doctrines, as from Christ, about the forms and models of kingdoms and commonwealths, or to adjust the limits of the prerogative of the prince or of the liberties of the subject' was 'every whit as indecent...as it would be for him to determine titles of land in the pulpit'.

We meddle not with politics [he went on], we meddle not with prerogative or property, we meddle not with the disputes and controversies of law that may arise about these matters. But we preach a company of plain lessons of peaceableness and fidelity, and submission to our rulers, such as the law of nature teaches, such as both Christ and the Apostles did preach in all places.[14]

He then considered the form of obedience the clergy ought to enforce, and here he was quite explicit:

Let the form of government in any country be what it will, in whomsoever the sovereign authority is lodged (whether in one, or in many) they are the principalities and powers to whom we are to submit.

This submission was defined by 'the standing laws of every country', and it is difficult to believe that in his next remarks he was not glancing at the Toleration Act:

Whatever laws are made by just authority, whether in civil matters or in matters relating to religion, if they be not contrary to God's laws, there the subject is bound in conscience to obey them, even though he apprehends they are inconvenient...[for] it is in the power of the legislature, when there is reason, to bind our consciences to obedience, as well as to award punishments to our disobedience.

If the subject doubted the propriety of such legislation he must still obey; only if he were convinced that it was against God's law could he disobey, and then only passively, of course.[15]

He admitted that this was nothing less than 'that doctrine of passive obedience which of late hath made so ill a sound among many of us', but he denied that it was made for tyranny. In its nature it was not servile, but supportive and preservative, and the subject's submission was only 'as the laws and constitution require'. In the present case its function was 'to preserve and secure the national Settlement in the same posture and upon the same foot in and upon which it is already established'. Nor had he the least doubt that such obedience was owing to the present government, as to all established governments under the law:

That there is such a submission due from all subjects to the supreme authority of the place where they live as shall tie up their hands from opposing or resisting it by force, is evident from the very nature and ends of political society. And I dare say there is not that country upon earth, let the form of their government be what it will (absolute monarchy, legal monarchy, aristocracy or commonwealth), where this is not a part of the constitution...And this is so true, that there is not a commonwealth in the world so free, but that these doctrines of non-resistance and passive obedience must for ever be taught there, as necessary even for the preservation of their liberties...Subjects must obey passively where they cannot obey actively, otherwise the government would be precarious, and public peace at the mercy of every malcontent...Nor is this a state doctrine only, but the doctrine also of Jesus Christ.[16]

Sharp's unequivocal endorsement of constituted authority was of the first importance. If passive obedience and non-resistance were to be applied to a *de facto* monarch, then the distinction between *de facto* and *de jure* kingship was meaningless. His warning to the clergy not to indulge in political controversy was unqualified and unmistakable, though arguably it came late in the day. As it was, in the highly charged atmosphere of 1700 and 1701 his warnings went by the board.

The death of the Duke of Gloucester in 1700 reopened

the succession question; it was apparently closed in 1701 by
the Act of Settlement, which vested the succession after
Anne in the Hanoverians; but it was at least partly reopened
a few months later by the death of James II. (The com-
plexities of the situation are displayed in the last quarrel
between William and the Princess Anne, provoked by his
refusal to allow her to go into full mourning for her own
father.)[17] The new Jacobite claimant could not be less
attractive than his father, 'Old Popery', and despite the
lingering doubts about his legitimacy his emergence added
a new dimension to the political scene. This was at first
disguised by the outburst of nationalist rage which greeted
Louis XIV's decision to recognise James III as king of
England; but the introduction of a new oath to abjure him
and his title caused many Tories a serious crisis of
conscience.[18] According to Burnet, most of them took the
oath on the assumption 'that this abjuration could only
bind during the present state of things, but not in case of
another revolution, or of a conquest; this was too dark a
thing to be enquired after, or seen into, in the state matters
were then in'.[19] Meanwhile, the quarrel over the Partition
Treaties and the Grand Alliance, and the impeachment of
the Junto lords, lashed both parliamentary parties into a
frenzy, and a contentious first session of Convocation in
1701 underlined the discontent of the clergy.

The sudden accession of Queen Anne in March 1702 only
inflamed the situation further. In the last months of his life
King William had been moving reluctantly back towards
the Junto, but Anne's inclinations lay quite the other way.
She was known to be a staunch, even a fanatical Anglican,
and it was confidently expected that she would endorse the
High Church attack on occasional conformity. Her early
ministerial appointments included Nottingham, Rochester
and Sir Edward Seymour, who were all right-wing Tories.
At her coronation on 23 April Archbishop Sharp issued a
call for national unity and the abandonment of party
disputes. In an ideal world, he said, the queen's subjects
'would not, for difference of opinion about the methods

of the public conduct, break out into parties and factions. Much less, in case of such divisions, would they sacrifice the peace of the kingdom to their own private resentments, and mingle heaven and earth for the supporting of a side.'[20] This was always to be the queen's own view, but in the first heady months of her reign (so long postponed) her discretion lapsed, and she allowed herself to be jostled into a partisan attitude. She made a rather petty reflection on her predecessor in her first speech from the throne, her public conduct towards the Junto peers was slighting and contemptuous, and she allowed Nottingham, over Godolphin's protests, to slip into her speech dissolving parliament on 25 May the sentence 'My own principles must always keep me entirely firm to the interests and religion of the Church of England, and will incline me to countenance those who have the truest zeal to support it.'[21] It might almost have been the signal for a new High Church campaign, this time led not by Atterbury but by Henry Sacheverell.

Sacheverell was a man detested by most of his contemporaries, even by many who shared his views, and posterity, echoing Burnet's classic indictment, has dismissed him as 'a bold, insolent man, with a very small measure of religion, virtue, learning or good sense'.[22] But this does not mean that we can dismiss, or even diminish, the enormous influence he exerted on his times. To read his sermons and discourses is to recognise in him a preacher of great virtuosity and power with an unerring sense of timing, and a politician of no mean ability. He was certainly no original thinker, but he was a brilliant polemicist, whose pulpit style, even in an age of spectacular preaching, was acknowledged to be remarkable. 'He came into the pulpit', we are told, 'like a Sybil to the mouth of her cave, or a pythoness upon the tripod, with such an air of fierceness and rage, as is not possible to express.'[23] His enemies, at least, had no illusions about his importance; they gave him full credit for launching the whole campaign against the Dissenters in 1702. 'Sacheverell', said one, 'was the trumpeter of discord, and

the black generation took the alarm.'[24] He sounded
the tocsin in *The Political Union: A Discourse Showing the
Dependence of Government on Religion*, published in Oxford
a week after the dissolution of parliament, with the imprimatur of the Vice-Chancellor.[25]

Sacheverell fiercely rejected Sharp's picture of the supportive role of the church; its role in politics and society
was coequal with the state's. The core of the book is contained in this passage:

> The civil and ecclesiastical state are the two parts and divisions that both
> united make up one compounded constitution and body politic, sharing
> the same fate and circumstances, twisted and interwoven into the very
> being and principles of each other, both alike jointly assisting and being
> assisted, defending and defended, supporting and supported, in the
> same vital union, intercourse and complication.[26]

His philosophic view of man was curiously Hobbesian: 'All
the force of government', he said, 'is derived from and
depending upon the passions of shame and fear, and as
the first is ruled by conscience, the latter is guided by the
laws of it'; and the suppression of lawlessness and vice
hinged on the doctrine of the immortality of the soul, 'a
principle which reason and philosophy does but dubiously
conjecture at, and religion only proves'.

> Thus [he went on] we see how weak, impotent and unguarded human
> nature and human government are left, if stripped of that support,
> ornament and defence that they receive from religion. Nature, by itself,
> is a mere state of anarchy and confusion, of ruin, rapine and war; and
> though it be regulated, restrained and tied up by political laws, yet these
> reach not to the intellectual part, the most dangerous, active, busy and
> destructive part of man.

This Caliban was 'governed, directed and controlled by
nothing but the fears and promises of another life, the
precepts and insurances of a revealed religion'.[27]

This, of course, was why

> Atheism and anarchy have always gone hand in hand, they are the
> mutual spawn and genuine production of each other, and like vermin
> they are bred out of the same filth and corruption...Where the prin-
> ciples of religion come to be shaken, or ever happen to be subverted,
> the state never fails to follow it, and to take share in its misfortunes
> and ruin.[28]

Not content with accusing the Whigs of atheism and hypocrisy, he warned them against covetousness. There was grave danger, he argued, in England's very prosperity and her success in war, and in his hypothetical picture of a mercenary future he was obviously attacking present reality:

We should see nothing but an universal mart and trade of corruption, propagated and carried on both in church and state. We should see the posts and preferments of the one filled with mercenary little knaves, that would sell the liberty, honour and safety of their country for the vile gain of a pension; and we should find the holy offices of the other prostituted with an ignorant, mean and unworthy ministry, that would betray their own church, conscience and religion to serve the petty and scandalous designs of a secular interest. These are the noble effects of establishing government upon riches, exclusive of true piety, justice and religion.[29]

But the vials of his wrath were emptied upon the Dissenters:

Presbytery and republicanism go hand in hand; they are but the same, disorderly, levelling principle in the two branches of our state, equally implacable enemies to monarchy and episcopacy, and if the government does not severely find the truth of this in their indulgence, 'tis not beholding to their tenets. It may be remembered that they were the same hands that were guilty both of regicide and sacrilege, that at once divided the king's head and crown, and made our churches stables, and dens of beasts, as well as thieves.

He bitterly criticised the toleration at present extended to those, he said, 'whom no reason can ever yet convince, no kindness ever yet could win, no condescensions ever yet could oblige, and whom nothing but the corruption of our doctrine, the destruction of our discipline and the sequestration of our estates and revenues can satisfy'. They were, said he in a celebrated phrase, a party 'against whom every man that wishes [the church's] welfare ought to hang out the bloody flag and banner of defiance'.[30] As for occasional conformity, he characterised it as 'such a religious piece of hypocrisy as even no heathen government would have endured', and blessed God that 'there is now a person on the throne who so justly weighs the interest of church and state, as to remove so false an engine, that visibly overturns both'.[31]

A few months later he published (anonymously) another outburst of 'fluent and refined Billingsgate', this time directed against the Whig clergy and entitled *The Character of a Low Churchman*, which went into a second edition in 1706 and a third as late as 1714. (It was provoked by Richard West's *The True Character of a Churchman*, 1702.)

Can anyone believe the word of God [said Sacheverell] that thus distorts and wrests it to any meaning, and makes it speak what sense he pleases, to authorise and countenance a secular design? that can justify the Revolution out of the Apocalypse, and maintain Rebellion out of the 13th of Romans, resolve monarchy into popular power, and episcopacy into presbytery, out of Timothy and Titus?[32]

He did not lack for answers, of course. Perhaps the most notable, because it produced a new anti-clerical term of abuse, was *The Danger of Priestcraft to Religion and Government with some Politick Reasons for Toleration* (1702). Priestcraft, it said, 'comprehends all that the arts of designing men cause to pass for religion with the unthinking part of the world, though it is neither dictated by the law of nature, nor included in the written word'. It accused Sacheverell of wishing to break the Toleration Act, which in its turn would undermine the Act of Settlement, 'the security of the nation, and of the liberties of Europe', and it called on the clergy – not the first or the last time such a call was issued – to return to their pastoral duties: 'They ought not to pry into matters of state. They have an employment of a much larger extent, and of a much nobler consequence, and they must needs prove ill politicians if they are good priests.'[33] Meanwhile the *Observator* extravagantly denounced the lot of them:

This man speaks the sense of a party that cannot be matched but in France or Turkey; they are Capuchins, Mendicants, Cordeliers, Carthusians, Regulars, Irregulars, High Flyers, Tantivies, Bellswaggerists, Mufti and Priests... The followers of this party build their faith upon the tenets of Ignatius Loyola, and those in England take their opinions from Laud, Parker and Old Towser.[34]

But the tide was running hard against the Whigs. They fared badly in the first general election of the new reign, and it was known that the call for the banning of occasional conformity found favour with the queen. A bill for this purpose was passed by the Commons in December 1702, and the Whigs in the Lords, not feeling strong enough to reject it, could only amend it in a way they knew the Commons would not accept. It was generally recognised that, however sincere the feelings of many of its supporters, the queen included, the campaign against occasional conformity had a political basis. Not only was it intended to shake the Whigs' grip on certain marginal corporations, it was almost certainly, as the Whigs insisted, the prelude to an attack on the Toleration Act itself. The bishops argued, with some reason, that persecution would only reinvigorate the Dissenters, who were now a declining body, and hinder their eventual reabsorption into the church.[35] This infuriated the High Churchmen all the more, and early in 1703 Charles Leslie entered the lists with a pamphlet bearing the self-explanatory title *The New Association of Those Called Moderate Churchmen with the Modern Whigs and the Fanatics to Undermine and Blow Up the Present Church and Government.* In December 1703 a second Occasional Conformity Bill was sent up to the Lords, and this time defeated outright, and the following year Sacheverell returned to the attack. On 9 March 1704 he mounted the pulpit at St Mary's, Oxford, to give a rousing assize sermon, which he had the effrontery to entitle 'The Nature and Mischief of Prejudice and Partiality'. He launched another savage assualt on Dissent, under the name 'Phanaticism', and again traced its lineage back to the Civil Wars. In so doing he gave his party another catchword to succeed 'the bloody flag'. He said,

If we were to consider its progress, in all the series of rebellions, from its odious and never-to-be-forgotten era of transcendent villainy in the year forty-one, we shall find the same Jesuitical principles, like a plotter in masquerade, only changing their name, but carrying on the same machinations and wicked practices in church and state, to the subversion of our constitution in both down to the present day.[36]

The climax of the sermon was a call for the suppression of the Dissenting academies, whose sole purpose, he thundered, was 'the education of youth in all the poisonous principles of fanaticism and faction, and to debauch them with the corrupted maxims of republicanism'.[37] And though he uttered the usual denunciation of parties as the tools of 'skilful incendiaries in government, to make their ungodly stratagems and revolutions pass upon mankind', his preface, addressed to the staunchly Tory grand jury of Oxford, suggests that such considerations need not apply to his own followers:

The gentry of the whole nation must see their own interest involved in that of the clergy, and that whatsoever strikes at the church, must secretly undermine the state...[and] such open and ingenuous assertion of the good old principles of the Church of England will be no less a monument of your honour, who in this trimming age dare boldly defend its primitive truth, than of the lasting and indelible reproach of those temporising hypocrites who can have the confidence both to flatter and betray it, and under the pretence of its interest give it up to the insatiable malice and revenge of its most inexorable enemies.

On the other hand, in November 1704 the Whig journalist John Tutchin was arraigned at Guildhall for seditious libel and found guilty, for publishing in the *Observator* more than two years before what was really only a slightly exaggerated version of the standard Whig position. What he wrote was,

This is a prerogative of singular advantage to the people of England, in that their representatives are the judges of the maladministration of their governors, that they can call them in question for the same, and can appoint such to wear the crown who are fittest for government, which they have often done, and indeed which is the privilege of all free people, who are authorised by the laws of God and nature to choose their own governors.[38]

However, the High Churchmen could not consolidate their advantage. The queen was increasingly disenchanted by the propaganda cry that the church was in danger under her ministry and by the realisation that High Church agitation in Convocation was directed as much against her authority as against that of the bishops, and that whatever the merits of the arguments on both sides none of them justified splitting the church from top to bottom. The

Tories found to their cost that 'one facet of her character was an acid dislike of factious clergymen or of any discord in religion'.[39] She was also irritated by the opposition of the Tory ministers to Marlborough's war policy, and her uncle Rochester was forced to resign for this reason as early as February 1703.

Perhaps an early straw in the wind was the sermon preached before her on 31 January 1704 by Thomas Sherlock, son of the notorious William. She ordered it to be printed. Taking as his text Proverbs 24: 21, 'Fear thou the Lord and the King, and meddle not with them that are given to change', Sherlock strongly endorsed the arguments put forward by Sharp in 1700: 'To determine the original of civil power', he said, 'or how the prince's right to the obedience of the subject first began, is neither easy, nor at this time necessary. But whatever the original of government has been, or upon what account soever lawful authority has been gained, upon the same obedience becomes due.' Since God had never defined the state of obedience, only commanded its practice, Scripture could provide no rule, and in this vacuum, he said, 'The measure of power and authority must be the rule of obedience; whatever the prince can lawfully command, the subject is bound to obey', and 'to reason abstractedly upon the power of princes is a sign of weakness as well as of a troublesome temper'. On the other hand, 'to maintain the established form of government is the first and highest duty of men acting in society'.[40] He went on to castigate the High Church party with great vigour and in considerable detail. Change and amendment, he allowed, might be necessary from time to time in any institution which was partly man-made; but they were always a sign and a cause of weakness, and needed strong justification before they were attempted. This the High Churchmen had not provided. Indeed, he denounced their conduct as merely factious – 'When men dislike without reason, and obstinately condemn whatever has been settled by authority, when they disclaim the power and all the acts of the church, either their ignorance must be invincible, or their guilt un-pardonable.' He closed with a patriotic appeal for national unity in the face of the common enemy, with the queen as war leader:

We have an enemy strong and cunning to deal with, an ancient rival of the power and honour of England, an enemy to the religion of Protestants and the liberty of mankind; and if nothing else will, yet interest should prevail with us to unite for our mutual safety, and whilst our brave countrymen expose their lives to the hazard and fortune of war abroad, in defence of their prince and country, methinks the least that can be expected of us is to be quiet and peaceable at home. To save the sinking liberties of Europe is worthy a queen of England...and it will ever be the choice of an Englishman rather to die by his sword than live by his law.[41]

The comparison with Elizabeth I was one to which Anne was peculiarly susceptible; on her accession she had as-sumed Elizabeth's famous motto *semper eadem*. In May 1704 the Earl of Nottingham, the Earl of Jersey and Sir Edward Seymour were dismissed or forced to resign, and in August Marlborough more than justified the high hopes vested in him by his crushing victory at Blenheim. In the winter of 1704–5 a Tory attempt to tack yet another Occasional Conformity Bill onto the Finance Bill appeared as a blatant attempt to frustrate the successful prosecution of the war, and at the same time split the party. The tack was defeated after a damaging struggle, and subsequent voting figures on the bill itself, in Commons and Lords, showed an overall decline in support.[42] In the general election held that spring the Tory majority was clipped, and no more was heard of occasional conformity until 1711.

Meanwhile James Drake, a Tory pamphleteer as intem-perate as Sacheverell, finally tipped the balance against the High Church party. His *Memorial of the Church of England*, published in the summer of 1705, was a particu-larly aggravating assertion of the thesis that the church was in grave danger under the present ministry. It sharply criticised Anne herself for dismissing Nottingham and Seymour, and took Godolphin and Marlborough to task for their hypocrisy in voting for the Occasional Conformity

Bills of recent years while rallying their supporters to vote against them:

All attempts to settle [the church] on a perpetual foundation have been opposed and rendered ineffectual by ministers who owe their present grandeur to its protection, and who with a prevarication as shameful as their ingratitude, pretend to vote and speak for it themselves, while they solicit and bribe others with pensions and places to be against it.[43]

In September a London grand jury ordered the *Memorial* to be burnt as a seditious libel,[44] and the queen fully shared these sentiments. In her opening speech to the new parliament, described by Boyer as 'wise, pathetic and comprehensive', she told MPs, 'I cannot but with grief observe, that there are some amongst us who endeavour to foment animosities, but I persuade myself they will be found to be very few, when you appear to assist me in discountenancing and defeating such practices.' As for the libel that the church was in danger at that time, she forthrightly declared that 'They who go about to insinuate things of this nature must be mine and the kingdom's enemies, and can only mean to cover designs which they dare not publicly own by endeavouring to distract us with unreasonable and groundless distrusts and jeolousies.'[45] On 6 December, flushed with his success over the Regency Bill, Lord Halifax forced the High Church peers out into the open by moving to debate the commonly held notion that the church was in danger. The resultant debate, held in the queen's presence, produced considerable entertainment but not much enlightenment. Rochester, the queen's uncle, took a leading part, and had to suffer yet again at the hands of Wharton and Burnet for his role on James II's Ecclesiastical Commission. Bishop Compton of London, now a High Tory, was also twitted for his aggressive resistance activities at Nottingham in November 1688. It was made to appear as if the cry of 'Church in Danger' had only been raised because of the dismissal of the Tory ministers; on the other hand Burnet, Simon Patrick Bishop of Ely and John Hough Bishop of Lichfield vigorously complained of the insubordination of the lower clergy at the instigation of the

High Flyers. In the end the Lords carried a thumping resolution:

That the Church of England, as by law established, which was rescued from the extremest danger by King William III (of glorious memory), is now, by God's blessing, under the happy reign of her Majesty, in a most safe and flourishing condition, and that whoever goes about to suggest and insinuate that the church is in danger under her Majesty's administration is an enemy to the queen, the church and the kingdom.[46]

This was unanimously accepted by the House of Commons, and by a proclamation dated 20 December it was distributed to magistrates, with instructions to prosecute those who argued the contrary.[47] After a stormy session of Convocation that winter the queen further defined her attitude in a letter of 25 February 1706, in which she rebuked the Lower House for its conduct and affirmed her intention 'to maintain our Supremacy and the due subordination of Presbyters to Bishops as fundamental parts of the constitution of the Church of England'.[48]

Three years into the new reign, the political situation was still confused. Under William III both parties, if they could be said to have existed in any real sense, were weak; that is why the Country interest remained strong, perhaps unnaturally so.[49] Party weakness was encouraged at the same time by a strong system of 'management' operated by the Earl of Sunderland up to 1697[50] and by an ideological uncertainty which affected both sides. There is considerable truth in an apocryphal remark of Sunderland's. He is supposed to have told William 'that it was very true that the Tories were better friends to monarchy than the Whigs were, but then his Majesty was to consider that he was not their monarch'.[51] The Whigs were billed as inveterate opponents of monarchy, and this was an impression which, despite the efforts of the Junto, the Whig radicals did a great deal to confirm. Unfortunately, their appropriation of credit for the Revolution encouraged the idea that this too had been some kind of republican plot. The Tories, on the other hand, found it difficult to give unqualified allegiance to William III, and their difficulties were brought into sharp focus by the Abjuration Act right at the end of the reign.

Anne's accession strengthened the Tories enormously, and allowed them to discard the *de facto* theory and give their wholehearted support to a hereditary queen. They were encouraged in this attitude by the High Church revival, which gave them a spiritual rallying point and enabled them increasingly to discount the Revolution. But, with the Duke of Gloucester dead, and Sophia of Hanover increasingly a Whig candidate, this kind of Toryism had no long-term future; by the logic of their own theories they must all be Whigs or Jacobites. Unfortunately, most of them lacked the resolution to be either, except for Francis Atterbury – and his Jacobitism was little more than a *pis aller* – and the Earl of Nottingham, whose unbending logic and stern moral courage in the end drove him to oppose the Schism Act and take office under George I. Others flirted either with Jacobitism (like Bolingbroke) or with Whiggism (like Hanmer), but lacked the necessary resolution. Like the men of Laodicea they were neither hot nor cold, and the Lord spat them out of His mouth.

To the Whigs also the years 1700–5 were a turning point. The vicious attack on the Junto lords in 1701, followed by the clean sweep of them and their supporters on Anne's accession, followed by a noisy public campaign against Dissent, convinced the Whigs that there was now a determined attempt on foot to eliminate them altogether. They tightened their discipline, with results seen in the regency debates of 1705–6, and mounted a vigorous defence of William III and what they conceived to be William's war policy, which meant Marlborough's. The need to defend the Revolution itself was not yet apparent.

REVOLUTION PRINCIPLES
Whiggism under Queen Anne

The Tories certainly sustained a defeat in 1705, but it is difficult to assess its nature or its extent in political terms, and it did not imply a Whig victory. The concept of 'alternative government' had not yet emerged, and if it had Queen Anne was the last monarch to pay attention to it; she disliked party rancour of any kind, and she had a particular antipathy for the Junto leaders. Some contemporaries even thought that her attitude towards Whiggism in general was dictated by a belated guilt for her own share in the Revolution.

In Robert Harley she found a minister who echoed and reinforced many of her own ideas. Bred a Dissenter and raised as a Country Whig, Harley regarded the bigotry of the High Churchmen and the power-hunger of the Junto lords with equal aversion. To him political parties were an unwelcome and unnatural accretion on the constitution, antithetical to 'the ancient liberties of England and the good of this poor nation', and he envisaged the queen as playing a strong regal and managerial role in a multi-party or non-party administration devoted first to winning the war, then to making a just peace.[1] His increasing influence on Anne, up to his fall in 1708, frustrated the ambitions of the party leaders and thus intensified the fury of the propaganda battle.

This continued without pause. Though a proclamation was already out for James Drake for his *Memorial of the Church of England* (1705), early in 1706 he was indicted on another charge, in connexion with a short-lived periodical he had founded called *Mercurius Politicus, or An Antidote to Popular Misrepresentations.* In this he narrowed 'Revolution Principles' to two: 'That kings are but ministers of the people, and therefore accountable to them for their administration; the second, that the sovereignty is in the people, who may therefore confer the administration of it upon whom they please.' He went on,

These two are [the] ground and foundation of what some at present dignify with a new name, and call *Revolution Principles*; a sort of principles that will justify all the rebellions, treasons and conspiracies that ever have been, or ever shall be raised or formed...According to these principles, a few men of any sort may declare or agree their prince to be a traitor, and if the rest of the nation should not agree with them so far as to enter at least into judgment, they may give judgment and do execution by themselves. Those that convene to act as a people are to be looked on as the people, and according to these principles may act for the people. For if the absolute sovereignty be in them, their warrant legitimates the form, be it never so irregular or extravagant.[2]

The bearing of this on the Convention of 1689 was obvious enough, but the following week he went even further: 'By those principles', he said, 'the Revolution put an end to the English constitution, and consequently all our rights thereupon ceased with it.' He reasoned, in fact, that either England had been conquered by William in 1688, or sovereign power had reverted to the people. So 'Whether the king was a conqueror, or the mob, in one of them all the civil rights of England centre, and what that one has not granted out again, rests there still, and is but precariously exercised or enjoyed by those that have not an express grant since that time.'[3]

At Drake's subsequent trial there was a significant exchange between the bench and Sir John Hawles, defence counsel. Hawles remarked, ''Tis uncertain what Revolution Principles are.' That staunch Whig Lord Chief Justice Holt replied, 'Every man in England understands what Revolution Principles are', but Hawles went on to argue that they 'are new, and have as yet obtained no fixed and general construction'.[4] There is no doubt that he was right, though this was now an era in which the term was being used more freely than ever before. There was no accepted or agreed definition of what had been accomplished in 1689, or on what grounds. Had King James really abdicated, or had he been deposed? Who had accomplished the act: the Whigs, the Tories or both? What was the responsibility of the church, and was 1689 an irreparable fracture of its principles?

The party leaders – or at least, the Whig party leaders – had not been unduly disturbed by these disputes, or any other. One cynic later remarked, 'These distinctions of Whig and Tory do properly belong to the second class, or inferior rank of men; for persons of the first rank, who either by their birth or abilities are entitled to govern others, do not really list themselves in those parties, but only put themselves at the head of either of them.'[5] But the question of the succession made it increasingly difficult to ignore the debate on the Revolution. To many the claims of the Electress Sophia, though endorsed by parliament, were indirect and roundabout, and Anne's steadfast refusal to invite her to England put her under something of a cloud. The Pretender was a more direct and more attractive candidate; at the moment he was seriously disadvantaged by the patronage of Louis XIV, the national enemy; but the end of the war might well bring a reconciliation with France, as in 1698, and what then? It is significant that in the negotiations for a Barrier Treaty, beginning in 1705, successive Whig ministers, supported by Marlborough, insisted that the Dutch guarantee the Hanoverian succession, and in the final treaty of 1709 this was the first effective article.[6] The novelty of inviting a foreign power to intervene in English politics naturally caused adverse comment, not least from Swift.

The Tories' attitude was ambiguous, and the refusal of their right wing to admit that Anne had a parliamentary as well as a hereditary title to the throne was ominous, for Sophia would be entirely a parliamentary monarch. In 1701 a Whig pamphlet was published giving what was now the party line: that even if the Stuart Pretender were legitimate and Protestant he had no claim to the throne, since parliament, in 1689 and again in 1701, had deliberately diverted the succession another way without even enquiring as to his religion or the circumstances of his birth.[7] This involved the assertion that Anne's title, too, was one hundred per cent parliamentary. In this context the insistence of non-jurors like Charles Leslie that she reigned by hereditary succession could be read as an oblique endorsement of the Pretender. The strong and widely believed rumours that if William III had not died unexpectedly the Junto had planned to put Sophia on the throne at once, bypassing Anne altogether, were another straw in the wind.[8] In 1705 the question was brought to the fore by the parliamentary debates on a Tory proposal to invite Sophia to England, which resulted in the Regency Act, and by the Scots Act of Security, which gave Scotland the option of rejecting the Hanoverian succession altogether when the time came.[9] In his *Advice to All Parties* (1705), Defoe warned that the High Churchmen were already talking of repealing the Act of Settlement as well as the Toleration Act.[10] This was, of course, an important implication of the campaign against Dissent. There was a strong presumption, shared by Tories like Nottingham, that the reform legislation of 1689 was eternal and immutable, as was the Act of Settlement – it was even argued in 1716 that this immutability embraced the Triennial Act – but if one piece of legislation, the Toleration Act, could be repealed the rest was at risk.

Such matters were very much the concern of the journalist John Tutchin, who published the first number of his newspaper the *Observator* on 1 April 1702, less than a month after Anne's accession. Tutchin was an unreformed Country Whig; he had been out with Monmouth in 1685, and had been lucky to escape with his life at the Bloody Assizes; he frequently denounced all parties as destructive of the constitution, excepting only 'the party of our country, men of Revolution Principles', and it is doubtful if this definition embraced the Junto.[11] Scattered references in the state papers suggest that he was working as an informer for Nottingham, then Secretary of State, as late as November 1703; thereafter he was impartially persecuted by each successive administration.[12]

Much of the *Observator's* space was devoted to reviling the High Church clergy: 'The Black Generation', with their 'hackney consciences', their 'hocus-pocus divinity' and their 'fanatical whimsies, the product of slavish fancies'. Tutchin's view of English history owed something to the researches of Petyt and Tyrrell, but he also incurred an unacknowledged debt to the Levellers. 'We are not to look into the Scriptures for the English constitution', he said, 'nor our free birthright and privileges. The Apostles and penmen of the Scriptures were none of them Englishmen, and knew not the modes and forms of our government.'[13] On the contrary, to him the English constitution was founded on the law of nature, which allowed of no distinction between persons, all being equal, and it gave the people the natural right to change their ruler; in fact, a government, he said, 'is actually dissolved which tends to the destruction of those for whose good it was first instituted'.[14] Nor was he mean with his natural rights: 'The law and constitution of England', he wrote, 'is according to the law of nature, and prescribed by it. Nor are the rights of Englishmen in point of natural rights different from the rights of all mankind. The furthest corners of the earth, and the nearest parts to us, have all the same privileges.' Therefore, all nations ought to have constitutional rulers like Anne, and receive the blessing of the Common Law, though he made no positive proposals for bringing this about.[15] As for the Revolution, this, he argued, was a reaffirmation of the Englishman's natural rights, and in attacking it the Tories were sabotaging their own birthright:

They endeavour to undermine the foundations of the Revolution, on which this government is built, and which we must maintain with hazard of our life and limb. A blessing so dearly purchased must be highly valued. Revolution Principles were the principles of our ancestors;

without them we had never been able to defend those rights to our own use, and to leave them to our posterity.[16]

To him the most dangerous aspect of Tory propaganda, of course, was the insistence that Anne reigned by virtue of her hereditary title alone, and he was willing to go to extreme lengths to counter it, along with the parallel argument that William III owed the crown to his wife's title and to his own descent from Charles I. He even denied the hereditary principle altogether. In June 1702 he wrote, 'Never anyone yet was born a king or queen, otherwise than by the previous consent and settlement of the people, for it is contrary to the nature of any government to have offices hereditary.' In the next issue he pursued the same theme:

Without doubt, no throne can be established upon a better foundation than the consent, approbation and election of the people...[and] 'tis hard to convince men how a king drops down from heaven, and how one man is born with an authority to govern another man, without his own consent...Now Queen Anne has a right to the crown by the consent of the people, which settled the crown more firmly on her head than if she had come to it by a hundred old hereditary successions, or had been sprung from the loins of an antediluvian monarch.

A few months later he went further, arguing that

No office is hereditary, nor is it consistent with the nature of government it should be so; the qualification of the person is the first step to the office...The crown of England (by which is freely meant our constitution) was first made by the people, and has for many hundreds of years been supported and maintained at their expense, and therefore it highly concerns them to support it as best suits their convenience for the common good of themselves, and this of late they have done.[17]

Like so many Whig writers, he was decidedly touchy about the Norman Conquest; naturally, since some Tories, adapting Brady's theories, were now arguing not only that by the Conquest William I had secured absolute rights over the English people, which he had transmitted to his successors, but that William III had no such rights, because he had *not* conquered England in 1688. Tutchin thought this was 'within a hair's breadth of downright blasphemy', for 'if conquest gives a right to the estates and liberties of Englishmen, our crowns are always precarious'. Thereafter he was always careful to refer to William I as 'William the Norman', or 'William (commonly and falsely called) the Conqueror'.[18] Yet 1066 was not the only pitfall in medieval history; in the autumn of 1703 he detected a concealed attack on the Revolution in the argument that the barons' revolt against John and Henry III had been a rebellion. He quoted with approval a treatise called *A Vindication of Magna Charta*, which he may well have written himself:

It is well indeed for us that our ancestors lived before us, and with the expense of their blood recovered the English rights for us, and saved them out of the fire; otherwise we would have been sealed up in bondage, and would have had neither any English rights to defend, nor their noble example to justify such a defence...For in all the steps the barons took, we [in 1688] followed them...and if we had miscarried in our affair we had not been called rebels, but treated as such; and the Bishop of London and all our worthies had made but a blue business out of it, without putting on the Prince of Orange's livery. And therefore it is a great ingratitude in those that receive any benefit or protection by this happy Revolution, to blemish the cause of the barons, for it is the same they live by.[19]

Indeed, he concluded that

Our government at present, and the Settlement of the succession of the crown, are founded on Revolution Principles, which neither is a new Settlement, nor contrary to the ancient constitution of this realm, but is conformable in every point to the laws, customs and practice of our ancestors.[20]

But this needed proving, for even a Whig historian like Tyrrell considered that the barons opposed to John, 'notwithstanding all their pretences, minded their own interest and grandeur more than the common good of the nation', and that de Montfort was in 'open rebellion' against Henry III, and that his rule was more tyrannical than the king's.[21] So, although in December 1703 Tutchin remarked, 'I would not lead my readers into the archives of this kingdom, and tumble over to their view the musty roles of antiquity; I would rather argue from things within memory, which more easily come within the bounds of common conception', the following April he embarked on a constitutional history of England which occupied six successive issues, leaving room for little else; and even then it did not reach the end of the Middle Ages.[22] In response to the protests of angry readers that he was filling the paper with 'old stories' he then broke off, but the same summer he devoted another five issues to a detailed account of the rise and fall of William Laud, which he obviously regarded as appropriate to the times.[23]

It may, of course, be that Tutchin found past history safer than present speculation, for he was a much harassed man. In May 1703 he was presented at the Old Bailey for issue no. 17 of the *Observator* (2 June 1702), which was a savage attack on the Catholics; but the grand jury returned a bill of *ignoramus*. He celebrated by devoting five successive *Observators* (II, nos. 37–41) to a history of trial by jury, the duties of jurymen and the function of grand juries. His busy year was 1704: first the House of Commons pursued him for publishing accounts of debates on the Occasional Conformity Bill; a proclamation was issued against him, with a reward of £100, and when he surrendered in May his bail was set at an intimidating £1000. The government then decided to proceed against him for seditious libel, with the result we have seen;[24] after months of argument the Queen's Bench judges set aside the verdict 3:1. In the meanwhile, he was badly beaten up in October at Rowe's Coffee House, near London Bridge. He was still bound over, and his recognisances were not cancelled until June 1705; then in September of the same year he was bound over again on the direct complaint of the Imperial Envoy, for referring to Joseph I as 'emperor *jure diabolico*'.[25]

But professionally, so to speak, his chief opponent was Charles Leslie, who not only kept up a running barrage of criticism in his own periodical, *The Rehearsal*, which ran from 1706 to 1709, but also published several pamphlets directly addressed to Tutchin. The Whigs and Dissenters, he sneered,

have set up a screech-owl *Observator*, which goes abroad twice a week with the newspapers, and is read by some sort of people more than any of them, and with more delight; and the professed subject of this paper is the deposing doctrine. It is his constant theme, not by inference, or

hiddenly, but bare-faced and in express words he justifies the calling
of kings to account, to depose them, and even take away their lives. He
boasts and glories in it.[26]

The ghost of Charles I was still walking, and Leslie warned his readers,

There is still a set of men amongst us who are visibly driving on...the
ruin of these nations by setting up the principles, and carrying on the
same pretences, which began and at last completed the bloody revolution
of forty-one.

Incoherent as he often was, he was acute enough to realise the deficiencies of Whig theory:

The root and foundation of all our republican schemes and pretences
of rebellion is this supposed radical power in the people, as of erecting
government at the beginning, so to overturn and change it at their
pleasure...[But] it was never yet known, nor ever can be, what is meant
by the word 'people' in this scheme of government. For the whole people
never chose, and a part of the people is not the whole.

To support 'this ridiculous scheme of government' the Whigs had revived 'the traitorous and long since exploded notion of their predecessors in the rebellion of forty-one', that the king was one of the three estates of parliament. As for the Original Contract, his view was:

There are limitations of concession, and limitations of coercion. The first
sort as well as the last are always given by superiors to their inferiors
...and thus kings may limit themselves to their subjects, by granting
them such and such laws, and giving them the assurance of their solemn
oath to observe them. And this is all the Original Contract can be showed
between king and people, but it is neither original nor a contract.

He then stood Whig medieval history on its head by lauding the concessions that English monarchs had made to an ungrateful people:

No commonwealths or what they call popular governments (though no
such ever truly was, or can be in the world) have granted such limitations
of concession as monarchs, at least ours, have. And no subjects in the
world may be so happy and easy as we, if that rebellious principle of
coercing our kings, and making ourselves co-ordinate with them, were
once rooted out from amongst us.[27]

Tutchin's reaction was near hysterical; indeed the year
1704 sees a distinct decline in his powers, perhaps owing
to the persecution he was experiencing.[28] 'The Scots

Levite', as he persisted in calling the Irishman Leslie, speedily reduced him to gutter rhetoric:

The Scots priest talks of nothing but forty-one, rebellion and revolution. He's a mere parrot or magpie. What o'clock, Meg? Six o'clock...What sayest thou, Leslie? Forty-one, rebellion and revolution! A hundred times over and over. This is the chief note of the Scots buzzard...This 'forty-one' is the strangest thing that ever was; it blackens revolution, and blanches Ethiopian negroes, it answers books, and knocks down parties; 'tis the shibboleth of the High Church, and the confusion of the Low Churchmen. 'Tis an amusement or charm, an unfathomable something, a long time ago reduced to oblivion, and now trumped up by the Scots Levite. Take his forty-one from his book, and you won't have forty-one words of sense left in it.[29]

The queen's decision to ditch the High Church party in 1705 did little to ease the situation; in fact, the chorus of Tory complaint only grew shriller. In the ensuing uproar much abuse was hurled around, but little fresh was said, except perhaps by the Dissenters, whose confidence was enhanced by the queen's attitude and the improved position of the Whigs in the new House of Commons. John Toland published a long reply to James Drake, entitled *The Memorial of the State of England* (1706), in which he restated the Whig position in extreme terms:

The Whigs maintain that all good governments are (under God) originally from the choice of the people, for whom and by whom they are established; and that no government is good which does not consist of laws, by which the magistrates are restrained and regulated no less than the subjects, for their common happiness. This end of all society they think may be encompassed by several methods, means and forms, since the sovereign authority is safely and commodiously lodged in a few or many hands; and among the rest they like none so well as our own mixed form, of king, Lords and Commons, the latter being purely elective, the second absolutely hereditary, and the first partaking of both.[30]

However, though Toland was eager to disabuse the public of the notion that the Whigs were all Dissenters, and vice versa, John Shute (later Viscount Barrington) gloried in it. In *The Rights of the Protestant Dissenters, in a Review of Their Case* (1705) he argued that the Dissenters were in fact more representative of the nation than the Anglicans, 'being entirely disengaged from all foreign interests', and that

their religious freedom, built upon the Revolution Settlement, was inviolable. Shute also argued that the Dissenters
were not lineal descendants of Cromwell's regicide Puritans, and called attention to their important role in the
Revolution. The fact that the pamphlet was dedicated to
the queen only gave greater offence, and Sacheverell
focussed on it the full power of his invective. He called the
Dissenters 'resolute sinners, who have the impudence to
call the Grand Rebellion in '41 an old story, who arrogate
to themselves the sole merit of the Revolution, and yet
charge the Church of England's compliance with it as
treason, and represent her doctrines of obedience as pernicious to Kings'. He even accused them of setting fire to
London in 1666, on 'the celebrated lucky day of Oliver' (3
September).[31] At the same time the author of *An Address
to the Clergy of England* (1705) warned of the dangers of the
projected Union with Scotland, which would swamp the
church with Presbyterians.[32]

It is possible to sympathise with the High Church divines,
or at least see what they were objecting to, when we turn
to *Seculum Davidicum Redidivum, or the Divine Right of the
Revolution, Scripturally and Rationally Evinced and Applied*,[33]
published in 1706 by Robert Fleming, a Scot by birth who
had emerged as one of the most influential Presbyterian
ministers in London. Fleming compared the Revolution to
David's deposition of King Saul, and argued that in such
cases the voice of the people was in a literal sense the voice
of God; divine right to rule was properly evinced only by
'national choice'. Indeed, he handsomely approved of
revolutions in general, as a creative or propellent force in
history. Fleming went unscathed, though Drake had been
prosecuted for saying rather less on the other side. (In fact,
the only clergyman to be prosecuted up to 1710 was the
maverick William Stephens, rector of Sutton, for a libel on
Marlborough.)[34]

Moreover, the efforts of Tutchin in the *Observator* were
now seconded by those of Defoe in the *Review*. The *Review*
began, in fact, in February 1704, but it was not until 1705

or 1706 that it amended its previous moderate stance, perhaps in reaction to the attacks on it by Charles Leslie, perhaps because of a change of attitude on the part of Defoe's patron, Harley.[35] Indeed, if Defoe was as closely wedded to Harley in this period as his biographers assume, this could be said to throw new light on Harley's own political ideas.[36]

By June 1706 Defoe was arguing emphatically that by the doctrine of divine right Anne had no title to the throne at all, and that she owed her position entirely to the Bill of Rights. But his main contribution to the debate was his attempt to define the sovereign 'people', left so vague by Locke and Sidney.[37] Beginning with the common Whig premise that God had decreed government but not defined it, and it was therefore carnal and rational, a product of man's unaided intellect, he went on to argue that property-holding was the qualification for political power:

God gave man the earth for his possession; in that possession He included the government, for to have given a body of men the possession of a country, but give the dominion of it away from them, had been not to give it them at all; in this possession is their original power seated. Lords of the soil are always lords of themselves; if it be otherwise 'tis by usurpation and invasion, and that is a force upon reason, and thwarts the order of nature.

Therefore in England political power in the ultimate, as well as the immediate, parliamentary sense, rested with the freeholders:

The freeholders are the foundation branch of the constitution; and here all the governments in the world began; the right of possession always had the right of government, which is the band and guard of that possession. Reason, thus finding itself possessed of property, dictated government for its regulation and security, and this is a right whose divinity cannot be disputed.[38]

He was fully conscious of the novelty of his arguments, and though he referred to Locke and Sidney with approval, he disdained their support – 'I am arguing by my own light, not other men's.' His ideas were reinforced and extended in a long satirical poem, *Jure Divino*, published about the same time, in 1706:

He had the justest title to command,
Whose property prevailed and owned the land:
And so elective power commenced its reign,
Where equal right of property began.
The land divided, right to rule divides,
And universal suffrage then provides.
The government lay in the general voice,
They only had the power who had the choice...
They had the right because the land's their own,
And property's the basis of a throne.

In these circumstances, according to Defoe, the attitude of God was quite irrelevant:

Consent of nations is the sovereign call,
The best, the first, the true original.
The great *Vox Dei*'s in the public choice,
And always Heaven concurs with general voice.[39]

However, he was now prepared to allow the sanctity of rights gained by conquest, which he had previously dismissed as being against 'the order of nature'. The divine right of possession was now paramount in his mind:

He that had all the land, had all the power;
The property the title must secure

and he swept aside all Tyrrell's painful arguments for the sanctity of kingly election in the Middle Ages. To him the Anglo-Saxon kings were not the leaders of a free society but a pack of robbers whose sketchy rights were sanctified by force:

In robbery and blood they fixed the right divine,
The sword possessed the banished Briton's right,
The sword that vanquished innocence in fight...
The strongest king the weaker's crown possessed;
Conquest was always law, descent's a jest.

As for William the Conqueror, he was even worse:

Of foreign breed, of unrelated race,
Whore in his scutcheon, tyrant in his face,
Of spurious birth, of intermingled blood,
Neither our laws nor language understood;
But foreign to the nation and the line,
Upon his sword engraved the right divine.[40]

Nor did he share Tutchin's affection for John's barons, though he shrewdly allowed that their appeal to the Dauphin Louis was comparable with the invitation to William in 1688, and he observed that if James had had an acknowledged son, like John, and if he had not fled abroad, he would have kept the crown.

This was a degree of realism unusual in this period, and it is evident again in Defoe's treatment of Charles I. Sweeping aside all equivocation, he said,

The parallel between the Civil War, or Parliament War, or Rebellion, call it what you will, and the inviting over, joining with and taking up arms under the Prince of Orange, against King James, seems to me to be very exact, the drawing such a parallel very just, and the foundation, proceeding and issue just the same. I have nothing to do here with the consequences of the action: the parliament men, and others concerned in that war, could no more have it in their design to destroy the person of King Charles I, or the English gentry that invited over the Prince of Orange have it in their design to form the Revolution that followed, than either of them could foresee the subsequent issues of their undertaking before it was begun.[41]

It is not surprising that he rejected with contempt 'the old abdicated doctrine', and insisted that James had been deposed. He argued that the only defence against tyranny was a community of property, vesting in the people a community of choice:

People may crown the man that they approve,
And what they like below is always liked above

and he continued to press his opponents to acknowledge the *jus divinum* of the Revolution.[42]

Meanwhile the thunder from the pulpits deepened, with Henry Sacheverell in the lead. On 25 July 1706 he stormed into the pulpit at All Saints', Leicester, to deliver another assize sermon, this time on 'The Nature, Obligation and Measures of Conscience'. He was in fine form. Of occasional conformity he said,

Thus villainously are our laws abused, and this sacred name played upon, to the foul dishonour of God, and the disgrace of religion, which nowadays is made the pharisaical and Puritan cloak, like Samuel's mantle to amuse the witch and cover the Devil, and consecrate all infidelity, injustice, pride, lust, avarice and ambition, and the most execrable vices of hell, with the holy title of conscience; which in truth is nothing else but the vizor mask of cozenage, knavery and hypocrisy; it is the spiritual tool to serve the turn of all wicked designs, mere party cant and fanatical jargon, the very sound whereof should be a warning piece to alarm every honest man to stand upon his guard, and look about him.

The Dissenters, he went on, had inherited Naaman's crime,

more odious and stinking than his leprosy, who to keep in the government, could bow down in the House of Rimmon, and yet acknowledge the God of Israel; in a word, they outdo that amazing and irremissible sin of the son of perdition, the arch-traitor Judas himself, in that they daily sell and betray their Saviour for money.[43]

Francis Atterbury was not far behind. Preaching before the Lord Mayor of London in September 1706, he told him,

We live in evil days, when the most important and confessed truths, such as by the wisest and best men in all ages have been revered, are by licentious tongues questioned, argued against, derided; and these things not only whispered in corners, but proclaimed upon the house tops, owned and published in defiance of the common persuasion, the common reason and the common interest of mankind; and of all authority, both sacred and civil. Libertinism hath erected its standard, hath declared war against religion, and openly listed men of its side and party.[44]

The following spring, again before the Lord Mayor, he even launched an attack on the personal impurities of the Junto lords:

They that sat at the gate (some even of the men of greatness, and business, and gravity) spake against us, and we were the song of drunkards, of vain, idle, dissolute companions. The House of God itself hath been profaned by riots; abominable impurities, not to be mentioned, have been openly and daringly practised: we have declared our sin, as Sodom, and have not hid it.[45]

But by now the Whigs had acquired their own clerical champion in the person of Benjamin Hoadly. Hoadly is now chiefly remembered as the prime mover in the Bangorian Controversy of 1717, but his famous sermon before King George I to the text 'My church is not of this world' was only the climax to a career of militant unorthodoxy; and he has never received his due as the most powerful and effective, if not the most original, Whig propagandist of his generation.[46] He was not a pleasing man, physically, socially or mentally. He was not loved, even by those whose beliefs he expressed, whose cause he espoused. But it is difficult to withhold respect from a man who summed up the course of his life like this:

I have used my best endeavours to serve a cause upon which the Gospel, the Reformation and the Church of England, as well as the common rights of mankind, entirely depend...It is a cause in which I could more willingly spend the rest of my life, and a cause in which I could with more certain and well-grounded satisfaction suffer all that this world can bring upon me, than in any with which I have ever been acquainted. I have done, and resolve to do, everything in my power for its support. And I now offer up the whole of what I have done, and can do, to the glory of God, the honour of Christianity, the interest of the Reformation, and the good of human society.[47]

Hoadly was already debating matters of Christian belief and church government early in Anne's reign, but he first crossed the vague frontier between theology and politics in 1705, when he was invited to preach before the Lord Mayor and Aldermen of London on 29 September at St Lawrence Jewry; he was then rector of St Peter Poor, Broad Street. He chose to grasp the nettle of Romans 13: 1, 'Let every soul be subject to the higher powers', that famous text which was the principal scriptural justification for the doctrine of passive obedience.[48] He agreed that rulers were 'ordained of God', but he denied that the apostle's words were anything but conditional. According to Hoadly, 'the sole end and business of all governing power is to consult the good of human society, by maintaining peace and virtue in it', and all St Paul had meant was 'that it is the indispensable duty of subjects to submit themselves to such governors as answer the good end of their institution'. Any ruler who infringed this proviso, who misused his God-given power for the purposes of tyranny, at once forfeited his right to obedience:

For though his authority in carrying forward the end of his power cannot be resisted without the highest guilt, yet his power in acting contrary to that end may be opposed without the shadow of a crime; nay, with honour and glory...There is nothing in nature, or in the Christian religion, that can hinder people from redressing their grievances, and from answering the will of Almighty God, so far as to preserve and secure the happiness of public society.[49]

This sermon, at once printed, and reprinted twice before the end of the year, caused a sensation. Compton, Bishop of London, even denounced it obliquely in the Lords' debate of 6 December on the state of the church. (To which Burnet retorted, 'If the doctrine of that sermon was not good, he did not know what defence his lordship could make for his appearing in arms at Nottingham.')[50] John Haslewood rushed into print with *St Paul No Mover of Sedition; or A Brief Vindication of That Apostle from the False and Disingenuous Exposition of Mr Hoadly*, and Atterbury followed with *An Enquiry into the Nature of the Liberty of the Subject.* Hoadly replied with *A Review of the Doctrine of the Sermon*, and for good measure republished the offending sermon itself, with a further commentary, under the title *The Measures of Submission to the Civil Magistrate Considered.* Certainly, if Hoadly's ideas were shallow and unoriginal, he had a mind of great power, and the lucidity and logic with which he presented his own theories and ruthlessly dissected those of his opponents made him a difficult man to face; according to an admiring Burnet, he displayed 'a visible superiority of argument to them all'.[51] Atterbury took refuge in Convocation, where he had no trouble persuading the Lower House to pass a resolution that Hoadly's sermon was 'contrary to the doctrine of the church expressed in the first and second parts of the Homily against Disobedience and Wilful Rebellion'.[52] The Upper House took no notice, but when Convocation rose in the spring of 1706 Atterbury composed a highly ten- dentious account of its proceedings, including a violent personal attack on Hoadly, whom he accused of 'imputing rebellion to the clergy in the church while he himself preached it in the state'.[53]

There followed something of a lull, though even this was enlivened by a furious controversy between Hoadly and Atterbury on a purely theological question, the doctrine of the after-life and the proper interpretation of 1 Corinthians 15: 19. But on 26 July 1708, at Hertford Assizes, Hoadly returned to that unexpectedly whiggish apostle St Paul, and in the course of a re-examination of Acts 22 demonstrated that he had declined to recognise the government of Rome when it persecuted him illegally, whatever he may have written to the Christians of that city; indeed, he had 'plainly thought that laws were designed as a curb to the arbitrary will of the executive power'.

But in vain did he contend in his days [lamented Hoadly], in vain have the wisest of men discoursed in all ages, and in vain is absolute power controlled by success of arms in our own times, if we can live to be persuaded that there is no difference in governments, or that there is no guard in laws against arbitrary power.[54]

This published, amid a predictable storm of disapproval, he launched an immediate attack on the new Bishop of Exeter, Offspring Blackall.

Blackall is something of an enigma. A man of obscure origins, he had the reputation of a High Churchman; indeed, it was said of him that he had delayed taking the oaths to William and Mary for two years. Nevertheless, William appointed him one of his chaplains. He had a pamphlet tussle with John Toland in 1699, on the apocryphal books of the New Testament, from which he emerged much the worse for wear, but this seems to have confirmed his reputation as a right-winger. In 1705, however, preaching the sermon at St Dunstan-in-the-West on the anniversary of the queen's accession (8 March), he uttered sentiments which with very little amendment could have come from the lips of Hoadly himself. In fact, he modelled himself very closely on Archbishop Sharp: supreme power was granted by God, but the manner of its exercise, whether by one man or many and how, was a matter of earthly concern only, and therefore an unequivocal and truly religious allegiance could be given to parliament. He went on to say that a sovereign power could repeal laws as well as make them, and could alter the whole frame of government; and though he warned that such alterations must be very prudently considered – 'it being very rarely that any considerable change can be made in the form of a government that has been long established...without more danger of hurt than hope of good' – he made it clear that he thoroughly approved of the Revolution.[55] His general tone was admonitory – he took as his text Proverbs 24: 21, 'Fear thou the Lord and the King, and meddle not with them that are given to change' – but it is difficult to reconcile this sermon with the attitude he adopted a few years later, and he irritated and mystified the High Church members of his audience. One of them wrote, 'It may be questioned whether Dr Blackall's late sort of pulpiteering tends not to heighten the differences amongst us... Is it not more advisable to let the civil differences wear off in silence, than seek to eradicate them by popular arguments, which can never be framed satisfactory to all parties?'[56]

However, in January 1708 Queen Anne insisted on raising him to the see of Exeter, probably because he was rated one of the best preachers of his generation, and the sermon he delivered in her presence on her accession day two months later was a quite different thing. Published at the queen's command as *The Divine Institution of Magistracy and the Gracious Design of Its Institution*, it firmly asserted that monarchy was of divine origin, it had never been erected by the community at large or any part of it, and monarchs were responsible to God alone. They were appointed for the good of the people, but they were directly appointed by God. Perceiving that Blackall had deserted to the High Church camp, Hoadly felt it incumbent upon him to set his ecclesiastical superior right, which he did in *Some Considerations Humbly Offered to... the Lord Bishop of Exeter* – a remarkable performance, considering that the sermon had been received by the queen with evident satisfaction. Blackall published a rather petulant *Answer*, with the epigraph 'Faithful are the wounds of a friend, but the kisses of an enemy are deceitful' (Prov. 27: 6). Hoadly came back with *An Humble Reply to... the Lord Bishop of Exeter's Answer in Which the Considerations Lately Offered to His Lordship Are Vindicated, and* [with heavy sarcasm] *an Apology Is Added for Defending the Foundation of the Present Government*.

In the annual Latin sermon to the London clergy, on 17

May 1709, to the text of Romans 13: 1, Atterbury leaped to Blackall's defence (and St Paul's). He pointed out that resistance to constituted authority was an undoubted sin, and no Christian teacher ought to go about finding instances in which sin was permissible. Like Sacheverell, he considered that the promptings of man's carnal nature gave him ample excuse and opportunity to err:

Nor is there occasion for any man to prompt or advise the people to that which they are naturally too studious about of themselves. Their inclinations, too much bent on sedition, call rather for a bridle to rein, than a spur to quicken and provoke them... Where's the necessity, then, of our being taught by others that which corrupt nature teaches, and which without the dictates of a tutor we greedily imbibe? The subtle disputes of some moral authors are highly worthy of rebuke. For instead of deterring men from vice, they instruct them how far they may approach the confines of sin without incurring the guilt.

Thus he came down firmly in favour of passive obedience, to prevent political and social chaos:

It would be more for the common good to submit to the cruellest tyrant, than to break out into open rebellion, obey no power, and put our last refuge in arms and violence. For this is of all conditions the worst and most miserable that can be imagined; in which, the reins of government being wrested out of the prince's hands, his laws subverted, and his authority trodden underfoot, the populace are at liberty to run headlong into any mischief, and act with impunity whatever their lawless extravagancies prompt them to. 'Tis therefore of universal benefit not to resist evil princes, lest the rebellion prove of worse consequence to the public than the unjust administration itself.[57]

Blackall himself felt it prudent not to re-enter the controversy, but by now it had generated its own momentum, and continued notwithstanding. Much of the pamphlet literature it provoked was mere abuse, and none of it made any significant contribution to the matters under debate. The High Church party was dismayed and enraged that a clergyman should publicly preach whiggery – since the early 1690s Whig churchmen like Lloyd and Burnet had remained surprisingly quiet – and its sense of status was outraged by his attack on a bishop. The epigraph to one pamphlet read 'And one of them that stood by smote him on the mouth, and said, "Revilest thou God's high priest?"';[58] and in another annual sermon, this time to the sons of the clergy, Atterbury referred with sorrow to 'men sprung from the loins of Levi, and yet enemies to the tribe', and admitted that 'those among Christians who have been best educated, and principled in their youth, if they once break through such restraints...arrive at the utmost pitch of impiety'.[59]

Nor was this the only cause of High Church disquiet. In the same year, 1709, the long-time non-juror William Higden suddenly reneged, took the oaths and published a distinctly whiggish apologia. Government, he said, was subject to 'the suffrage of reason', and 'was instituted for the security and welfare of all members of civil society'.[60] Moreover, he had discovered that between the Norman Conquest and 1485 only six kings out of nineteen had succeeded with a hereditary title and indefeasible right; therefore the facts of history did not support the non-juring position. His conclusions had important implications for the High Churchmen, and as one critic remarked, 'Though he may satisfy himself in it, yet if his arguments prevail he will unsettle thousands.'[61]

Meanwhile the Whig journalists continued to pour out their poison. John Tutchin died in September 1707, beaten up by a Tory gang in the street, but his *Observator* continued, and grew if anything more radical. It was soon asserting 'that God gave power to the people to choose and limit their kings, to judge if they broke the Original Contract, and to renounce their allegiance if they would not govern accordingly, which justifies the late happy Revolution'. The Original Contract was now located in 1066, between 'William the Norman' and the English people, and 'the subjects [were] then sworn to the kingdom, as well as to the crown, and might be capable of treason against both'. Yet it was not the author of the *Observator* who was arrested but Charles Leslie, for his editorship of the *Rehearsal*, in May 1709.[62] Moreover, with Harley's fall in February 1708 Defoe slipped the leash, and the *Review* became more pronouncedly Whig than ever. By May 1709 it was telling its readers,

The present government stands upon the foot of the Revolution; every act of government her Majesty exerts, every step the present ministry takes in the present administration...everything done in the state, whether it be [by] Parliament, Council or Convocation, all recognise the Revolution; all set their seal, and give a sanction, to this principle established by the Revolution, that the people of Britain have an original right to limit the succession of the crown.

When Defoe went on to speak of 'the principle of revolutionary liberty', his writing took on a distinct Jacobin tinge.[63]

The trend was sustained by a famous pamphlet of 1709, probably written by the Whig publisher Thomas Harrison, which bore the significant title *Vox Populi Vox Dei: or True Maxims of Government*.[64] It contained nothing very original, but it was well written and cogently argued, and it was reprinted eight times in the first twelve months. What distinguished it from most of its predecessors was its aggressive self-confidence. A great deal of Hoadly's work, even, had fallen into the defensive mode usual in Whig propaganda; but *Vox Populi Vox Dei* was offensive, in the literal sense of the word, an attitude summed up in a rubric added to the title-page in later editions:

Recommended as proper to be kept in all families, that their children's children may know the birthright, liberty and property belonging to an Englishman. And that they may have a just notion of government and obedience, according to Scripture, law and undeniable reason.

Similarly, whereas Hoadly had devoted half of his own book on government to a refutation of Filmer, as had Locke and Sidney, the author of *Vox Populi Vox Dei* scarcely mentioned patriarchalism at all. He merely said,

We must suppose all mankind to have been infatuated, and to have become distracted, if they should have submitted themselves to the jurisdiction of one who had not antecedent right to command them, merely in order to their being in a worse condition than they previously were. And therefore, seeing the extent and latitude of the magistrate's power must owe its original to some grant of the people, it does from thence lie incumbent upon him to prove and justify the several degrees and measures of authority and prerogative which he pretends to claim. And what he cannot derive from some concession of society must be acknowledged to remain still vested in the people, as their reserved privilege and right.

As for the spectre of Charles I, that was exorcised briskly enough. The only real treason was to the constitution, and resistance to the ruler could only be treason if he was in fact fulfilling his proper function of defending and upholding the law.[65] (This was an argument used by the Long Parliament in 1642.)

The author went on to state categorically that ultimate power lay with the people; their contract with the ruler was defined by law, and the law was properly interpreted by parliament. As for absolute monarchy, as implied by the doctrine of passive obedience, that was simply 'inconsistent with civil society, and therefore can be no form of civil government, which is to remedy the inconveniences of the state of nature'. Indeed, he said,

No power can exempt princes from the obligation to the eternal laws of God and nature. In all disputes between power and liberty, power must always be proved, but liberty proves itself, the one being founded upon positive law, the other upon the law of nature.[66]

His attempt to portray the Revolution of 1688 as an act of resistance leading to the application of the Original Contract was not a success, because the facts were all against him; but he defended the general and continuing right of resistance in a stirring passage:

The greatest and wisest of nations, and the best of men of all ages, have reckoned it not only lawful for the people under the most absolute governments to do themselves justice in case of oppression, but have thought the doing of it a duty incumbent on them, and which they owed to themselves and their posterity; and the chief instruments of the great revolutions and changes that have happened in the world from slavery to liberty have always been accounted as heroes, sent by God Almighty from time to time for the redemption of man from misery in this world. They were accordingly honoured and respected while they lived, and their memories have been and will be held in veneration by all posterity.[67]

Answers were slow to come, and when they did they were feeble. *An Appeal to Thy Conscience As Thou Wilt Answer It at the Great and Dreadful Day of Judgment* (1710) was a mystical-religious tract dredged up from as far back as 1643, though its rubric, in imitation of *Vox Populi Vox Dei*, gave it some topicality:

Recommended as proper to be kept in all families, that their children's children may never become rebels against, or murderers of their lawful sovereign.

Charles Leslie certainly scored a point when he enquired of an imaginary Whig lord, 'Was your lordship's noble family first raised to that honour by the people? Did the mob first summon your ancestor to parliament? And is that the tenure by which you hold your baronage?' But Atterbury's *The Voice of the People No Voice of God* was stronger on assertion than argument, and ended on a note of hysterical abuse. He accused the author of being 'a Leveller, and consequently an implacable enemy to anything above himself, which is the most dangerous of enthusiastical delusions, or rather, a desperate contrivance of the needy to bring all things into common, or under that colour to thrust themselves into estates they have no title to.'[68]

But hysteria was an emotion not inappropriate to a High Churchman at this juncture. Hoadly had posed questions which it was really impossible to answer except, as Charles Leslie did, from a Jacobite standpoint. In fact, Thomas Hearne remarked that it was 'most absurd and ridiculous for those to speak against Revolution Principles who were for it [sic] when the Dutch Pretender came to England'.[69] Moreover, ever since they had lost the queen in 1705 the Tories' political fortunes had been going downhill. The Union with Scotland had not had the dire effects on the church which some had predicted, but it had strengthened the Whigs in both Houses of parliament; a bungled invasion attempt by the Pretender in February 1708 also reacted in the Whigs' favour at the elections that spring. The Junto lords were now so indispensable to Godolphin and Marlborough that not even the queen's prejudices could keep them from power. The Earl of Sunderland had already been forced upon her in 1706 as Secretary of State, together with the more moderate Whig, William Cowper, as Lord Keeper. The fall of Harley in 1708 made way for further changes: Robert Walpole was made Secretary at

War, and John Smith took the Exchequer. In November 1708, after a considerable struggle, Somers emerged as Lord President and Wharton as Lord Lieutenant of Ireland. After an even fiercer struggle, lasting the best part of a year, Orford at last returned to the Admiralty in November 1709.[70]

It is apparent to historians that the Whigs had seriously overplayed their hand. The long-drawn-out disagreement between the queen, Godolphin and the Junto over the appointment of three new bishops in 1707 wounded Anne's deepest sensibilities, and showed her that the Whigs could be just as great a nuisance in church affairs as the Tories.[71] The pressure that then had to be exerted on her to make her accept the new Junto ministers was counterproductive, and she had increasing doubts of the feasibility of Marlborough's war policy.

But the true situation was not apparent to outsiders at the time, not even to junior ministers. It seemed that the Whigs were riding high, and if they were still a natural minority in the country at large, the electoral system now seemed to be biassed the other way. The Act of 1709 naturalising foreign Protestant refugees, a measure proposed several times before but always defeated by the church lobby, could be regarded as a straw in the wind.[72] There were rumours of a new bill to repeal the sacramental clause in the Test Act of 1673, making occasional conformity unnecessary, and another to reform the universities, particularly by abolishing the requirement that Fellows of colleges take holy orders.[73] With the Whigs firmly in the saddle, a continuation of the war guaranteed by Townshend's Barrier Treaty, and the existing parliament due to last until 1711, none of these things were impossible, or even unlikely. In the light of this glorious dawn Defoe contemptuously dismissed the attacks of the High Church preachers, even Sacheverell:

Let them girn and snarl and rail, the Mountain stands sure, the Glorious Pillar is raised; Revolution is the basis, Protestant Succession is the column, and Union is the capital; Liberty, Religion, Peace and Truth are the beautiful carved work around it; and the Queen, supported by Justice on the one hand, and Strength on the other, is its guard and defence.[74]

But to other Whigs, and particularly Whig churchmen, it was almost terrifying that, with the queen sinking into premature old age, the church should still be committed to a supine obedience to the powers that be, and deplorable that the most important act of state in English history, on which the legality of all succeeding governments depended, should still reside in a kind of moral limbo, its legal and constitutional respectability tainted by its association in the public mind with popular *émeutes* and mass rebellion. As White Kennett told the clergy of Huntingdon in May 1709,

It is...to all considering men a great wonder, that after such a happy Revolution desired, promoted, brought about, submitted to and defended by the clergy in general as well as by the people; confirmed and established by the Providence of God to the apparent benefit of these kingdoms, and to the common good of the Protestant cause and the liberties of Europe; [it is] I say, a wonder that after all this there should arise a murmuring in the church, as if the Revolution were upon a wrong bottom, as if the principles of it were not to be defended.[75]

Later the same year Hoadly made the same point with some passion, in his final rejoinder to Offspring Blackall:

The case of the Revolution is a public national case of conscience, and the lawfulness or unlawfulness of the like practice is a case in which both the clergy and the laity of this land have long before my time thought their conscience extremely concerned. Were it only on this account, it could not be inexcusable in any clergyman to debate this matter in a theological manner. But on the former it hath, I think, become absolutely necessary that one way or other it should be put as much out of doubt as possible. For the matter is now reduced to this, whether we lie under a national guilt, or not. If the nation sinned against God in inviting over the arms of resistance, or in joining themselves to them when they were come, or in casting off their allegiance to one king, and fixing it to another by illegal methods, this is a national guilt.[76]

These two forces, Tory hysteria about toleration and Whig neurosis about the Revolution, found a common focus, yet again, in Henry Sacheverell, who climbed into the pulpit of the new St Paul's Cathedral on 5 November 1709 to deliver one of the most celebrated of eighteenth-century sermons, 'The Perils of False Brethren, Both in Church and State'.

8

BLACK AND ODIOUS COLOURS
Sacheverell's trial

Sacheverell's famous sermon was one he had delivered as long ago as 1705 at St Mary's, Oxford, at the height of the High Church revanche.[1] There were, however, important differences. For one thing, this was at the height of the Whig revanche; for another, he was not now addressing a sympathetic flock of parsons and pedagogues in a university noted for its old-fashioned orthodoxy, but the governing body of the nation's capital.[2] It is still not established whether the Lord Mayor invited him to print it, but whether or not, it sold in alarming numbers.[3]

The body of the sermon was commonplace enough: the usual studied rant against the Toleration Act, against occasional conformity and against the Dissenters in general, pictured as the heirs of the regicides. It was more serious that he took up, or simply repeated, the outcry of 1705, and accused the government of being infiltrated by the professed enemies of the church, forming a kind of Presbyterian fifth column. The reference to these men as 'wily Volpones' is supposed to have swayed the judgment of Lord Treasurer Godolphin, but this would be strange in a man often likened in the public prints to Judas, 'the apostle who carried the purse'.

In fact, though Sacheverell's attitude to Dissent was taken up in the subsequent impeachment, there was never any doubt that the gravamen of the charge against him rested on his interpretation of the Revolution of 1688; and here it was important that his words were uttered on the solemn anniversary of William III's landing at Torbay. Hitherto

5 November had posed as much difficulty to High Church preachers as had 30 January to their Low Church colleagues; witness Atterbury's sermon before the queen in 1704, and William Beveridge's before the Lords the same day. In these long discourses (thirty-five and twenty-eight pages respectively) each could find room for only a paragraph on 1688.[4] Sacheverell's approach was quite different: after heaping his usual scorn on the Dissenters, he made only a token thrust at the Papists, then launched a head-on assault on the Whigs:

Our adversaries think they effectually stop our mouths, and have us sure and unanswerable on this point, when they urge the Revolution of this day in their defence. But certainly they are the greatest enemies of that, and his late Majesty, who endeavour to cast such black and odious colours upon both. How often must they be told that the [late] king himself solemnly disclaimed the least imputation of resistance in his declaration; and that the parliament declared, that they set the crown upon his head upon no other title but the vacancy of the throne: and did they not unanimously condemn to the flames (as it justly deserved) that infamous libel, that would have pleaded the title of conquest, by which resistance was supposed? So tender were they of the regal rights, and so averse to infringe the least tittle of our constitution![5]

This much is famous, but the full flavour of his argument only appears in the passage immediately preceding this, in which he said,

The grand security of our government, and the very pillar upon which it stands, is founded upon the steady belief of the subject's obligation to an absolute and unconditional obedience to the supreme power in all things lawful, and the utter illegality of resistance upon any pretence whatsoever. But this fundamental doctrine, notwithstanding its divine sanction in the express command of God in Scripture, and without which it is impossible any government of any kind or denomination in the world should subsist with safety, and which has been so long the honourable and distinguishing characteristic of our church, is now, it seems, quite exploded, and ridiculed out of countenance as an unfashionable, super-annuated, nay (which is more wonderful) as a dangerous tenet, utterly inconsistent with the right, liberty and property of the people; who, as our new preachers, and now politicians, teach us (I suppose by a new and unheard-of gospel as well as laws) have in contradiction to both the power invested in them, the fountain and original of it, to cancel their allegiance at pleasure, and call their sovereign to account for high treason against his supreme subjects, forsooth; nay, to dethrone and murder him for a criminal, as they did the royal martyr by a judiciary sentence; and, what is almost incredible [they] presume to make their court to their prince by maintaining such anti-monarchical schemes. But, God be thanked, neither the constitution of our church or state is so far altered but that by the laws of both (still in force, and which I hope for ever will be) these damnable positions, let them come either from Rome or Geneva, from the pulpit or the press, are condemned for rebellion and high treason.[6]

The implication was, of course, that the Revolution *had* involved resistance, and was therefore wrong. Even if his words were taken at their face value they meant that the Revolution had implied nothing revolutionary, that it was an unfortunate and regrettable accident which had established no new principle of government. This had important implications for the nature of Anne's title. The Whigs, said Sacheverell, 'have the impudence to deny and cancel' her hereditary right, 'to make her a creature of their own power; and by the same principles [on which] they placed a crown upon her, they tell us, they (that is, the mob) may resume it at their pleasure'.[7]

The sermon had a mixed reception. The Lord Mayor hastened to disembarrass himself of all responsibility, and though William Fleetwood is no unbiassed witness, his comment on what he found when he arrived in London later in the month is probably not far wide of the mark:

I may safely affirm that there were not ten men of sense and character in all the city but did not absolutely condemn that discourse as a rhapsody of incoherent, ill-digested thoughts, dressed in the worst language that could be found. They said it became not a minister of the gospel for the spirit with which it was composed, nor a Doctor for the argumentative part of it, nor a tolerable Englishman for the style and expression. In a word, neither the matter nor the manner of the sermon pleased anyone.[8]

If the Whigs were displeased, Tories like Nottingham must have been even angrier, to hear the Comprehension Bill of 1689 described as 'a scheme so monstrous, so romantic and absurd, that 'tis hard to say whether it had more of villainy or folly in it'.[9] Defoe forcefully argued that given enough rope the Doctor would hang himself, and his party with him: 'Let this beast break wind, for it is no other; let him belch, his breath stinks so vilely it will make the whole cause smell of it.'[10] After all, he had been mouthing similar sentiments from the pulpit and in the press ever since 1702, and though the Whigs were apparently stronger now than at any previous time in the reign, no one expected him to suffer for them yet. This makes the decision to impeach him for 'high crimes and misdemeanours', reached after a month's delay, the more difficult to understand.

This difficulty has largely been cleared away by Geoffrey Holmes. A direct challenge, in the nation's capital, was something the Junto could no longer afford to ignore, and though some, like Somers, had grave doubts, the resentment and fury of the rank and file made some such action inevitable. The obscurity of Sacheverell's thought and words would probably protect him in a Common Law action, and the House of Commons in its judiciary capacity could only imprison him for the unexpired portion of the session and order the sermon to be burnt by the common hangman – a procedure usually calculated to increase sales. The remedy was an action for impeachment, which, it was thought, could be expeditiously got under way, and swiftly concluded.[11] The impeachment of Roger Manwaring in 1628 was a case in point, and an account of his brief trial was obligingly republished.[12]

Outside the Cabinet – whose members were well aware of Anne's growing hostility – the feeling of the Whigs was one of ebullient optimism, an attitude reflected many years later by Edmund Burke, who wrote of this trial, 'It rarely happens to a party to have the opportunity of a clear, authentic, recorded declaration of their political tenets upon the subject of a great constitutional event like that of the Revolution. The Whigs had that opportunity, or to speak properly, they made it.'[13] It was a clear opportunity to disable their chief adversary, establish their own view of the Revolution, which would give the nation a prospective as well as a restrospective right to overthrow tyrannical or popish rulers, and support their great champion, Benjamin Hoadly. The connexion with Hoadly was acknowledged on 14 December 1709, when the Commons resolved on Sacheverell's impeachment, and in the next breath took the unprecedented step of recommending Hoadly to the queen for preferment, 'for having often strenuously justified the principles on which his Majesty and the nation proceeded in the late happy Revolution'.[14] The leading Tories were abashed and pessimistic, the Whigs exultant, even those who had advised against impeachment. As Defoe said, 'Here the validity of the Revolution will be tried, and the whole body of the people of Britain will determine whether it was a legal, just transaction, or a plain rebellion against God and the king.' He called for a parliamentary resolution endorsing the validity of the Revolution, affirming the parliamentary nature of the queen's title, and outlawing the preaching of nonresistance. The *Observator* called for a public investigation of the universities, and other pamphleteers joined in the cry for a statutory affirmation of Whig dogma: 'Let the Act of Union and the Hanover Succession be made irreversible; let the Revolution be declared honourable; let the necessary means, the resistance then made, and in such deplorable cases hereafter to be made, be allowed lawful and honourable.'[15]

Of course, all these ambitious dreams perished in the reality of Sacheverell's trial. The Whigs won a Pyrrhic victory, and by the autumn were swept from office. Though the queen ordered all Hoadly's books to be brought to her, either she did not read them or what she read did not please; it was the Whig Duke of Bedford who gave him a chaplaincy and a living at Streatham.[16] (Some Commons Whigs had always thought it improper to recommend him to her favour when he had so strongly and publicly attacked a sermon published at her command, and it was said that Nicholas Lechmere, one of the most violent of the Commons' managers and Wharton's personal lawyer, thought the same.)[17]

Geoffrey Holmes has admirably described how the trial got out of hand, and instead of being briefly staged at the Lord's bar, was transferred to the public arena of Westminster Hall, and how the delaying tactics of Sacheverell and his lawyers postponed the opening until 27 February. This allowed support for the Doctor to be mobilised on a large scale, and over Christmas and into the new year the pulpits of London rang with denunciations of the Dissenters and praise for the new martyr, reaching a climax, naturally, on 30 January. At St Saviour's, Southwark, the preacher 'breathed nothing but axes and halters against those who are not of arbitrary and tyrannical principles', while Luke Milbourne provoked the Whigs 'almost to an outrage'.[18] Meanwhile, it was now considered propitious to publish *The Black Memorial*, a broadside listing Charles I's judges, and a poem on his martyrdom entitled *Exequiae Carolinae*.

The Commons Whigs struck back by nominating as their preacher for 30 January Richard West, the controversial author of *The True Character of a Churchman* (published in 1702 and now reprinted). Nor did he disappoint them. He launched a brisk attack on the High Churchmen for perverting the true doctrines of their own communion, and reprimanded them specifically for comparing Charles I's execution with the Crucifixion: 'We may be allowed to abominate the vile practices of wicked men against their sovereign', he said, 'without presuming to blaspheme for his sake.' He also reprimanded them for the use to which they commonly put this solemn day: 'We are not to fast', said he, 'for strife and debate.' He went on to accuse the Tories of wilfully confusing the Revolution with the Great Rebellion:

A people's preservation by defensive arms, when they are absolutely necessary for their preservation, is very far from the nature of rebellion; the design to uphold a constitution is very different from those black contrivances that subverted the foundations of it; and the means made use of to save the nation, at the happy Revolution, were founded upon principles that will no way defend those wicked men that reduced it to a heap of ruins.

He closed with an appeal commonplace enough in twentieth-century pulpits, but unusual then; it is a reminder that the Whigs were the war party par excellence:

Whilst our brave countrymen are willingly hazarding their lives for supporting her Majesty on the throne and her people in their liberties, let us be cautious of maintaining any doctrines that may be interpreted to violate the rights of either. Whilst some are asserting the cause of liberty with their blood it is a strange sort of employment for others to be acting in direct opposition to them, and betraying it by their opinions and doctrines.[19]

A moderate enough performance, it might be thought, certainly when compared with Stephens's sermon in 1700,[20] but when the House reassembled next day the customary motion of thanks was challenged, and though it passed on a division by 124 votes to 105, this is in contrast to a straight party vote of 182 to 88 on a reply to Sacheverell's Answer to the articles of impeachment later the same day.[21] Clearly the Anglican Whigs were wavering, and could be stiffened only by a decisive party victory.

Unfortunately, the outcome of Sacheverell's trial was not decisive, and especially not on Article I of the impeachment, which accused him of impugning the right and justice of the Revolution. For this article, and for no other,[22] the Whigs brought up their political and legal big guns: Stanhope, Walpole, Lechmere and Sir Joseph Jekyll (Somers's brother-in-law); but none of them was able to prove that resistance had been used in 1688, or that contract theory had affected the outcome in 1689. Jekyll was the boldest, but even he dared not assert that James II had been deposed; he merely argued that his 'abdication' implied an involuntary and obligatory renunciation. 'The word "abdicated"', he said, 'was insisted upon and carried, for that it included in it the maladministration of King James, which the word "deserted" (desired to be used instead of it) did not, and this appears by the Journal.'[23]

Lechmere offered the most lucid summary of Whig theory, from which it emerges that his Original Contract was still a historical phenomenon:

The nature of our constitution is that of a limited monarchy, wherein the supreme power was – by mutual consent and not by accident – limited and lodged in more hands than one; and the uniform preservation of such a constitution for so many ages, without any fundamental change, demonstrates to your lordships the continuance of the same contract. The consequences of such a form of government are obvious; that the laws are the rule to both, the common measure of the power of the crown and of the obedience of the subject; and if the executive part endeavours the subversion and total destruction of the government the Original Contract is thereby broke, and the right of allegiance ceases, and that part of the government thus fundamentally injured hath a right to save or recover that constitution in which it had an original interest. Nay, the nature of such an Original Contract of government proves, that there is not only a power in the people, who have inherited its freedom, to assert their own title to it, but they are bound in duty to transmit the same constitution to their posterity also.[24]

So far so good, but it was a different matter when he went on to argue that if the Revolution were held out to involve the Original Contract, or if it were legally invalid, then every act of state since 1689 was similarly invalid:

The denying the Original Contract is not only to disavow the whole proceeding at the time of the Revolution, but to renounce the constitution itself, to disclaim those many and undeniable proofs and testimonies of it which almost every part of our history, our records and memorials of antiquity will furnish. To deny the Original Contract of government is to contradict and condemn the voice and tenor of all our laws, of every act of the supreme legislative power, the force and efficacy of which exist upon the consent of the crown, Lords and Commons.[25]

And this thesis was put much more bluntly and immediately by the other managers. Robert Eyre, the solicitor-general, said, 'If resistance at the Revolution was illegal, the Revolution [was] settled in usurpation, and this Act [the Bill of Rights] can have no greater force and authority than an Act passed under a usurper'; and he was seconded by the Chancellor of the Exchequer (John Smith), who said,

The Acts of Settlement of the crown depend upon that legality; if that be illegal, the others in consequence are void, and though her Majesty has a hereditary right to the crown, yet I take those Acts to be her great security, and I can make no question but that if the foundations of those Acts were shaken the Doctor would soon find another hereditary right to resort to.[26]

Stanhope put it with his usual vigour:

If they be in the right, my lords, what are the consequences? The queen is not queen; your lordships are not a House of Lords, for you are not duly summoned by legal writ; we are no House of Commons, for the same reason; all the taxes which have been raised for these twenty years have been arbitrary and illegal extortions; all the blood of so many brave men who have died (as they thought) in the service of their country, has been spilt in defence of a usurpation, and they were only so many rebels and traitors.[27]

This was an astonishing and highly dangerous doctrine. Since it was the Whigs, not the Tories, who were applying contract theory to the Revolution, and since Sacheverell and his counsel now admitted that they, too, accepted and upheld the Revolution, their only quarrel with the Whigs being on the manner of its accomplishment and the justification for it, the Whigs were open to the accusation that it was they who were undermining the constitution, not their opponents, and that it was they who were encouraging anarchy and were therefore indirectly responsible for the famous Sacheverell Riots, which swept London in the middle of the trial, on the night of 1–2 March.

Indeed, when it came to the defence, Simon Harcourt admitted that his client had denied the legality of resistance to the supreme power, 'But it can't be pretended', he went on, 'there was any such resistance used at the Revolution; the supreme power in this kingdom is the legislative power, and the Revolution took effect by the Lords and Commons concurring and assisting in it'; and he referred his audience to Archbishop Sharp's sermon of 31 January 1700.[28] Following him, Constantine Phipps was glad to seize upon a loophole in the prosecution's case, and admit that 'The Doctor entirely concurs with the gentlemen of the House of Commons that the Revolution is an exception; and is not adversary to one of the learned managers, who was pleased to admit it was the only exception from the general rule.'[29]

The reference was to Sir John Hawles's speech, which according to a hostile witness was resented by his fellow managers.[30] He did, in fact, pre-echo Harcourt's argument that passive obedience was owing not to the monarch alone, but to queen, Lords and Commons. Dolben followed, and though he was briefed for the second article of the impeachment, on religious toleration, he declared that the general aim of the prosecution was 'To avow the principles and justify the means upon which the present government and the Protestant succession are founded and established, and this more out of a generous concern for posterity than our own security.' Echoing the sentiments of Commons leaders back to Queen Elizabeth's reign, if no further, he heaped Anne with praise, but stressed that it was necessary to take precautions against the possibility of a successor less pious, Protestant and well-intentioned.

We hope [he said] the record of this proceeding will remain a lasting monument to deter a successor that may inherit her crowns but not her virtues from attempting to invade the laws or the people's rights; and if not, that it will be a noble precedent to excite our posterity to wrestle and tug for liberty, as we have done.[31]

But it was left for Sir Thomas Parker, coming last, to point the moral that Sacheverell was really a concealed Jacobite. Since Sacheverell argued that resistance to the supreme power was illegal, but never defined that term or included the queen in it, his audience was meant to infer that he condemned resistance only to James II, in the past, and the Pretender, in the present. In fact, if his ideas were taken to their logical conclusion the Jacobites were the only men of principle, and in undermining the Revolution Sacheverell was deliberately trying to exalt the Pretender. 'As long as the Revolution stands unimpeached', said Parker, 'that person [the Pretender] can have no title, let his pretence be as favourable as he pleases. If the Revolution stands, the laws which are founded upon it stand too; and those laws concerning the right and succession of the crown are absolutely binding.'[32]

On this key point Simon Harcourt's reply was far from convincing. He argued that there was no reason to suppose that by the words 'the supreme power' Sacheverell meant monarchical power alone, and as for his Jacobitism, of that he said, 'This is diving into the secrets of his heart, and searching into his thoughts, which God alone knows.'[33] Phipps was on safer ground when he said,

I did not think that the Doctor, who asserts the hereditary right of the queen, could be charged with an intention to bring in the Pretender. I am in your lordships' judgment whether the denying her Majesty's

hereditary right be not the most likely way to bring him in? For I submit
to your lordships whether the denying the hereditary right of the queen
be not to suppose a hereditary right in somebody else.[34]

The basic defence was either that the Revolution had
been effected by passive obedience (to the supreme power
of parliament), or that the Revolution was an exception to
the general rule, and that in arguing such moral precepts
as 'Keep the Sabbath holy' or 'Honour thy father and thy
mother' preachers could not be expected to explore hypothetical instances in which it was proper to break them.
The Revolution was clearly such an instance, said Harcourt,
and he paid the prosecution the compliment of returning
their arguments upon them:

We are hearty well-wishers to the Revolution, and to the happiness of
England that is in a great measure built upon it. We agree that the law
of the land is the measure of the prince's authority and the people's
rights; that in the case of the Revolution, when the laws were overturned,
when popery was coming in upon us, and property signified nothing,
the people of England being invited by his late Majesty did resort to
the last remedy, that of necessity, and that necessity did induce resistance, and justify them in it, and upon that fact the Revolution
succeeded.[35]

It must be doubted if Sacheverell really accepted these
sentiments, but he was not anxious to court imprisonment
or the pillory, and his final speech, in which he drew on
all his gifts of obfuscation, was at once evasive and
conciliatory, and he did at one stage commit himself to this
unambiguous statement: 'I neither expressly applied my
doctrine of non-resistance to the case of the Revolution, nor
had the least thoughts of including the Revolution under
my general assertion.'[36]

All this took the wind out of the managers' sails. Jekyll
tried to turn the occasion into a triumph by saying, 'These
are concessions so ample, and do so fully answer the drift
of the Commons...and are to the utmost extent of their
meaning in it, that I can't forbear congratulating them
upon the success of their impeachment; that in full parliament this erroneous doctrine of unlimited non-resistance
is given up and disclaimed.'[37] But the fact is that Sache-

verell's capitulation underlined what to many people had always been obvious enough, that this great trial, with its attendant expenses of £60,000, not to mention the public disorder and excitement roused, had been largely redundant.

This feeling was strong amongst the Lords, whose business had been at a standstill for over a fortnight. They met to consider their verdict on 16 March. The old Duke of Leeds, whose part in the Revolution, as Earl of Danby, made him something of an authority, declared that the whole thing hinged on success. He said succinctly that 'They ought to distinguish between Resistance and Revolution, for Vacancy and Abdication was the thing they went upon, and therefore Resistance was to be forgot. For had it not succeeded it had certainly been Rebellion, since he knew of no other than hereditary right.' He went on to say 'he never thought things would have gone so far as to settle the crown on the Prince of Orange, whom he had often heard say, he had no such thoughts himself'.[38] His old companion in arms the Duke of Shrewsbury supported this commonsense view, and so, more predictably still, did Lord Nottingham and the Young Earl of Anglesey. 'As to the Revolution', said Anglesey, 'the vacancy of the throne was properly the thing, and therefore the mentioning the necessary means was mere nonsense.'[39] Lord Haversham, a rather undisciplined Tory who had sat in the Convention as a Whig, heartily agreed:

Means, my lords, is a relative term, and refers to some end; and the design of the Prince of Orange in his coming hither, and of those that joined him when he was here, being to have the nation and rightful succession secured by a free parliament, it follows that whatever force was at that time made use of, could not be made use of as a means to bring about an end which was never intended.

He pointed out that it was the Jacobites who had insisted in 1689 that King James had been driven out by force, and,

On the other side, those that were friends to the Revolution made it their business to persuade the world that all this was but a colour and pretence, and that the fact was quite otherwise; that the sense and conviction King James had of what he had done prevailed upon him rather to throw off the government than concur with a free parliament.

Now, he went on,

> It is very strange to see...those very men, and that party, who en-
> deavoured to place the Revolution then upon King James's voluntary
> desertion, which they called 'abdication', should now, without any
> reason given, be for changing that foundation, and do all they can to
> put it upon King James's foot of force and resistance.[40]

Somers, Wharton, Halifax, Devonshire and Cowper
spoke for the prosecution, naturally, but only Wharton's
speech is recorded at any length.[41] He said, fairly, that
Sacheverell's speech at the trial was irreconcilable with his
sermon. He denounced his doctrine of non-resistance as
'ridiculous and false', and pointed to the many specific
instances of armed resistance to James II in 1688. 'If the
Revolution is not lawful', he concluded, 'many in that
House, and vast numbers without, were guilty of blood,
murder, rapine and injustice, and the queen herself is no
lawful queen, since the best title she had to the crown was
her parliamentary title, founded on the Revolution.'[42]

A remark of Wharton's that the doctrine of passive
obedience was 'not reconcilable to the practice of churchmen' stung Hooper, Bishop of Bath and Wells, into a
defence of his own conduct in 1688. Hooper defended
passive obedience and agreed that in a desperate emergency resistance might be necessary.

> But that this ought to be kept from the knowledge of the people, who
> are naturally too apt to resist, and that the opposite doctrine ought to
> be maintained and enforced. That the Revolution was not to be boasted
> of, and made a precedent; but we ought to throw a mantle over it, and
> call it a Vacancy or Abdication; and the Original Contract were two very
> dangerous words, not to be mentioned without a great deal of caution.
> That they who examined the Revolution too nicely were no friends to
> it, for at that rate the crown would roll like a ball, and never be fixed.[43]

Several bishops followed, notably Burnet, who treated the
Lords to a detailed account of his own conduct in 1688, and
went on to argue that non-resistance had never been an
accepted part of church doctrine until after the Civil Wars,
which he admitted were 'plainly a rebellion'. He castigated
Charles Leslie, justified Hoadly's sermons (which had been
severely criticised earlier in the debate by Lord North and

Grey) and accused the High Church party of crypto-Jacobitism, finishing with a strong restatement of the Whig case:

Since resistance was used in the Revolution, and that the late king invited all the subjects to join with him, which was in them certainly resistance; and since the lawfulness of the Revolution is so much controverted, the condemning all resistance in such crude and general terms is certainly a condemning the Revolution.[44]

But the Whigs were not well served by other defenders, like the Duke of Argyll, who 'spoke very severely against churchmen meddling with politics and of their insolent expressions as he had heard of the restoring to them church lands',[45] and Lord Haversham probably spoke for many when he drew the Lords' attention to the fact that the prosecution had signally failed to mention at any point 'the divine appointment or institution of government', which obliged men to submit to it 'for conscience's sake'.

And I the rather mention this [he went on], because of notions that some people have of late advanced of their own (and have found their advantage, too, in so doing) of a discretionary obedience only. That is [to say], in my opinion, [that] whilst the government is for them they will be for it, and [otherwise] think themselves bound to obey no longer.[46]

It took all Wharton's considerable political skill to secure a firm verdict against Sacheverell, and even then the size of the majority, sixty-nine to fifty-two, was a slap in the face to the Whigs, and the sentence, that the sermon be burnt by the common hangman and that Sacheverell refrain from preaching for three years, fell far below the prosecution's imaginings, which had extended as far as imprisonment. They had to content themselves as best they could with burning the Oxford decrees of 1683 and several extreme pro-Sacheverell publications, and the whole crisis 'seemed to terminate with these small flames'.[47]

Indeed, the Whigs had gained technical acceptance for their view of the Revolution, and even bullied the defendant into accepting it, but only at the expense of modifying the general right of resistance almost out of existence. So anxious had the Whig managers been to fend off the accusation that they were supporters of popular rights that they had confined the application of contract theory to the Revolution alone and virtually forsworn its future use. Lechmere had explained the anxious care with which they had chosen the words 'the necessary means' to describe their resistance to James II, and had stressed that it had been legalised only because of the circumstances of supreme emergency in 1688.[48] Jekyll eagerly denied any wish on his part 'to state the limits and bounds of a subject's submission to the sovereign', or to 'put any case of a justifiable resistance, but that of the Revolution only'.[49] Walpole was 'very sensible of the difficulty and nicety that attends the speaking to this point', and feared that he might be 'misconstrued and misrepresented, as maintaining anti-monarchical principles'.[50] Sir John Holland would not have it thought that he was 'pleading for a licentious resistance, as if subjects were left to their own good will and pleasure when they are to obey and when they are to resist'.[51] And so on. And it is noticeable that when *Vox Populi Vox Dei* was republished in the wake of the trial it bore the milder, though heftier, title *The Judgment of Whole Kingdoms and Nations concerning the Rights, Powers and Prerogatives of Kings and the Rights, Privileges and Properties of the People...*[52]

In this guise it scored another success; the British Library catalogue lists six editions in 1710, an eighth in 1713 and an eleventh in 1714. Though the term 'edition' in the eighteenth century was far from precise, this was clearly a bestseller. Yet it seemed in 1710 that the judgment of this kingdom had gone against the Whigs. Beginning in 1710, a flood of jubilant propaganda denounced the Whigs for the very faults they had so strenuously denied, and the process continued to the end of the reign. One mock political glossary defined the term 'Revolution Principles' thus: 'Revolution comes from the Latin word *revolvere*, which signifies "to turn about", so that by "Revolution Principles" are meant such principles as, under the specious pretence of justifying the last happy Revolution, prepare mankind for any, and allow of the same proceedings, without the same necessity.'[53] Another twitted the Whigs for their blind devotion to 1688:

If your mouth be ever, on all occasions, in all places and company, full of encomiums of this Revolution, if your tongue be well turned to speak but those two words, REVOLUTION PRINCIPLES, with a grace; if you derive the very bread you eat, and the bed you lie upon, from thence, and do really profess yourself to believe that if it had not happened you would have been starved of course, or lain in a barn, or upon a hurdle; then you are truly sound and perfect...But if at the mention of Revolution, though it be one to come, you shake your head, shrug your shoulders, or look down; nay, if you allow one to have been attended by very good consequences, and to have been justifiable because it was necessary, yet if you spoil all with an IF or a BUT, there is no further need of witness, you are condemned from your own mouth.[54]

The same scribe also remarked,

Our forefathers, it seems, for many generations were so dull, illiterate and undiscerning as to derive all government and authority from God alone, [and] to imagine that the supreme power bore His immediate commission...and was accountable to none but Him...But these quick-sighted and ingenious gentlemen have made us happy in discovering another account of the original right of government, quite different from all this. They make government and authority to ascend from the people, tell us of an Original Contract made, no one knows where, or at what time, or by whom; but from them it comes, to them is the *dernier ressort*, and the last appeal to be made. Thus in their scheme the very splendour of the crown is like a shining vapour drawn up from a dunghill, which may blaze for a time, whilst the same exhalation continues to feed it, but if the jakes be covered, or refuse to send up a steam, the meteor drops to the ground from whence it was taken.[55]

Still more were simply horrified at the result of the debate.

I think [wrote one] the Revolution is in a very miserable condition if its only support is resistance. When we are reduced to that extremity as to have no better warrant for deposing the son than beheading the father, I'm afraid the difference between death and exile will prove but a very trivial excuse...To preserve our laws and constitution inviolable we have totally subverted them. King James only went about to alter them from what they then were to what they had been for above 700 years together from Egbert to Edward VI. To prevent this, we have changed them to what they never were since the beginning of the world.[56]

Another, masquerading as a pretended Whig, asserted that
'The late Revolution has made such a thorough change as
to have altered the fundamental laws of the land, the
constitution of our government, nay even the doctrine of
the Scriptures and the unchangeable nature of things.'[57]

The way in which the common people had turned
on their self-styled champions created unseemly mirth.
Edward Ward sneered at the Whigs' predicament,

> So unexpectedly to find,
> The sovereign people so unkind;
> Who had so long been soothed and flattered,
> Hoadly'd, Review'd and Observator'd

and the Addresses later in the year roused John Oldmixon
to fury. 'It could not but be provoking', he said, 'to see a
set of illiterate, intoxicated mechanics and peasants compliment the queen on her hereditary right, when even that
right was founded on the Revolution, which they branded
with the odious name of anti-monarchical principles.'[58]

On the other hand, the Whigs were freely and predictably blamed for the riots of 1710:

Hoadly was to tell the people that they were the original of government,
that kings and queens were creatures of their making, and when any
part of the government was displeasing to them it was their duty to rebel,
to bind their king in chains and their nobles in links of iron...Now, when
care is taken to instil such principles as these into the minds of the people,
when they are persuaded that they are to speak and that none is lord
over them, is it to be wondered at that they act in conformity to the
doctrine which they have learned; that they take upon them to express
their resentment by such insurrections, when their governors by any
maladministration, as they think, become obnoxious to it.[59]

Immediately after the riots Hearne observed,

The Whigs and all the party may by this time see the ill consequences
of the doctrine advanced by them of the original of government's being
from the people, and their chief writers, such as Hoadly, the Review,
Kennett, etc., ought to be punished with the utmost rigour for maintaining such arguments as give the people a power of taking up arms
when they shall think fit.[60]

This is the rhetoric of the gutter, of course, but the same
attitude was shared by better-educated and better-balanced

men. Francis Hare, a clergyman who despised Sacheverell and owed many obligations to the Marlboroughs, told the Duchess that the Whigs had laid too much stress on 'the liberties and properties of the people... without those limitations and reserves that the mixture of kingly government makes necessary', though he did not find this surprising in a party which according to him was still that of Ludlow and Ireton, and included too many 'men who have drawn their politics from books, and have their heads filled with the ideas of the Greek and Roman governments'.[61] Charles Hornsby, in mock-solicitous vein, advised the Whigs 'to lay aside those dangerous principles of rebellion which they still seem so fond of, which tend not so much to support the late Revolution as to draw us from the basis of our government into an eternal whirl of fresh revolutions'.[62]

In short, the impeachment of Henry Sacheverell, intended to strengthen the Whig position, had only weakened it. The importance of the Revolution, its centrality to the constitution, had been publicly reaffirmed, but serious doubts had been cast on the right of the Whig party to function as guardians of this heritage, and the party leaders had been forced into a more conservative interpretation of the Revolution than they would previously have avowed. This threw them onto the defensive at a decisive juncture in Anne's reign.

9

THE FOUR LAST YEARS
Whiggism on the defensive

In the last four years of Anne's reign it seemed that the Whigs had shot their bolt. They had failed to establish their political orthodoxy; indeed, Sacheverell's trial had tarred them even more indelibly with the brush of republicanism and irreligion. Nor had the verdict given 'a lasting sanction to the Revolution', as they tried to insist; they had been pinned back to the wretched 'abdication' compromise of 1689, and forced to admit that it had been a once-for-all-time event. This would only make it the more difficult to employ similar techniques on Anne's death, if it were then a case of resisting James III – whose hereditary title they had themselves confirmed.

Moreover, they had signally failed to clinch the question of Anne's own title, whether it was hereditary or parliamentary or both, though this had been the subject of debate for most of her reign, and at least one passage in Sacheverell's sermon gave them the opportunity to incorporate it in the articles of his impeachment if they wished.[1] Inevitably, the question arose at the trial, and the Whigs themselves seemed far from unanimous on the matter. Sir John Hawles argued that Anne had a stronger title than King William because hers was hereditary as well as parliamentary, but there was no reason, he said, why the exact proportion between these two elements should be defined, and the one need not exclude the other. He accused Sacheverell of advising her 'to quit that title she claims from her people, and to rely upon her title by inheritance'.[2] Constantine Phipps, for the defence, denied the charge, and remarked, 'If the queen, who has an hereditary right, and also a right confirmed and established by Act of Parliament, cannot be said to be a *jure divino* queen, I do not know who can.'[3] As we have seen, at the close Wharton asserted, in contradiction to Hawles, that her parliamentary title was her 'best title', and that if the Revolution was not lawful she was 'no lawful queen'.[4] Anne's own position was ambiguous. Later in 1710 she told the Duke of Shrewsbury that she objected to the idea that she ruled by divine right, and 'having thought often of it she could by no means like it'. This is well known. But there is a difference between ruling by divine right and succeeding by hereditary right, and the fact that she resumed the practice of touching for the King's Evil, a practice abandoned since the Revolution, suggests that she thought she had a better title than William III, with an element of the divine in it.[5]

The failure of the Convention, or any subsequent parliament, to pronounce on the legitimacy of the Prince of Wales was now coming home to roost. Burnet, in his memoirs and in a sermon preached at Salisbury on 29 May that year, lamented the omission, though in 1689 he had been one of those who were against an enquiry.[6] Moreover, too many Whigs had in recent years argued for the Pretender's legitimacy, in order to make his exclusion from the succession the more resounding. As Robert Molesworth said, 'A right Whig lays no stress upon the illegitimacy of the Prince of Wales; he goes upon another principle than they who do carry the right of succession so far as upon that score to undo all mankind.'[7] There is some evidence that even Lord Wharton had adopted this notion.[8] This did not seem so clever now, and one hopeful pamphleteer put as his case *The Assertion Is that the Title of the House of Hanover to the Succession of the British Monarchy...Is a Title of Hereditary and of Divine Institution* (1710). On the other hand, Somers, Halifax and Sunderland were so worried by all the adverse publicity that they sent a joint letter to the Hanoverian Resident in London, asking him to make it clear to the Princess

Sophia that they were not in favour of a republic, nor an elected monarchy.[9]

The queen's attitude to these party disputes remained in doubt. It was confidently said in some quarters that she resented Sacheverell's impeachment because it obliged her to sit day after day in Westminster Hall hearing her own title discussed and her father and grandfather freely criticised.[10] But she was not obliged to attend, and though her conduct was vigilantly scrutinised she gave little away. On 16 March, for instance, she caused a sensation by leaving in the middle of an aggressive speech by Nottingham's brother Lord Guernsey, which 'so confounded him he had much ado to proceed'; but it was, after all, ten at night.[11] Other indications were more decisive; when a preacher in her chapel at Whitehall presumed to pray for Sacheverell as one under persecution, the Clerk to the Closet, the Bishop of London, was peremptorily told to dismiss him, and a similar fate overtook one Dr Hesketh, who preached 'a very high-flying sermon' before her in July.[12] Charles Leslie, who had pleaded a royal pardon the previous year for rank incendiarism in *The Rehearsal*, was now laid by the heels, and after a spell in prison left to join the Pretender in Lorraine. It is significant that he was arrested not by Sunderland, but by his Tory successor as Secretary of State, Dartmouth. Most notably, when Lord Chief Justice Holt died in the middle of Sacheverell's trial Anne moved with unusual speed to replace him with Sir Thomas Parker, who had just completed the case for the prosecution to general applause.[13] She was willing to retain Somers and Walpole in the new government formed later in the year by Harley, and her refusal to grant Sacheverell preferment and her reluctance to appoint Atterbury bishop of Rochester are well known. Indeed, Sacheverell was regarded with general contempt. His own chief counsel at his trial pleaded the obscurity of his sermon: 'I must confess', said Harcourt, 'I can't easily comprehend him myself, but it may be a man's misfortune to express himself in such a manner as to make it decent and fit for him to explain himself.' The very lords and bishops who voted for him did so because they 'never knew nonsense to be a crime': 'In their warmest debates they said he was a madman, in their coolest they said he was a fool; and those that spoke best in his cause had more modesty than to attempt his defence any other way than by endeavouring to prove that his sermons were nonsense.' On top of all this, he was regarded as having reneged on his own principles in the course of the trial.[14] If he had not been symbolic of things other than religion – such as war-weariness and the growing antagonism to the monied interest of the City – his fame would have vanished in weeks. Its survival was a short-term advantage to the High Church party, though in the long term his incoherence, his self-contradiction and his hypocrisy became associated with the party as a whole.

Whatever the rights and wrongs of the case, the queen was left to face the results, and Cowper did not advance the Whig cause by arguing, 'If the difference of party advanced higher, it would break in upon all relative duties, it being at that pitch already, to produce differences between the most near relations, so that by progress of this all practical religion must be laid aside, and bitterness of mind succeed.'[15] Unfortunately, this was as much an indictment of his own party as of the Tories. If the Whigs had been willing to abandon Marlborough, throw over William III's war policy (or what they imagined that policy to be) and make peace, they might have survived. As it was, their obstinacy compounded their own defeat, which unwound over the period April to October 1710. The Whigs, Marlborough and his Duchess left Anne with no choice but to dismantle her ministry and assemble another at a period of maximum political excitement.

The piecemeal dismissal of the ministry over the summer, beginning with Shrewsbury's appointment as Lord Chamberlain in April and ending with Godolphin's dismissal in August, is well enough known; so are Harley's efforts to form a bipartisan cabinet.[16] But Harley's and the queen's attempts at moderation were undermined by the enormous upswell of Tory emotion which followed the Sacheverell trial and the beginning of yet another campaigning season in Europe. The arguments used at the trial were rehearsed and re-rehearsed in a chattering stream of pamphlets and a thundering tide of sermons all that summer. Many were alarmed at the disposition of the working classes to join in these controversies, and for them this was sufficient reason to call a halt. As one pamphleteer put it,

Both sorts [Whigs and Tories] are enemies to the public peace, by filling the minds of the vulgar with notions of liberty and passive obedience, which they are not able to digest...One leathern-attired coxcomb has heard of Hoadly, another read Sacheverell's sermon, others those firebrands the *Observator* and the *Review*...One purblind old sot tells you he has read the sermon, and truly he can see no harm in it, when a thousand to one his ignorance is so great that he understands not his own affair, or how to govern a family of four souls; yet he finds fault with the parliament, and wonders they'll make such a noise about nothing. Thus fools turn statesmen, and blacksmiths and tinkers turn regulators and vindicators of the church.[17]

Or as a poetaster wrote,

> The oyster wenches lock their fish up,
> And cry 'No Presbyterian bishop!'
> The mousetrap men lay save-alls by,
> And 'gainst Low Churchmen loudly cry.
>
> Some cry for penal laws instead
> Of pudding, pies and gingerbread;
> And some from 'Brooms, old boots and shoes'
> Roar out 'God bless our Commons House'.[18]

Ever since the Revolution, parties had been bitterly criticised as conducive only to political strife and social chaos; indeed, even the most committed partisans, like John Tutchin, paid lip-service to this idea. In 1710 a minority are found calling for a party truce or a coalition of moderates, notably in that famous pamphlet *Faults on Both Sides*, attributed at the time to Harley himself.[19] As Abigail Harley wrote to her brother Edward, 'The extravagance of every party is to be dreaded.'[20]

But Harley needed the very violence he deplored if he

were to unseat Godolphin and the Whigs, and in any case, neither he nor anyone else could control it. Sacheverell's triumphal progress across the country to take up a lucrative living offered him by a well-wisher in Shropshire was the occasion for wild rejoicing. Hoadly's books were burnt, and sometimes his effigy, and it was soon apparent that one of the Junto's chief aims in impeaching Sacheverell, to silence the High Church divines, had signally failed. If anything, their sermons were now tuned to a higher, more outrageous key.[21] The dispute invaded the private sector, and Abel Boyer records that 'Several private quarrels also happened on the same account, in which many were killed or wounded' – clearly a reference to duels.[22]

In the spring and early summer party spleen found a new focus in the device of Addresses to the queen, not seen on such a scale since 1701, and before that 1679. They were ostensibly provoked by the queen's final speech to parliament on 5 April, though why this should be so it is difficult to say. Here Anne referred to Sacheverell's trial as 'so necessary an occasion', and went on to say, 'I could heartily wish that men would study to be quiet, and do their own business, rather than busy themselves in reviving questions and disputes of a very high nature, and which must be with an ill intention, since they can only tend to foment, but not to heal our divisions and animosities.' She concluded with the hope that 'There may remain no other contention among you, but who shall exceed the other in contributing to advance our present happiness, and secure the Protestant succession.'[23]

In fact, the first Address, from the grand jury of Gloucester, was presented that very day, and had been drawn up on 18 March. It did not answer Anne's expectations, but it certainly set a pattern. It affirmed the petitioners' loyalty to the Protestant succession, gave an undertaking to defend the church 'against all republican, traitorous, factious and schismatical opposers', and undertook to choose Members of a like mind 'in the ensuing parliament'.[24] Meanwhile Sir Samuel Garrard, the Lord Mayor who had invited

Sacheverell to preach at St Paul's the previous November, had pushed a staunch Tory Address through Common Council by a slim majority of 114 to 95. It was presented on 13 April, closely followed the same day by a Whig Address from the Commissioners of Lieutenancy, undertaking to defend Anne 'against all that shall go about to prejudice the late happy Revolution, your Majesty's present most gracious administration in church and state, the succession in the Protestant line, the Church of England as established by law, or the Toleration'. In the same way the Address from the grand jury of Gloucester was countered a week later by the mayor and burgesses of that city, who hoped that by the interposition of royal authority 'we may everywhere hear the sound of the gospel, unmixed with the noise of politics'.[25]

But even the Whig annalist Abel Boyer had to admit that the High Church Addresses were more numerous, and 'according to the general opinion, received with more graciousness and countenance'. The University of Oxford was not backward in affirming its loyalty to the Hanoverian succession, but it condemned 'that popish republican doctrine of resistance to princes' as well as 'the damnable sin of schism', and undertook not 'to call in question any title by which your Majesty holds your crown, particularly that which is hereditary'. The county of Oxford was not far behind, affirming that its loyalty would be transmitted to the next generation, being as hereditary as the queen's title, and hinting broadly at a dissolution.[26] Similar hints appeared in other Addresses: from Minehead and from Henry St John's borough of Wooton Bassett (understandably, since St John had failed to gain election in 1708). The Whigs struck back with an Address from Hampshire supporting the queen's 'just title, founded upon the late happy Revolution'; the grand jury of the same county, sponsored by the Duke of Bolton, uttered similar sentiments, as did the cities of Norwich and Hertford. Kent, like Gloucester, was hopelessly divided. On 30 July the two county Members presented a violently worded Address

signed by twenty-six Deputy Lieutenants and fifty-two
Justices of the Peace, which denied that Anne had any title
at all except that which was 'founded on the happy
Revolution, and confirmed by the undisputable authority
of parliament'. The same day came another Address, from
the sheriff and grand jury, in precisely opposite terms.[27]
By this time Sunderland had been dismissed, and the
pattern of the future was apparent. By August the dissolution of parliament was being openly mooted, and the
clergy of London, under Compton's direction, sent up one
of the most discussed of all the Addresses. Sitting firmly
on the fence, it asserted Anne's hereditary right, but also
declared that the House of Hanover had the only undisputable right of succession, and gave a very firm assurance
with regard to the Pretender:

We thank God from the bottom of our hearts, for the legal provisions
made in this regard from popery and arbitrary power, which we once,
through the Divine Assistance, vigorously and successfully withstood
when they were breaking in upon our constitution; nor shall we fail to
manifest an equal zeal against them whenever, and by what means
soever, they shall meditate a return.[28]

The effect was rather spoiled, however, by the fact that
several of the High Church clergy refused to sign it. The
comments of that doughty Jacobite Thomas Hearne are
pertinent:

This address is finely drawn up in smooth, flattering words; but should
the time once come when God should think fit to settle one who has the
true right, notwithstanding his being a Papist, these men may perhaps
as readily strike in with him, and fall from their protestations, as they
did in the late Revolution.[29]

Indeed, the paradoxes of the Revolution, a living revolution in the sense that it was part of the memory of all men
over thirty-five, were infinite. 'Jack' (John Grubham)
Howe, a fierce Exclusionist in 1679 and an 'Old Whig' ten
years later, was now an aggressive Tory; in fact, he had
crossed the floor of the House under King William, and
he told the Commons in 1694, 'I have never changed party;
if others have left me, let them answer for it.'[30] Bishop

Compton, one of the signatories of the invitation to William, had undergone a similar transition. Mercifully, his share in the invitation was unknown; he was twitted enough for his flight to Nottingham with the Princess Anne in November 1688, just as Burnet was twitted for the 'Turkish' sermons he had delivered at Whitehall under Charles II, and Rochester for his part in James II's Commission for Ecclesiastical Causes. As late as 1712 a Tory prelate like Trelawney of Winchester still kept 30 June as a day of thankful rejoicing, it being the anniversary of his acquittal as one of the Seven Bishops in 1688.[31] Well might a cynical rhymester quip,

> Among the High Churchmen I find there are several
> That stick to the doctrine of Harry Sacheverell.
> Among the Low Churchmen too I find that as oddly
> Some pin all their faith in Benjamin Hoadly.
> But we moderate men do our judgment suspend,
> For God only knows where these matters will end.
> For Sal'sbury Burnet and Kennett White show,
> That as the times vary so principles go.
> And twenty years hence for ought you and I know,
> Twill be Hoadly the High, and Sacheverell the Low.[32]

This added spice to a controversy which continued all summer long. Unfortunately, little new was said, and it would be tedious to recount old arguments. The impression is that both sides had talked themselves into a state of exhaustion. The Addresses, indeed, produced a curious sub-literature, whose titles, and often contents, were calculated to deceive, like *The True Genuine Modern Whig Address* (actually Tory), *The True Genuine Tory Address* (Whig), *The Whigs' Address: Exploding Their Republican Principles* (Whig) and, capping it all, *The True Genuine Tory Address and the True Genuine Whig Address Set One against Another* (Tory).[33] The only original note was struck by *Four Letters to a Friend in North Britain*, which boldly stated what even the managers at Sacheverell's trial had only hinted, that the Doctor was a subsidiary agent in a far-ranging Jacobite plot to change the succession.[34] Harley apparently commissioned a reply, but thought better of publishing it.[35]

By the time parliament was finally dissolved on 21 September, the Whigs must have known they were doomed; in fact, the Tory majority in the new House of Commons was 151.[36] The election propaganda again makes it clear that Sacheverell was only a symbol; the real impetus was towards peace, low taxation and the curbing of the monied interest. Hostility to the monied as against the landed interest had always been part of the opposition to Whiggism, at least since 1695,[37] and it was particularly weakening to the Whigs in 1710 that men could be bitterly opposed to Sacheverell and the High Church interest, but equally critical of the Junto and the financial interests in the City they were thought to represent.[38] *A Letter to a New Member of the House of Commons*, published in October or November, commented,

Is it not a strange and wonderful thing, that while the nation is almost bankrupt, wealthy men should shoot up in several offices, like mushrooms, and that while the government was endangered to be beggared, that all its servants should riot in such wealth and plenty that the bare handling of a brush in any office was the way to a plentiful fortune.[39]

Swift took up the same theme in *The Examiner* as soon as parliament opened, and returned to it in *The Conduct of the Allies* the following year, though the Commission for Accounts appointed by the new House of Commons could discover no serious improprieties.[40]

By 1711 the Whigs were in serious disarray, and their morale blasted. Swift remarked almost casually,

It sometimes happens for a cause to be exhausted and worn out, as that of the Whigs in general seems at present to be. The nation has had enough of it. It is as vain to hope [of] restoring that decayed interest as for a man of sixty to talk of entering on a new scene of life that is only proper for youth and vigour. New circumstances and new men must arise, as well as new occasions, which are not like to happen in our time.[41]

Indeed, it was the burden of much of Swift's argument, not only in *The Examiner*, but in *Some Advice to the October Club* (1712) and *The Four Last Years of the Queen*, that the words 'Whig' and 'Tory' had lost all effective meaning and should be discarded.[42] This was the theme, of course, of *Faults on Both Sides*, which was followed by a number of other pamphlets which adopted a 'centre' position.[43] It was only natural that Harley's pensioners, like Swift and Defoe, should take a similar line, but it is rather surprising to find John Toland joining them.[44]

But it was one of the weaknesses of the Whigs that they were losing their left wing, which was disillusioned by the compromises offered by the prosecution at Sacheverell's trial, and by the drift of recent Junto policy. Contemporaries made a distinction between the 'Old Whigs' (among whom even Robert Harley might plausibly be listed – by others, not himself) and the 'Modern Whigs', the government group associated particularly with the extreme leadership of the Earl of Sunderland.[45] The nature of the division can be inferred from Robert Molesworth's *The Principles of a Real Whig*, written in 1711. Molesworth began by denouncing 'nominal' Whigs as 'worse than any sort of men', and defined a 'real Whig' as 'one who is exactly for keeping up the strictness of the true old Gothic constitution under the three estates of king (or queen), lords and commons; the legislative being seated in all three together, the executive being trusted with the first, but accountable to the whole body of the people in case of maladministration'. He boldly declared that the Great Rebellion was an example of justifiable resistance to a tyrannical ruler – contradicting the idea put forward by Burnet that the incident was an aberration, brought on by original sin. In fact, echoing the Duke of Leeds, he admitted that 'When subjects take up arms against their prince, if their attempt succeeds it is a revolution, if not it is called a rebellion.' He regarded the legitimacy or otherwise of the Pretender as irrelevant, because 'The exercise of an arbitrary, illegal power in the nation, so as to undermine the constitution, would undermine either King James, King William, or any other.' As for the operation of the constitution, here Molesworth's attitude was pure Country. He called for annual parliaments, he defended 'a whiggish army' in the present emergency, but looked to 'the arming and training of all the freeholders of England' in a citizen militia; and on the subject of qualifications for MPs his attitude is indistinguishable from that of the October Club.

An Old Whig [he said] is for choosing such sort of representatives to serve in parliament as have estates in the kingdom, and those not fleeting ones, which may be sent beyond seas by bills of exchange by every packet boat, but fixed and permanent. To which end every merchant, banker, or other monied man who is ambitious of serving his country as a senator should have also a competent, visible landed estate, as a pledge that he intends to abide by [his constituents], and has the same interest with theirs in the public taxes, gains and losses.

Finally, he evinced a missionary attitude towards the principles of Whiggism which was certainly not shared by the Junto:

No man can be a sincere lover of liberty that is not for increasing and communicating that blessing to all people; and therefore the giving or restoring it not only to our brethren of Scotland and Ireland, but even to France itself, were it in our power, is one of the principal articles of Whiggism.[46]

In contrast to this sturdy radicalism, the ambiguities of the official Whig position come through in John Withers's *History of Resistance*:

We count no curses, no execrations too bitter for him who shall involve the nation in blood and confusion because his ambitious expectations are not gratified, or even because there may be mistakes in government. We look upon magistrates as God's vice-gerents upon earth, and that they ought to be respected and obeyed by us in all lawful things. We think nothing but extreme necessity can justify resistance to them.[47]

The trouble is, what constitutes 'extreme necessity'? What 'mistakes in government' should be considered penal, and what 'ambitious expectations' should be regarded as legitimate? The effect of 1710 – Sacheverell's trial followed by the October election – was to put the succession in greater doubt than ever. William Fleetwood, Bishop of St Asaph (disguised as 'a curate of Salop') was not the only clergyman who still had difficulty defining the nature of Anne's title:

I tell my people that she is the Lord's anointed, that she possesses the throne as well by the Act of Settlement as by an hereditary right, as being the daughter of King James, the title and the hopes of the Pretender (be they what they will) having been extinguished by an Act of Parliament; so that nobody can or ought to come between the crown and her.[48]

But this left the situation wide open. One who rejoiced at the whole imbroglio was Charles Leslie. In *The Good Old Cause: or Lying in Truth* and *The Good Old Cause Further Discussed* (1710) he hinted pretty broadly that the Pretender's was the only true title, and that he was in the same state as the young Charles II, in forced exile from his rightful kingdoms. The Whigs he castigated unmercifully:

> All the last reign they gave the Pretender no other name than Perkin and Imposter. Now they plead for his birth and own it. Abdication is now run down, and the Revolution must be all resistance...Having made the Revolution resistance and given up the birth of the Pretender, if the church should preach any more her old doctrine of non-resistance she must be against the Revolution, and if she owns heredity she must be for the Pretender.[49]

So seriously did the government regard such stuff that Leslie was arrested on a Secretary of State's warrant, and released only to go abroad. Warrants were also issued for the author of *The Hereditary Right of the Crown of England*, a learned folio on medieval history published in 1713. Innocent as it might seem, medieval history was dangerous ground, especially since the author affected to prove that every king since the Conquest had ascended the throne by direct hereditary succession. The drift was obvious enough, even without the closing text from Ezekiel (17: 15), 'Shall he prosper? Shall he escape that doeth such things? Or shall he break the covenant and be delivered?' The author was George Harbin, but another non-juror, Hilkiah Bedford, was found guilty, fined one hundred marks and imprisoned for three years.[50]

On the other side, though the volume of Whig polemic against the government was unprecedented, driving Oxford in the end to pass the Stamp Act of 1712 levying an increased duty on newspapers and journals, its quality, despite the efforts of Addison and Steele, was not high.[51] Moreover, it was directed not so much to the discussion of constitutional problems as to conventional attacks on the High Church position as popish and Jacobite and on the Peace of Utrecht as popish and francophile. And in response the Whigs had to face the brilliant and sustained invective of Swift, whose *Conduct of the Allies* (1711), a brilliant demolition of Junto war policy, was one of the most compelling pamphlets of the century. This was followed by *Some Remarks upon a Pamphlet Entitled a Letter to the Seven Lords of the Committee* (1711), the devastating *Short Character of Thomas Earl of Wharton* (1711) and (most telling of all) *The Public Spirit of the Whigs* (1714).

Nor was Swift alone, though the skilled polemicists who supported him are overshadowed by his posthumous fame. One such was Charles Hornsby. Hornsby's *A Caveat against the Whigs in a Short Historical View of Their Transactions* was published in four parts between 1710 and 1712; together they make a substantial book, which went through at least four editions up to 1714. In a long review of Charles II's reign (Part I) he tied the first Whigs firmly in with Oliver's Puritans, and in Part II he ascribed James II's fall to a deliberate plot on the part of the second Earl of Sunderland, whose relationship to the third Earl, the Junto peer, was naturally not underplayed. As for the Revolution itself, this was part of the same conspiracy, a gigantic fraud perpetrated on a supine nation:

Thus was this amazing Revolution accomplished, in which, to the glory of the fabricators it must be allowed, that the whole machine was so exquisitely contrived, and the parts so duly adjusted, that when it was set together and put in motion it went off with little exterior assistance, in that order and regularity that many of those who were moved by it knew not they were leaving their old government till they were quietly seated under a new one, and then, awakening out of their lethargy, wondered to find themselves in a strange place.

As for the famous Original Contract, he said of the Commons' resolution of 28 January 1689,

I shall not question but those who gave their affirmative to it had diligently perused the Original Contract, and nicely examined every clause and covenant in it, whatever is become of it since.[52]

In Part III he accused some of the Revolution Whigs of plotting to bring in a republic – 'a new Babel fabric', he called it – and said that they all 'rejoiced to have deposed a monarch, and made the crown once more elective, which they hoped at another opportunity to improve to their further advantage'.[53] In Part IV he accused them of stressing Anne's parliamentary title the better to depose her when their plans were ripe, and if Sacheverell had not put a spoke in their wheel they had planned not only to impose a political test on the clergy and repeal the sacramental test, but to take control of the army in order to give backing to the people's right of resistance.[54] He meant the Whigs no harm personally, he assured his readers, but he thought they ought to be quarantined:

If these gentlemen were separated from the rest of this nation, and assembled together in their fancied primitive state of equality in one of Mr Hoadly's wildernesses, we here should not trouble ourselves about them; they might be welcome to put in practice their closet notions (as they call them), and establish their reasonable form of Utopian government, their free state of No-Land, according to such a model as they could agree amongst themselves, and if they should never agree (as most certainly they would not), if they should behave themselves like the Cadmean brethren, and fight it out to the last man, each in defence of his own darling whimsy, we should not be angry; they would only be objects of our pity, and a fresh instance of popular frenzy, and the miserable condition of men left to themselves without law and government, and infatuated with such notions as tend to the destruction of that order and subjection by which both are constituted and preserved.[55]

A similar publication was Joseph Trapp's *The Character and Principles of the Present Set of Whigs*, which was published in 1711 and reached a third (and enlarged) edition the following year. Trapp branded all the Whigs, without distinction, as 'inveterate republicans' – 'as to their scheme of government, it is of the old chaos make, without form and void, and darkness is upon the face of it'. Under that scheme, *horribile dictu*, 'all distinctions are lost, all ranks and degrees of men confounded', for 'the governed are the governors, and the governors are the governed; or, more properly, there is no such thing as any government at all'. As for the famous Revolution,

The use the Whigs make of the Revolution is to disprove the doctrines of the Scriptures, and alter our form of government; and to put it upon such principles as the late king of glorious memory, and those who joined and assisted him, expressly disclaimed. We have had a revolution; therefore (according to the Whigs) we must talk and think about nothing else. The government, upon a very extraordinary occasion, once received a shock; therefore it must never return into its right course. Revolution Principles must be industriously propagated, and that single transaction must be of more force and authority than a dozen acts of parliament, and the constitution of our government.[56]

The pulpits had been surprisingly quiet meanwhile, to judge by the sermons published, but in March 1713 Sacheverell's three years were up. On the 29th, Palm Sunday, he preached himself back into form at St Saviour's, Southwark, with a vigorous sermon on 'The Christian Triumph, or The Duty of Praying for Our Enemies', taking as his text Luke 23: 34, 'Father, forgive them; for they know not what they do.' Apart from a lengthy excursus on the execution of Charles I, this was relatively uncontroversial, but two months later, on 29 May, he preached to the House of Commons on a more congenial theme, 'False Notions of Liberty in Religion and Government Destructive of Both', which needs no gloss.

The surprising thing is the passivity of the Whigs at this juncture. Certainly Whig pamphlets continued to be published,[57] but they entirely lacked the fire and the impact of Swift's work, or even Trapp's and Hornsby's. Their best writers, Addison and Steele, were occupied with the *Tatler* and *Spectator*, which had a huge following but only a mild political influence. The task of answering Sacheverell in 1713 devolved on an ordinary clergyman, Francis Squire.[58] It was not until late 1713 and early 1714, with the founding of Steele's *The Englishman* and the publication of his pamphlet *The Crisis*, that the Junto apparently woke to the need for some forceful propaganda on their side. They may have been waiting for the general election of 1713, which they expected to reverse the verdict of 1710, and in general they probably considered that time was on their side. Anne was in poor health, and the logic of the Peace of Utrecht had driven the Elector George of Hanover into the Whig camp. By the end of 1712 Oxford and Bolingbroke were patently at loggerheads, and the ministry seemed on the point of breaking up. Neither man had much of a future except with the Pretender, and unless James could be induced to change his religion his chances of succeeding to the throne were slim. Even the most besotted of the High Churchmen would be reluctant to hazard James III after their experiences with James II.

But the bishops did not agree; and it was they who sounded the tocsin. Jonathan Trelawney wrote to Wake of Lincoln in March 1712, 'I have hardly had a quiet night or a cheerful day since the advance of peace to a certain people's liking. I can't but fear the Pretender is next oars. If so, the coffin is bespoke for the queen, for popery is always in haste to kill when they are sure of taking possession.'[59] A few weeks later Fleetwood of St Asaph published a collection of sermons with a preface in which he lamented the unmerited discredit into which the Revolution had fallen, slighted the Peace of Utrecht, and observed that if Anne's son, the Duke of Gloucester, had survived, he 'had saved us many fears and jealousies, and dark distrusts, and prevented many alarms that have long kept us, and will keep us still, waking and uneasy'. On 10 June the House of Commons voted that the book be burnt, as 'malicious and factious, highly reflecting upon the present administration of public affairs under her Majesty, and tending to create discord and sedition amongst her subjects'. Fleetwood wrote to his friend Burnet, 'My heart is wounded within me, when I consider seriously whereabouts we are, and whither we are tending...Your lordship may now imagine you grow young again, for we are fallen, methinks, into the very dregs of Charles the Second's politics.'[60]

Gilbert Burnet is a curious figure. After the Revolution he never quite made the impact to be expected of a man of his character, learning and intelligence; perhaps this was because of his Scots nationality, perhaps because there was always something of the buffoon about him:

...A big-boned northern priest,
With pliant body and with brawny fist;
Whose weighty blows the dusty cushions thrash,
And make the trembling pulpit's wainscot crash.[61]

Moreover, though the meagre records suggest that he was an effective speaker and debater in the Lords, after parliament burnt his pastoral letter in 1693 he did not seem anxious to engage in public controversy. But to some extent Sacheverell brought him back, to fill the gap left by Hoadly, who remained silent from 1709 to 1714. On 29 May 1710 at Salisbury Burnet preached an important sermon, which was printed, elaborating on his speech at Sacheverell's trial. Together with another sermon, delivered on 5 November in the same year, they constitute a studied defence of the Revolution. He ended with the words

Thus I have deduced the grounds upon which the Revolution was carried on and established, which must be looked on as a continued usurpation to this day, if these principles are not true; all the oaths taken to support it are so many solemn perjuries, which are of no force unless built upon a sure foundation; and the prayers we have been offering up relating to it are an impious profanation of the name of God, if that for which we bless God was unlawful.[62]

When the queen consulted him on the peace negotiations the following year he told her that 'If any such peace should be made, she was betrayed, and we were all ruined; in less than three years' time she would be murdered, and the fires would be again raised in Smithfield.' 'I pursued this long', he tells us, 'till I saw she grew uneasy; so I withdrew.'[63]

Fleetwood's example spurred him to further efforts, and his manner of proceeding suggests that he was courting the same fate. In 1713 he published a collection of *Some Sermons Preached on Several Occasions*, with a twenty-five-page preface exhaustively justifying the Revolution and reaffirming Revolution Principles. (It was, in effect, an elaboration of his sermon at Salisbury on 5 November 1710). Later the same year he published a new edition of his *Discourse of the Pastoral Care* (first published in 1692), with 'a new preface suited to the present time'. This preface, which was also sold separately for the benefit of those owning previous

editions, contained explicit warnings of the danger from
the Pretender, and though it included a spirited attack on
the High Church party its general tone was one of gloom.
'I cannot look on without the deepest concern', he said,
'when I see imminent ruin hanging over this church, and
by consequence over the whole Reformation.'[64]

Early in 1714 he also published a separate introduction
to the third volume of his *History of the Reformation*, though
the complete book did not appear until 1715. This introduction was even more pessimistic; in fact, one of his
opponents rightly characterised it as the product of 'utter
despondency, fear and rage'.[65] He thought that England
was in the same danger now as in 1679 or 1681, when the
first two volumes of the *History* had been published:

> We are sunk in our learning, vitiated in principle, tainted some with
> atheism, others with superstition; both which, though by different ways,
> prepare us for popery. Our old breaches are not healed, and new ones,
> not known in former times, are raised and fomented with much industry
> and great art, as well as much heat. Many are barefacedly going back
> to that misery from which God with such a mighty hand rescued us.

He painted a hectic picture of England under a popish
successor, apparently regarding such a denouement as
inevitable. The church would be overthrown, the abbey
lands would be resumed, and, as he had warned the queen,
the fires of Smithfield would blaze again. (The fact that his
London house overlooked Smithfield must have been a
powerful stimulus to his imagination.)

> But [he admitted] none of these things will move an insensible and
> degenerate race who are thinking of nothing but present advantages.
> And so that they may now support a luxurious and brutal course of
> irregular and voluptuous practices, they are easily hired to betray their
> religion, to sell their country, and to give up that liberty and those
> properties which are the present felicities and glories of the nation.

and he ended on a note of near hysteria:

> God be thanked that there are many among us that stand upon the watch
> tower, and that give faithful warning; that stand in the breach, and make
> themselves a wall for their church and country; that cry to God day and
> night, and lie in the dust mourning before Him, to avert the judgments
> that seem to hasten towards us.[66]

This provoked many replies, of course, and Burnet being Burnet most of them were decidedly irreverent. He had characteristically given hostages to fortune by admitting the sloppy way he had composed the first two volumes of the *History of the Reformation* and blatantly 'plugging' the third; and the idea of his seriously preparing himself for death at the stake was eminently risible. One critic assured him,

Be easy, my lord, and disturb not the peace of your old age with vain and imaginary fears of taking the other turn to Holland, and sharing in a second Revolution. You are likely to enjoy a good bishopric as long as you live, and I dare say you will not die a martyr for your religion. If the worst comes, the Roman Catholics, you know, are not against episcopacy.[67]

But George Sewell struck a more serious note when he analysed the problems and paradoxes of Whig theory at this juncture:

I humbly beg of you [he asked Burnet] in the name of many of us, the ignorant people of Great Britain, that you will be pleased to give us an entire and complete set of Revolution Principles, that we may be better informed what they are; as also to direct us in the use of them, that we may apply them to all cases and incidents which may happen. But if that be not so convenient at this time, we desire to be instructed whether those principles that served us then may not be out of date at present, or by what alterations we may adapt them to any future emergencies. Because there was once a Revolution, both just and necessary, and we were forced (according to your confession) to depart a little from our constitution, must we therefore be continually insisting on that? Must we still be magnifying an act of necessity, and crying it up as the very basis and foundation of the government? Certainly it were more prudent to let such cases of extremity be taken as little notice of as may be; I mean such notice only as the legislature thinks proper, and not to be made the subject of every indiscreet writer that may think to parallel circumstances upon every whimsy of his own, and inflame the hearts of a people too prone to tumults and disturbances.[68]

This was the dilemma. Had the Revolution really produced any firm guiding principles for the future? After more than twenty years of debate it seemed not, and any future crisis of a similar nature must be met, as in 1688, by *ad hoc* improvisation.

In fact, just such another crisis was impending, on Anne's death, and the Whigs were ill prepared to meet it. The

Junto majority in the Lords was now precarious, and often non-existent, and the general election of 1713 was a bitter blow. Now that the Peace was signed, and the brouhaha over Sacheverell had died down, the Whigs confidently expected to recoup some of the losses sustained in 1710. Instead they lost ground again, the Tories emerging with a huge majority of 213.[69] Bolingbroke was now firmly in the saddle, and few doubted that he was in touch with the Pretender; and the Schism Act of 1714, suppressing the Dissenting academies, was the first statutory invasion of the Revolution Settlement. Looking back from the reign of George II, the Whig historian John Oldmixon viewed the whole episode with horror:

> From [1711] to the queen's death, the Whigs looked on themselves as in a state of impotence, incapable by any human help to prevent the subverting of our free and Protestant constitution...[and] had not the Providence of God delivered them by the demise of Queen Anne they had been in effect what the Tories called them in malice, a ruined party.[70]

In Commons and Lords, motions that the succession was in danger were fended off by narrow majorities, despite the defection of Sir Thomas Hanmer's 'Whimsicals' in the Commons and prelates like Dawes of York and Robinson of London in the Lords.

The Whigs' most effective spokesman emerged late in the day; it was not until October 1713 that the Junto engaged Richard Steele to edit a new periodical, *The Englishman.* Steele was as nervous of popery and the Pretender as any bishop, and in the first few weeks he returned again and again to those themes, sharply criticising Harbin's *Hereditary Right of the Crown of England* and those who read it.[71] At the same time he tried to draft a new historical theory which would take into account the growing conservatism of his masters. Issue no. 25 (1 December 1713) was rather defiantly devoted to a discussion of the excellencies of the Roman Republic,[72] but the following week he turned to the ancient Germanic tribes, those barbaric warriors who were 'masters of the great secret of governing all by all'. On the march their commanders consulted a council of officers, but on weighty matters the whole army was assembled to give its advice. After they had conquered western Europe these habits were carried over into civilian governments which were a mixture of monarchy, aristocracy and democracy, 'which in our language', said Steele, 'is called king or queen, lords and commons'. But such governments had survived only in England, because unless a due balance was preserved monarchy degenerated into tyranny, aristocracy into oligarchy, and democracy into anarchy:

Each of these have their proper spheres to move in, and whilst they continue within them the government is easy and the constitution safe. But if the motion of any one of them interferes with that of the other the whole frame is out of order, and the constitution immediately falls into convulsions, and without wise and speedy applications must expire in an apoplexy.[73]

The Normans, of course, had unduly enlarged the monarchical element in the constitution, until restrained by Magna Carta. In the late Middle Ages the barons tilted the balance too much in favour of aristocracy, until they were controlled by Henry VII:

Henry VII did prudently in lessening the power of the nobility and increasing that of the commons, by making a law to enable the lords to sell their estates; but the consequence of it was like to have proved fatal to our constitution both in church and state, by increasing too much the power of the commons, who purchased the estates the lords were once possessed of. The advantages arising from thence, and from immense riches gained also by increase of trade, made the democratical part of our constitution too powerful for the aristocratical, and was attended with the murder of King Charles the First and the fall of the Church of England.[74]

Switching abruptly to the present day, Steele seemed to assume that this imbalance had been rectified, though he did not say how. The popular element was still vital to the constitution, for 'the wider the foundation of it is, the longer will be its duration'; but the stress was on consent and support, not participation or control, and government was wielded by some undefined combination of monarchy and aristocracy: 'Government is the subjecting of power to authority: power arising from strength, which is always in those that are governed, who are many, to authority, arising from opinion, which is in those that govern, who are few.' The mainspring of government was 'the affection of those who are subject to it', and the prince was 'the common parent of all his people'.[75]

In the final issue of *The Englishman* (February 1714) Steele returned to Revolution Principles, which he defined as support for the Revolution and the Protestant succes-sion, as set out in the Bill of Rights and the Act of Settle-ment; this was a theme already set out in his famous pamphlet *The Crisis*, published the previous month. Most significantly, he now abandoned the Whig pose that the Pretender was legitimate, and revived the worst excesses of the 'warming-pan' theory.[76] For his pains he was ex-pelled from the Commons, and flayed by Swift in one of his most brilliant and corrosive pamphlets, *The Public Spirit of the Whigs.*

John Toland dismissed Swift as 'that profligate divine who, prostituting his sacred function, has sold himself for hire to iniquity, vilely turning state buffoon to a couple of the greatest state mountebanks in the world', but in *The Grand Mystery Laid Open* he had to admit that the picture was one of gloom. Ireland and Scotland seemed on the brink of rebellion, and the Pretender was enlisting vol-unteers even in London. On the passing of the Schism Bill, in June 1714, the Whigs began collecting money and arms, and distributing badges 'as a signal in the day of trial'.[77]

The denouement is of the stuff of fairy tales. On 9 July 1714 parliament was prorogued. Anne was a sick woman, but it was not until the 27th that she could be prevailed upon to dismiss Lord Oxford. Even then, she would not hand the Lord Treasurer's staff to Bolingbroke; on the 30th, dying now, she gave it to the Duke of Shrewsbury, who was reunited with his old associates of the Junto. Anne died at 7.30 on the morning of 1 August, and the machinery of the Regency Act of 1705, Wharton's creation, rolled into action. So smooth was the transition that the new King George I (his mother Sophia had died in April) could safely delay his arrival until 18 September. There followed a clean sweep of Tories; after a few weeks of Hanoverian rule Bolingbroke wrecked his reputation by fleeing abroad, and Oxford went to the Tower.

Yet nothing was owing to Whig principles, and less to Whig propaganda. Backstairs manoeuvring? Perhaps. But George's accession, and his bias against the queen's last ministry, ought to be ascribed to the workings of fate, not man's design, or man's intelligence. An exultant Burnet, preaching before the new king what was to be his *nunc dimittis*, had it right. It was all God's Providence:

And now, may we not challenge the whole tribe of infidels to reflect on this chain of Providence...? Can they reflect on it, and yet harden themselves in their impiety...? Those who are so obstinate in those libertine principles as not to be wrought on by all this deduction of providences, seem to be past the possibility of cure or conviction.[78]

Did he not remember the sermon he had preached in almost precisely these terms to the Convention, on 31 January 1689? Did it not occur to him that it was strange that after a quarter of a century of angry political debate, during which every possible justification for the Revolution had been put forward by one person or another, they were all reduced, yet again, to blind reliance on the random intervention of an inscrutable Almighty? It must have occurred to others.

IO

THAT TRIUMPHANT APPELLATION[1]
The deterioration of Whiggism

The accession of George I inaugurated a Whig ascendency of nearly fifty years, but in so doing it drove an even deeper wedge between the Old and the Modern Whigs, and modified the ideology of the Whig ruling classes almost out of recognition.

In his first ministry King George found room for only one leading Tory, the Earl of Nottingham, who was still regarded as a Junto ally. In his controversial proclamation for a new parliament the king called upon the electorate to reject the supporters of the last ministry, with the result that the Whigs secured a majority of 120; and this new parliament, on the report of a Committee of Secrecy headed by Walpole, decided to impeach Oxford for his part in the Treaty of Utrecht and attaint Bolingbroke, who had fled.

Bolingbroke's decision to join the Pretender, followed by the Jacobite Rebellion in Scotland, with muted echoes in England, finally damned the High Church interest as 'the party of popery and rebellion'. That is not to say that the clergy were entirely silenced, nor that the pulpits returned to sanity on political anniversaries like 30 January,[2] and Walpole for one did not rest until he brought down Bishop Atterbury in 1722; but with the next election not due until 1718, the Pretender repulsed and Louis XIV dead, it was an exploded force. The very fact that the archbishops and bishops felt it prudent to issue a public statement abhorring the Fifteen betrayed the fact that the church's loyalty was in doubt; Atterbury and Smalridge's refusal to sign confirmed it.

It might have been expected that the Whigs, operating now from a position of overwhelming strength, would inaugurate a reform programme of the kind advocated by their followers ever since 1688: a statutory affirmation of the legality of the Revolution, and perhaps an oath to the same effect as a new test on office-holders; the reform, leading to the laicisation, of the universities; strict controls on preaching; and the abolition of the sacramental test for office holders (the Occasional Conformity and Schism Acts having been repealed, of course).

Yet the Whigs' effortless victory only produced fresh tensions and divisions, which paralysed initiative. The great Junto leaders died on the threshold of the promised land; Wharton with appalling suddenness on 12 April 1715, followed by Halifax on 19 May. Somers lingered another year, until 26 April 1715, but he was critically ill the whole time, and never took office under the new regime. They were denied the time to arrange for the devolution of their authority onto acknowledged heirs, and the succession was left in dispute between four brilliant and ambitious men of the next generation, Sunderland, Stanhope, Townshend and Walpole. By rank, age and experience Sunderland had a slight advantage, but he was an unstable and erratic man; the old Junto leaders had betrayed their opinion of him when they tried to exile him to Dublin as Lord Lieutenant in 1714. An unsettled leadership, perhaps over-reacting to the Fifteen, had no time for reform.

It was unfortunate, too, that this leadership crisis fell in a period of some ideological confusion. The crushing defeat suffered by the Tories in the election of 1715 unexpectedly removed a powerful opposition which might have been expected to hold the Whigs together.[3] There was some public discussion of the propriety of taking the oaths to the new king, but it was insignificant compared with the controversy on the same issue early in the 1690s. The non-jurors were inadvertently to bring the Church of England to the verge of schism in 1717, but no one (with the important exception, perhaps, of Townshend and

Walpole) considered them to be of any political significance. The concept of party had never been fully accepted
by the thinking public, and since 1710 the manic irre-
sponsibility of both sides had lowered the prestige of both;
the basic message of Swift's great polemics, reinforcing
Harley's argument, was that party distinctions were now
meaningless, and were kept up, like the hallowed names
of Guelph and Ghibelline, out of ancient animosity or the
hope of unworthy advantage.

In 1710, reviewing the history of the last twenty years
for his patroness, the Duchess of Marlborough, Francis
Hare told her that the terms 'Whig' and 'Tory' were to be
ignored, for, he said, 'nothing but being in or out of court
is at the bottom of them'. It was as ludicrous to call the
Whigs republicans as it was to call the Tories Jacobites, a
point later endorsed by Lord Cowper, in a famous report
to George I. Even on lesser points of doctrine the difference
between the two parties had narrowed to the point of
invisibility. Hare pointed out that the Revolution showed
'that how much soever [the Tories] may...talk for unlimited obedience, when there is cause for it they can resist
with as little ceremony as their adversaries'; and since then
the Whigs had 'shown themselves as good courtiers as their
neighbours, and are for their principles no longer than
their principles are for them'. But by preaching unqualified
passive obedience on the one hand and the absolute
sovereignty of popular rights on the other, both parties
threatened that balance of power which Hare saw as 'the
great principle that affects the nation as to the disputes
between prince and people'.[4] Even Steele and Swift, locked
in one of the most bitter polemical contests of the age, had
realised that there was very little difference between their
political beliefs, and when Steele closed *The Englishman* in
February 1714 and Swift returned to Dublin in May it was
partly in disgust at the futility of their efforts.[5] In November
1713, groping for a more general ethos of politics, Steele
wrote, 'The distinctions of Whig and Tory are snares to
catch the unwary on both sides; but liberty and property

are substantial blessings, for which a man of honour and virtue will combat while he lives, and die with pleasure in the defence of them.'[6] In fact, the only substantial difference between the two parties now was their attitude to the Church of England, and in the last number of *The Englishman* Steele put the case, with great passion and vigour, that the Whigs were in favour of a closer, more equal church–state relationship.[7] All in all, a new dynasty might be expected to bring in a new age, and Alexander Pope voiced the thoughts of many when he wrote, 'A curse on the word *party*, which I have been forced to use so often in this period! I wish the present reign may put an end to the distinction, that there may be no other for the future than that of honest knave, fool and man of sense.'[8] Even Cowper, in the very biassed 'Impartial History of Parties' he wrote for George I, assumed that it was the king's intention 'to extinguish the being and the very name of party amongst us'.[9]

In these circumstances the attitude of the new party leaders was cautious. Several Whig writers understandably thought the moment ripe to reaffirm that the Revolution of 1688 had involved a deliberate change of ruler, if not the actual deposition of King James.[10] The accession of the Hanoverians was seen as an affirmation of the non-hereditary principle, and thus the culmination of 1688; at the same time it supplied the one thing lacking in the Revolution Settlement, an assured Protestant succession in perpetuity. 'The first Revolution', wrote one Whig, 'has not been the type of this only, but the parent of it.'[11]

The Whig leaders were not so sure. It had been evident since 1710, if not since 1701, that a doctrine which licensed and even sanctified rebellion was of greater advantage to the Jacobites than it was to them. Again Cowper's 'Impartial History' offers a clue to their thinking. His account of the Revolution does not even mention James II's departure, still less does it raise the question of his supposed abdication; the event is made to hinge on the outside intervention of William of Orange.[12] Their fears were intensified by the Fifteen, which, though in retrospect obviously doomed to failure, was infinitely alarming to live through from day to day. So worried was the government that it commissioned a reluctant Steele to defend its ideological position against the Jacobites, and in July 1715 *The Englishman* reappeared.[13] When Steele gave up in November, Addison took over with *The Freeholder*.

Steele already equated property with liberty as one of the proper goals of political society, and he now asserted that in the new scheme of things 1688 was the limit of political memory. The present Settlement was based on the Revolution, and by implication nothing else, and fealty was owing to George I because he had received a free and unforced invitation to ascend the throne. Furthermore, he said, 'The public good is the measure both of government and submission to it, and...every subject is obliged to defend the government under which he is born, without enquiring into the justice of its first institution.'[14] Addison in *The Freeholder* went on to confirm the new conservatism of Whig official doctrine. Rebellion was now 'one of the most heinous crimes which it is in the power of man to commit', and one which 'destroys the end of all government, and the benefits of civil society'. Government, moreover, was now supported by a divine sanction as strong as any Tory could have desired: 'As in the subordination of a government the king is offended by any insults or oppositions to an inferior magistrate; so the Sovereign Ruler of the Universe is affronted by a breach of allegiance to those whom He has set over us.' Nor was this incompatible with complete parliamentary sovereignty, for

Everyone knows, who has considered the nature of government, that there must be in each particular form of it an absolute and unlimited power; and that this power is lodged in the hands of those who have the making of its laws, whether by the nature of the constitution it be in one or more persons, in a single order of men, or in a mixed body of different ranks and degrees.

In other words, the Whigs had now adopted the proposition put forward by Simon Harcourt in 1710, that passive obedience was owed to parliament, which had an absolute sovereignty.

As for the people, Addison was completely disillusioned with them. One of the lessons of this rebellion, he wrote, was that

Nothing can be more contemptible than the scum of the people, when they are instigated against a king who is supported by the two branches of the legislature. A mob may pull down a meeting house, but will never be able to overturn a government...The authority of the Lords and Commons of Great Britain, in conjunction with that of our sovereign, is not to be controlled by a tumultuary rabble.

Finally, he rejoiced that the Whigs had had the opportunity 'of showing their abhorrence of several principles which have been ascribed to us by the malice of our enemies'.

A disaffection to kings and kingly government [he went on] with a proneness to rebellion, have been often very unjustly charged on that party which goes by the name of Whigs. Our steady and continued adherence to his Majesty, and the present happy Settlement, will the most effectually confute this calumny. Our adversaries, who know very well how odious commonwealth principles are to the English nation, have inverted the very sense of words and things, rather than not continue to brand us with this imaginary guilt; for with some of these men, at present, loyalty to our king is republicanism, and rebellion, passive obedience.[15]

In these circumstances it is perhaps understandable that the new ministers should adopt the stance of Bolingbroke in 1710. Bolingbroke, it will be remembered, confessed with disarming frankness,

I am afraid that we came to the court in the same dispositions as all parties have done; that the principal spring of our actions was to have the government of the state in our hands; that our principal views were the conservation of this power, great employments to ourselves, and great opportunities of rewarding those who had helped to raise us, and of hurting those who stood in opposition to us.[16]

The Whigs began with a campaign of revenge, for which the Fifteen offered a ready excuse.

Opening the government's case against the rebel lords on 9 January 1716, Nicholas Lechmere argued that this rebellion was merely the climax of a long campaign of treason.

He wished he could say [it was reported] that it was a plot just of yesterday, and that it had taken no deeper root than ordinary appearances would lead [us] to suspect; but he thought it plain that it was the effect of many years' labour, of the joint and united labour of great numbers, both Protestants and Papists, the plain and necessary consequence of the measures which had been carrying on for some years past.[17]

In fact, the preamble to the articles of impeachment harked back to a very ancient, almost Oatesian whiggery, with its picture of 'a most wicked design and contrivance', generations old,

to subvert the ancient and established government and the good laws of these kingdoms, to suppress the true Protestant religion therein established, and to extirpate and destroy its professors, and instead thereof to introduce and settle popery and arbitrary power, in which unnatural and horrid conspiracy great numbers of persons of different degrees and qualities have concerned themselves, and acted, and have joined themselves with professed Papists, uniting their endeavours to accomplish and execute the aforesaid wicked and traitorous designs.

King William, of course, 'of ever-glorious memory', had frustrated these designs, but only temporarily, for the whole conspiracy had been resurrected under his successor:

To accomplish these ends, the most immoral, irreligious and unchristianlike methods have been taken, but more particularly in the last years of the reign of the late Queen Anne; during which time all imaginable endeavours were used by the said conspirators to prejudice the minds of the subjects of this realm against the legality and justice of the said settlement of the crown; and for that purpose the Holy Scriptures were wrested, and the most wholesome doctrines of the Church of England perverted and abused, by men in holy orders, in the most public and scandalous manner, in order to condemn the justice of the late happy Revolution...false and dangerous notions of a sole hereditary right to the imperial crown of these realms were propagated and encouraged by persons in the highest trust and employments...[and] jesuitical and scandalous distinctions were invented and publicly inculcated, to enervate the force and obligation of those oaths which have been contrived in the plainest and strongest terms, by the wisdom of parliament, for the security of the said establishment...[and] groundless fears of the danger of the Church of England were fomented throughout these kingdoms, to disorder the minds of the well-disposed Protestants.

From a position of grave danger thus artificially created, the nation had been rescued only by the Providence of Almighty God, and there was a broad hint that this had been most signally manifested in the late queen's death: 'Under which most deplorable circumstances it pleased Almighty God, in His infinite wisdom, to call to Himself the late Queen Anne; and by a concurrence of most wonderful providences, to give a quiet and peaceable accession to his present most gracious Majesty.'[18]

In the preamble to the Land Tax Bill, in February, the government went even further, stating as accepted fact that their predecessors had 'contrived unnecessarily to encumber for a long time to come (if not for ever) several considerable branches of the public revenue'. This could be said to prejudge the trial of the former Lord Treasurer, Oxford, who was under threat of impeachment, and the Lords were furious. They considered rejecting the bill, but in the end contented themselves with a strongly worded declaration deploring such manoeuvres.[19]

Such violence subjected the ministry to increasing strain. Nottingham was dismissed in February 1716 for advocating clemency for the condemned Jacobite lords, and he was not alone. As early as July 1715, to Walpole's fury, Sir Joseph Jekyll publicly dissented from the Committee of Secrecy's recommendation that Oxford be impeached, and in March 1716 another stalwart of 1710, Lechmere, went clean against what was apparently ministerial policy by moving the repeal of the Occasional Conformity and Schism Acts, without effect. He was one of the leading opponents of the Septennial Act, and by the autumn he was openly acting with the Tories in the Commons.[20]

Much has been made in the past of the moral bankruptcy of High Toryism; not so much has been said of the moral breakdown of the Whigs after 1715, a breakdown whose beginnings some were inclined to date as far back as 1701, when Charles Davenant had crystallised in ideological terms an obvious division between Old and Modern Whigs. We know little of the internal structure of the Whig party during Anne's reign, but the idiosyncratic picture painted by Alexander Cunningham, and left unpublished until 1787, is not contradicted by other evidence, and accords with what we know of the character of the principals. According to him, the Junto's decision to oppose the suggestion that the Electress Sophia be invited to England in 1705 placed an insufferable strain on party discipline; even the young James Stanhope voted with the minority, who accused their leaders of forgetting 'their old principles'. The Regency Act only papered over the cracks, and in the years that followed, up to 1708, matters were made worse by the manoeuvres of the Earl of Sunderland, who 'associated to himself men of all parties, however scandalous their characters; he said with his father, "What is one man better than another?"' Somers took a decreasing share in policy decisions.[21]

These tensions were exacerbated by the Junto's decision in 1711 to purchase the support of the Earl of Nottingham in their fight against the Peace of Utrecht at the expense of ditching the Dissenters.

This is such a well-known incident that we are in danger of overlooking it altogether. Yet it was arguably a turning point in the history of Whiggism. If there was one principle with which all Whigs (Old or Modern) had always been associated it was religious toleration for Dissenters. It had preoccupied their fathers in the Exclusion Crisis; at the Revolution they had not only welcomed the Toleration Act, but sought to extend its privileges to refugees from Europe by sponsoring a series of bills to naturalise foreign Protestants resident in England, one of which finally passed into law in 1709, a period of maximum Whig ascendency. Meanwhile, in 1702, 1703 and 1704 they had resisted to their utmost the attempts to restrict Dissenters' access to office by outlawing occasional conformity. In 1709 there had been plausible rumours that the Whig-dominated government intended to repeal the sacramental test altogether, and as late as 1711, beleaguered as they were, the Whig peers secured the rejection of a bill to repeal the Act naturalising foreign Protestants. Yet during the next session, in November, Nottingham introduced an Occasional Conformity Bill which was not opposed by the Whigs and duly passed into law. In the same session the Act naturalising foreign Protestants was also repealed.

Some contemporaries put the blame on Sunderland, though it was Wharton and the Earl of Scarborough who sponsored the new policy in the Lords.[22] The Occasional Conformity Act was certainly milder than those proposed in the earlier years of the reign, and it was said that the chief London Dissenters had been talked into agreeing to it, lest worse befall; but the blow to Whig prestige and credibility was overwhelming. The horror and shock of many party supporters is mirrored by Defoe. Though he was now a supporter of the new government, and it was therefore in his interests to pillory the opposition, he still made a distinction between Whiggism and the Whig party, and his reaction cannot be dismissed as entirely false. At first he could not believe what was afoot, but when conviction finally dawned he lambasted the Whig leaders with impotent fury: 'Never open your mouths after this about public faith, the honour of treaties, justice to allies and standing fast to confederacies, and the like; whoever may speak of these things, it is not for those I am speaking of to open their mouths about it now.' This, he said, was nothing but a complete betrayal of Whig tradition and Revolution Principles:

Were our fathers to rise again from the dead, were my Lord Russell, the Earl of Essex, Algernon Sidney, Alderman Cornish, and the rest of the patriots of liberty on whose blood the Revolution was built as a foundation; were these to rise from the dead, and see their posterity, for a mere party interest, fly over to the most inveterate party that dipped their hands in the innocent blood of those days; were they to see the zealous patrons of Revolution Principles shake hands with the mortal enemies of the nation's liberty, and drink in the highest rectified spirits of Jacobite extraction, how would they stand amazed, and ask them if it was for this that they spent their blood? And if this be to be a Whig, or to be a renegade to professed principles.[23]

Burnet himself was at a loss to explain his friends' action. 'All the excuse that the Whigs made for their easiness in this matter', he said, 'was that they gave way to it, to try how far the yielding it might go towards quieting the fears of those who seemed to think the church was in danger'; or, to put it more broadly, they aimed to defuse the High Church agitation at the polls, which they blamed for the unfortunate result of the election of 1710.[24] Their second motive, of course, was to gain the votes of Nottingham and his friends against the Peace of Utrecht.

But both aims rebounded on them. There seems little doubt that Nottingham himself would have opposed the Peace anyway, and in the event he was alone; he could not even command the support of his brother Guernsey. He said, plausibly enough, that the Whigs had come over to him, not he to them.[25] As it was, his intransigence forced Oxford to break the Whigs' grip on the House of Lords by creating twelve new Tory peers, and it was their votes which eventually passed the Schism Act of 1714, a much more serious inroad on the Dissenters' position. Indeed, it could be argued that this unholy alliance between Nottingham and the Junto frustrated Oxford's efforts to keep his over-powerful right wing in check. Halifax told Lord Dartmouth frankly that 'he thought they paid too dear for him by disobliging many of their real friends to please a man that joined them in spite, and would be sure to leave them when he found it for his advantage'.[26] Nor did the Whigs improve their moral standing by broad hints that the Occasional Conformity Act would be repealed as soon as they came back to power.[27] As for any hoped-for electoral advantage, this proved totally illusory, though whether the disaster of 1713 can be attributed to a weakening of Dissenting support we do not know.[28]

But even in this last parliament of Anne's the Junto seized an almost casual opportunity to blacken their own reputation still further. On the plea that the new malt tax infringed the articles of the Union, the Scots peers moved for its dissolution. Sunderland, Wharton and Townshend joined them, and, even more amazingly, so did Lord Somers, one of the chief architects of the Union. It is now apparent that only Sunderland and Wharton were at all serious in this venture, and even they regarded it as a manoeuvre to embarrass the government. But contemporaries were denied such insights, and so, for that matter, were latter-day Whigs like Arthur Onslow and Lord Campbell, who were at a loss to explain their heroes' conduct.[29]

It might have been supposed that even those who acted irresponsibly and cynically in the face of defeat might regain their composure with victory. But King George's support was too strong, and so were the temptations of power. The new reign saw further surrenders of principle, and Atterbury's warning to the electors in 1715 showed remarkable prescience: 'If they can pack a House of Commons to their mind, they will leave [the king] no power to act but as they direct and prescribe; they will subject him to the arbitrary government of a junto, who cannot bear to be controlled even by the regal power, which, they say, is of their own creation'; and he went on to forecast that the Whigs would repeal the Triennial Act and maintain a standing army in time of peace, notwithstanding their vaunted Revolution Principles.[30]

He was proved right. Yet if there was a Whig principle even more sacrosanct than religious toleration it was the need for frequent elections, so that the will of the people could be more effectively brought to bear on parliament or the executive. The result was the Triennial Act of 1695, which, if it did not enjoy the unanimous support of the Junto, was backed by two of its most prominent members. (Somers was always credited with supporting it, and in 1693 Wharton had favoured annual parliaments.)[31] Frequent parliaments, of course, remained one of the cherished tenets of Country Whiggism. In 1711 Robert Molesworth wrote, 'A right Whig looks upon frequent parliaments as such a fundamental part of the constitution that no parliament even can part with this right. High Whiggism is for annual parliaments, and Low Whiggism for triennial, with annual meetings.'[32] Yet in 1716 a Whig government enjoying a plenitude of power unblushingly amended the Triennial Act, extending the life of each parliament to seven years.

The passing of the Septennial Act has been taken very much for granted.[33] But contemporaries were not slow to point out that it was a flagrant violation of constitutional proprieties, not so much in its general principles as in the fact that it extended the life of the existing parliament by four years without consulting the electorate. Indeed, it could be said to flout the wishes of the electorate, in that it shielded the existing government from an election it obviously expected to lose. This was a point which caused nineteenth-century Whig historians some unease.[34] It is not so often noticed that George I's support for his ministers in this policy, and his assent to the bill, was a remarkable invasion of constitutional rights by the crown; and he gained by it a considerable increase in his freedom of action and his prestige in Europe.[35] It is difficult to imagine his daring intervention in the Baltic being carried through under a triennial parliament, and it is equally difficult to imagine the Whig ministers allowing themselves the luxury of a disruptive three-year feud. Moreover, during the extended life of this parliament – illegally extended, many would say – the Whigs did not content themselves with the measures of consolidation and defence which were the excuse for the Septennial Act; they felt perfectly free to introduce a basic constitutional reform like the Peerage Bill.

The contemporary debate on the matter was fierce but short, since the government apparently gave little warning of its intentions before the simple bill 'for enlarging the time of continuance of parliaments' was introduced in the Lords by the Duke of Devonshire on 10 April 1716, and it passed its third reading in the Commons on the 26th. The government was obviously anxious to allow no time for public opinion to be mobilised – as it was the Commons received petitions of protest from ten boroughs – and the bill was accompanied on its course through parliament by a barrage of Whig pamphlet propaganda, obviously pre-concerted. Indeed, as early as 17 March Addison devoted a whole issue of *The Freeholder* to an apparently irrelevant discussion of the chronic instability of English government as a result of too-frequent elections.[36] This, and not 'fear of Newgate', explains why Tory response outside parliament was notably feeble.

That the ministry was wise to proceed in this way was confirmed by the initial reaction of the Whig rank and file, while the bill was still with the Lords. Walter Moyle admitted, 'No motion was at first treated with more coldness; the politicians of the Grecian and the neighbouring coffee houses, fired with uncommon warmth, bellowed loud against it. Time and good argument', he went on, 'made them espouse the quite contrary opinion', but it was obviously a hard struggle. Somers died the day the bill passed the Commons, but even his aid was invoked. Shortly before, so the story goes, Townshend heard that the dying man had had a lucid interval and rushed to his bedside. Somers embraced him and said, 'I have just heard of the work in which you are engaged, and [I] congratulate you upon it. I never approved the Triennial Bill, and always considered it, in effect, the reverse of what it was intended. You have my hearty approbation of this business, and I think it will be the greatest support possible to the liberty of the country.'[37]

Maybe so. The Duke of Leeds was another supporter of the Triennial Act who had publicly recanted, in 1710, and the measure had been the subject of constant criticism, and proposals for reform, down the years.[38] The arguments against it were given in some detail in *The Alteration in the Triennial Act Considered* (1716). The Act encouraged the maintenance of party divisions by obliging Whigs and Tories to maintain a permanent organisation. It subjected the constituencies every three years to riots and disturbances which were a threat to public order. It was even said that it undermined the administration of justice by making magistrates unwilling to give decisions against their supporters. (An unusual argument, this, but not implausible.)[39] It debauched the minds of the people, not only by bribery and corruption, but by drunkenness, disorder, swearing and every kind of vice, as well as sheer time-wasting. The author even blamed it for the decline in the woollen industry, and a fellow Jeremiah lamented 'a general disposition in men to leave the thoughts of diligence and industry in the business for the more agreeable entertainments of idleness and a luxurious beggary'.[40] From the candidates' viewpoint, the increasing expense was driving men to bankruptcy and ruining landed estates; many had had to sacrifice the portions of their younger children, others had become slaves to the corporations they served. One writer even said that a Member 'must spend a daughter's fortune at every election, for which reason the poor girl must go without a husband'.[41] Finally, the Triennial Act had rendered English government unstable and discontinuous, and had seriously prejudiced its dealings with foreign nations and its reliability in the eyes of its allies – a point driven home by the aftermath of the election of 1710.

These political and moral arguments were the ones used by Devonshire in presenting the bill on 10 April, but in a five-hour debate on the second reading, on the 14th, they were given scant attention. It was argued that election expenses were voluntary, separate legislation could be passed to deal with corruption, and the present measure was altogether too drastic. As the Duke of Buckingham put it, 'Pray, my lords, consider what you are doing: to prevent robbing on the highway you prevent travelling.'[42] On the other hand, Nottingham and Lord Powlet argued that the bill showed a distrust of the affections of the people which was in itself a disastrous blow to government prestige.[43] Others argued that the bill was an amendment to the ancient constitution, of which the Triennial Act was one aspect; to which the Whigs replied that the Act itself had been an amendment to that constitution, whose requirements were satisfied by annual sessions; it was not clear that parliaments grew more corrupt or less amenable the longer they sat. Atterbury sarcastically remarked that the bill was manifestly unseasonable, 'now especially, when we have a glorious standing army, and a ministry that knows how effectually to engage the affections of the people'.[44] However, it finally passed by seventy-four votes to thirty-nine, but not before thirty peers had entered their formal dissent.

The constitutional arguments broached in the Lords were taken up by the pamphleteers, and still more vigorously by the House of Commons. There the debate on the second reading, on 24 April, lasted from two in the morning until eleven at night; Shippen, the Jacobite, set the scene by arguing that a parliament elected by the people for three years could not possibly extend itself to seven,[45] and he delighted in turning the Whigs' former arguments for an enlargement of the liberty of the people against themselves. The Triennial Act, he concluded, was part of the original constitution, and 'grounded on the reasons of antiquity, and the original usage of parliaments'.[46] Bromley argued that in a government jointly exercised by king, Lords and Commons the people could make their opinions known only through their elected representatives, not directly; therefore, after the lapse of three years the present Commons would have no right to legislate; and he warned them that if they perpetuated themselves once, the temptation to do so again would be overwhelming. Similar arguments were voiced by other Tory MPs, and they were seconded by Lechmere, who said that 'it was unjust to continue themselves for any longer time than the people chose them for; they must then be esteemed not the people's but their own representatives, and what laws should be made by them after the time expired for which they were elected must be null and void'.[47]

In reply Stanhope painted a horrendous picture of the Jacobites' preparedness and Britain's weakness, declaring that no foreign power would ally with her in view of her present political instability. Steele agreed, likening the government to a vessel in a continuous state of distress: 'The pilot and mariners have been wholly employed in keeping the ship from sinking; the art of navigation was useless, and they never pretended to make sail.' He went on to argue, fairly enough, that there was nothing sacrosanct about the chosen period of three years, and to alter it to seven was not jeopardising the constitution in any fundamental way.[48] Richard Hampden said that if 'those great and honest men' who had passed the Triennial Act had foreseen 'how insufficient and cobweb a remedy' it would prove they would not have left it unamended for posterity. The implication that no parliament could bind its successors was driven home by others, who said that if the opposition arguments held, 'then we were a people that had not a supreme power, and so could neither make nor repeal any laws at all'. Nottingham's son, Lord Finch, termed them 'a lick-spittle parliament for coming into it', and there were as many as fifty speeches against it, but in the end it passed in an unusually full House by 264 votes to 121.[49]

There is no doubt that the Triennial Act had made the operation of government increasingly difficult, quite apart from its effect on the elections themselves. The Whigs had considered suspending it in 1708, and so had the Tories in 1713; in fact, Oxford thought of repealing it altogether in 1714, and might have done so had the queen lived.[50] The arguments for the constitutional propriety of such an action would probably be accepted without question today. But in an age when MPs were thought to have a much more direct link with, and mandate from, their constituents such arguments were much more open to dispute. The fact of the matter is, the Whig government had gone even further than the notorious Long Parliament, which in the first Triennial Act (1641) had presumed only to legislate for its successors. In more general terms, as its opponents pointed out, the Act was a craven admission of weakness; it was strange to see a Whig government unwilling to face the sovereign people – and stranger still to see a sturdy radical like Defoe supporting them. Nottingham was right when he said they 'showed a distrust of the affections of the people, and an intention of governing by fear'.[51]

Its effect on elections was if anything adverse. It was argued at the time that competition for seats would only increase, for 'an annuity for seven years deserves a better consideration than for three',[52] and so it proved, especially since the Hanoverians proved unwilling to use their prerogative to dissolve parliaments early, as William III had done in 1700 and 1701, and Anne had done in 1710. Not until 1747 was a septennial parliament dissolved before its full term, except on the demise of the sovereign.[53] It was argued that the Triennial Act had increased the relative influence of the Lords by rendering the Commons unstable and impermanent, and by laying their elections open to increased interference,[54] a suspicion which was enhanced when the Lords vetoed a tough bill to prevent bribery and corruption at the hustings in 1708.[55] Yet the decline of the House of Commons, even as a money-voting body, continued after 1716.

The immediate political aspects of the bill remain an enigma. On the evidence we have it is surprisingly difficult to be sure whether there was a real Jacobite threat in 1716 or not, or whether the government believed in it. There is evidence that Townshend emphatically did, but he always stands out as the most naive of the Whig ministers,[56] and Stanhope's assertion in the Commons that an alliance with any European power was impossible in the present circumstances was disingenuous in view of the secret negotiations proceeding with France, and the treaty of guarantee just concluded with Holland.[57] Walpole was ill in the country throughout, and Sunderland's attitude is unknown, though later he was to show himself remarkably relaxed in his dealings with Jacobitism.[58] All of them must have known what parliament did not, that the Jacobite cause had reached its nadir. Returning from Scotland in February 1716, James III dismissed his only able minister, Bolingbroke; the Regent Orleans then cashiered all James's followers who held commissions in the French army and ordered him out of France, and since no other European state was willing to grant him asylum, he had to take refuge in the papal enclave at Avignon. His agents, no doubt imbued with their usual optimism, numbered his supporters in this parliament at twenty-three peers and eighty-three MPs.[59] There is no evidence to suggest that an election in 1718 would have encouraged a Jacobite revival, and if there had been, the time to deal with such an emergency would have been in 1717, and then not by outright amendment but temporary suspension, for which there was every precedent in the suspension of the Habeas Corpus Act in 1689 and 1715. It is impossible to acquit the Whigs of the suspicion that they and the king were using Jacobitism as an excuse to throw Whig principles to the winds and consolidate their power for a further term of years. One result of giving George I more rope was an aggressive, expansionist foreign policy in the Baltic and the Mediterranean, which called for the maintenance of a large standing army. This brought several protests, especially from the Lords on the passing of the Mutiny Bill in 1718. While continuing to pay lip-service to the Bill of Rights, eighteenth-century Whig governments consistently ignored the proviso declaring a standing army in time of peace illegal.[60]

By even greater damage was done to the public image of Whiggism by the party split in 1717. The quarrel between Stanhope and Sunderland on the one hand and Townshend and Walpole on the other was occasioned by their conflicting opinions on foreign policy, and it was related to the growing animosity between the king and the Prince of Wales; but basically it was a dispute over the division of profits and power.[61] This made the decision of Walpole and his followers to go into formed opposition to the ministry, in alliance with the Tories and even avowed Jacobites like William Shippen, the more reprehensible. Over the next two years they made it their business unscrupulously to oppose every measure embodying basic Whig principles which the government brought forward, even the belated repeal of the Schism Act and the reform of the universities. Townshend and Walpole were cynical enough even to block the impeachment of Oxford, their arch enemy, simply to score points off the Sunderland–Stanhope ministry, a tactic they pursued on quite minor issues, too. For instance, Walpole unblushingly seconded Sir William Wyndham's proposal that Dr Andrew Snape, a notorious High-Flying divine and Hoadly's chief adversary in the Bangorian controversy, be invited to preach before the House in May 1717. Lechmere said he

could not but wonder that a Member who had been one of the managers against Dr Sacheverell should now speak on behalf of a divine who had asserted the same notions of passive obedience and non-resistance for which the other had been prosecuted, and who had lately attacked a strenuous and worthy champion of the Revolution and the Protestant succession.[62]

J. H. Plumb admits that though Walpole's conduct set a pattern for all eighteenth-century oppositions, it was 'a pattern which it is difficult for men versed in the politics of recent times to judge sympathetically'.[63] Contemporaries were even less sympathetic, because there was no precedent for such an abandonment of party principles and reversal of political alliances; even the 'Tackers' and the 'Sneakers' or the 'High Flyers' and the 'Whimsicals' had divided only on specific issues, and as one Whig pamphleteer pointed out, the apostasy of Nottingham in opposing the Peace of Utrecht and the Schism Act had been pointedly ignored by his political allies, even his own brother.[64] Much of the propaganda vilifying the dissidents was obviously inspired by the government, but it expressed views which were widely held. A pamphlet like *The Defection Considered* was largely unanswerable. It accused Walpole, who had soon emerged as the principal target, of dividing the Whig party and rendering it vulnerable to the Tory/ Jacobite menace; in fact, he was threatening that very public unity which had been made the excuse for passing the Septennial Act. Worse still, he was committing the unforgivable crime, the 'criminal conspiracy', of trying to coerce the king in an unconstitutional manner, not only by withdrawing his own services but by trying to unseat the king's chosen servants and even fomenting discord within the royal family.[65] And for these scandalous actions no proper reason had ever been given; merely 'such horrid things to be done as they dare not so much as name', or 'senseless stories about foreign divorces, new marriages, and I know not what idle tales'.[66] In view of Walpole's continued silence on this point, it is not surprising that the worst construction was put on his conduct. One writer hit the bull's-eye when he remarked that the sole origin of the whole dispute was 'that old, ridiculous question that even divided the disciples of Christ, who should be greatest?'; another backdated it to the squabble in 1716 over clemency to the Jacobite rebels, when according to him the noble Stanhope had frustrated 'those vindictive and inhuman bloodsuckers' Walpole and Townshend.[67] But the simplest and apparently the most natural explanation to contemporaries was that Walpole's insatiable lust for power and money had simply grown too much for George I and the other ministers. He was now accused of gross corruption at every stage of his career to date, as Treasurer of the Navy, Secretary at War, Paymaster-General and First Lord of the Treasury, and his supposed eagerness to fill the administration with relatives and friends was freely denounced. He was even accused of selling pardons after the Fifteen. One writer rejoiced that 'the tyranny of the Robinocracy' was ended, and another went so far as to say, 'Had a certain gentleman died about the time the report of the Select Committee came out, he might have made his exit with more reputation than he must expect for the future.'[68]

Indeed, Walpole's reputation took a nose-dive in 1717 from which it never really pulled out, and with the South Sea Bubble the descent became steeper. It needed a new generation of men coming into parliament in 1722 and 1727 to gloss over his faults. The several vindications of his conduct published by him or on his behalf in 1717 were uniformly feeble, largely because of his reluctance to explain what the crisis was all about. He argued, quite rightly, that any minister could resign if faced by measures he did not like, but he was vague as to what these measures were in the present case; in fact, in one pamphlet he said outright that he was not prepared at this stage to explain the points at issue.[69] Worse still, some of his defenders showed a disposition to whitewash the Tories as well as him. *The Resigners Vindicated: Part I* (1718) called for a general reconciliation with the Tories, absolved them from complicity in the Fifteen, and compared their conduct under James II favourably with that of the Dissenters. *Part II* of the same work even put up a strong defence for the retention of 30 January and 29 May as days of religious observance.[70] In fact, the more respectable Tories were as disgusted with the situation as the Whigs. When Oxford's impeachment came up in the Commons in June 1717, Shippen pointedly remarked that Walpole's interest in the matter 'was very much abated since he was out of place'; on which Walpole 'made a very faint apology for himself'.[71] As one critic remarked,

When people find that he can play fast and loose, be of either side or party, as it may best suit his interest or resentment, call himself the king's friend in place, and when out of place to form new alliances... in the defence of the church, and under pretence of honesty clog and distract public business, all he can say after such behaviour will go for little, or for nothing more but to expose himself.[72]

However, no sooner had one wing of the Whig party covered itself with obloquy than the other hastened to follow suit. At the end of February 1719 the Stanhope government suddenly introduced in the House of Lords one of the most controversial measures of the eighteenth century, the Peerage Bill. It proposed to limit the number of the English temporal peers to 184 (six above their then number); when that limit was reached new creations could be made only when existing peerages became extinct through failure of the male line. At the same time the sixteen elected Scots peers established by the Union in 1707 were to be replaced by twenty-five hereditary peers whose seats would descend in the male line in the usual way.

The crisis that followed is well enough known, and it would be otiose to recount the various arguments for or against the Bill in any detail here.[73] On the other hand, it is too easy to pass it over as an aberration on Stanhope's part, an over-cunning move in the party game. In fact, it would have introduced a change in the constitution more significant than any attempted in 1689. The ostensible motive was to arrest the steady increase in the peerage in recent years, which threatened to devalue the dignity of a peer, and to prevent the kind of gerrymandering which had enabled Oxford to pass the Peace of Utrecht by the creation of twelve new peers in one day. Behind this lay the fear that the Prince of Wales, now totally alienated from his father and his father's ministers, might succeed to the throne in the near future and overturn Sunderland's and Stanhope's majority in the Upper House by mass creations. But contemporaries were quick to scent other motives. It was argued (baselessly) that it would perpetuate the present ministry's majority in the Lords for generations.[74] It was feared that it would make the Upper House a closed oligarchy, separated entirely from the Commons, and with a permanent veto on its decisions. Perhaps Walpole and his associates would in the future be in a position to take advantage of this new 'system', but at the moment this seemed unlikely; in January 1719 his reputation reached its nadir when he opposed the ministry's bill for the repeal of the Occasional Conformity and Schism Acts.

However, such was the reception of the measure by the public, and such was the known attitude of the House of Commons, that Stanhope adjourned the third reading in the Lords beyond the end of the session, allowing the summer for debate. The debate was certainly intense. It fostered at least three new periodicals, each of which ran for four issues: The Plebeian (by Steele), The Old Whig (by Addison) and The Patrician (possibly by Molesworth); and nearly thirty separate pamphlets.[75] The dispute did not generate much excitement in the public at large, but it exacerbated the divisions in the governing class; for instance, it severed the long-standing friendship between Addison and Steele.

The debate centred on the legality and propriety of introducing such a measure at all. Similar arguments had been used against the Septennial Act; there was a strong feeling at this time that parliament could not, or ought not to, undertake such fundamental alterations to the constitution except in extreme emergency. Many ingenious arguments were employed on the bill's behalf; for instance, that the Commons had already restricted their own size in the 1670s by forbidding the creation of new boroughs, and the Lords were only following suit; that the bill would stop the drain of talent from Commons to Lords; that the greater the number of the Lords the greater their electoral influence.[76] But this did not meet the argument put by Walpole in *Thoughts of a Member of the Lower House* (1719), that the measure would not only kick away the ladder of preferment, and take away one of the crown's most handsome and beneficial prerogatives, but also destroy the delicate balance between king, Lords and Commons, monarchy, aristocracy and democracy, without which the constitution could not subsist.[77] Also the changes in the Scots peerage provoked what seems at first a disproportionate amount of attention, but this was because they infringed the Act of Union, which was regarded as one of the immutable factors in the British constitution; if this could be amended, so could the basic provisions of the Act of Settlement and the Bill of Rights.[78]

Stanhope, in Germany with the king, was so worried by the drift of the controversy that he suggested bribing the Commons by offering to repeal the Septennial Act, leaving them to be dissolved only on the king's death – a proposal eloquent of the extent to which the Whig oligarchs were prepared to go in jettisoning Whig principles, or indeed the general principles on which the constitution was supposed to rest.[79] He was dissuaded only by the young Duke of Newcastle. At the beginning of the next session, on 23 November, the king recommended the Peerage Bill in his speech from the throne, and it was reintroduced in the Lords. But the celerity with which it passed that House, in less than a week, reinforced one of the main general arguments against it; that if the Lords were so blindly and unanimously in favour, with only the Earl of Oxford dissenting, it boded no good. On the second reading in the Commons it was handsomely defeated, though here the turning point was a great oration by Walpole in which he laboured the argument that the bill would frustrate for ever the laudable ambitions of commoners for social advancement: 'If this bill passed into law one of the most powerful incentives to virtue would be taken away, since there would be no coming to honour but through the winding sheet of an old decrepit lord, and the grave of an extinct noble family.' He was not appealing to the Commons' sense of public responsibility or to constitutional convention; instead, in the words of his biographer, he 'played admirably on the secret ambitions of men and their jealousy of power'.[80]

Meanwhile, the Church of England had fallen into confusion. The death of Burnet and the dismissal of Nottingham removed the two men who might have fashioned a new church policy; their successors, preoccupied with questions of safety and power, allowed their programme – if programme they had – to drift. It was generally agreed that the Dissenters should be given complete religious toleration once more, but apart from Lechmere's solitary démarche in 1716[81] nothing was done. Of course, the question was not as straightforward as it might appear. Many Whig churchmen, lay and cleric, had always been opposed to occasional conformity, and were content that the Act of 1711 should continue; some bishops who were otherwise staunch party men, like Nicholson of Carlisle, supported the Act vociferously, and were horrified at the idea of repeal.[82] All the same, it was strange that the Schism Act (a much more serious infraction of the Toleration Act), which was not being seriously enforced, and which had produced a formidable written protest in 1714 signed by thirty-one lay peers and seven bishops including William Wake, now Archbishop of Canterbury, should still be on the statute book four years later.[83]

In the same way, reform of the universities had been confidently expected on all sides; by Atterbury, for instance, and Bishop Trelawney, as well as by John Toland, who also demanded that the clergy be disabled from being magistrates.[84] A bill to vest control of university patronage in the crown for a term of years (though it did not abolish the requirement that Fellows be in holy orders) was under discussion by Townshend, Stanhope and Sunderland in 1716, but it was overtaken not only by the split in the ministry but by the Bangorian Controversy.[85]

Benjamin Hoadly, whose reward for his labours on behalf of Whiggism had been the poor and junior Bishopric of Bangor, had been drawn into the current dispute on the status of the non-juring clergy – a dispute which was now sharper than ever because of the prospective permanence of the present regime in church and state. From arguing the non-validity of non-juring orders, however, he went on to argue the irrelevance of all holy orders. Taking as his text 'My kingdom is not of this world', he preached before George I on 31 March 1717 a celebrated sermon which was immediately published at the king's command under the title *The Nature of the Kingdom or Church of Christ.* Here he transferred to the church a familiar whiggish notion concerning the origins and the nature of the state: that God had decreed church government in general terms, but had not laid down any specific forms, and though He remained the head, indeed the only head, of the church, He took no part in its operation. The structure of church government was therefore only an administrative convenience, and to suppose otherwise was to partake of the impudent blasphemy of the Roman Catholic Church, for 'He [Christ] had in those points left behind no visible, human authority; no vice-gerents who can be said properly to supply His place; no interpreters upon whom His subjects are absolutely to depend; no judges over the consciences or religion of His people.'[86]

The furious controversy which ensued split the church crossways, at right angles to the High Church/Low Church axis, and considerably weakened moderate support for the Whig ministry. Convocation threatened to become a beargarden, and had to be adjourned indefinitely (it did not meet again until 1854). This was a welcome bonus; but the defensive attitude of the Low Churchmen, coupled with the factiousness of the dissident Whigs, made any generous or constructive reform impossible. The bill 'for strengthening the Protestant interest' which Stanhope introduced in the Lords in December 1719 proposed not only to repeal the Occasional Conformity and Schism Acts but also to absolve the Dissenters from taking the sacramental test altogether. However, the opposition of the bishops and the dissident Whigs, joined by ex-Lord Chancellor Cowper, forced him to drop this last clause. Even then, Walpole factiously opposed the measure in the Commons on the far-fetched grounds that it heralded toleration for Catholics, which would 'reverse the Revolution'. The Dissenters had to be content with Stanhope's Act for 'quieting and establishing corporations', the first of a series of Indemnity Acts which in effect allowed Nonconformists to retain their posts in local government unless challenged within six months of entry. The bill for reforming the universities, though it was mooted again in 1719, was quietly shelved in the aftermath of the Peerage Bill.[87] Whig reform of the universities was confined to the establishment of regius chairs of history at Oxford and Cambridge in 1724.

The attitude of the Whig politicians to the Bangorian Controversy was one of some embarrassment; in the House of Commons John Aislabie said it was 'a controversy that did not properly belong to their cognisance'.[88] Hoadly, for whom a brilliant career might have been forecast as a political theorist and a prince of the church, found his promotion slowed down. He moved to Hereford in 1721, another poor, bucolic see, and Salisbury in 1723; in 1730 he was kept out of Durham, on which he had set his heart, and reached a safe and prosperous haven at Winchester in 1734 only through the intervention of Queen Caroline. He lived until 1761, but neither Walpole nor Pelham had any use for the most aggressively Whig churchman of the century.

But the ferment in the church was accompanied by a virtual stagnation in political and constitutional debate. While the Old Whigs continued to peddle old-fashioned Whig notions of the Revolution as establishing individual liberty and the right of resistance, establishment whiggery was concerned to play down such principles, now they seemed likely to benefit only the Jacobites.[89] There was an increasing disposition to see 1688 as the 'year one' of English history, when a state of affairs had been established so perfect that it required no amendment.[90] As we have seen, the idea that the Revolution Settlement was immutable was a very strong one, and of long standing; even the Tory peers who protested against the Abjuration Act in 1702 believed that the Bill of Rights had been 'enacted to stand, remain and be the law of this realm for ever'.[91] In 1713 and 1719 vocal elements protested that the same sanctity protected the Act of Union from the least amendment, and in 1716 the supporters of the Septennial Bill tacitly accepted the sanctity of the Revolution Settlement by arguing that the Triennial Act was not part of that Settlement; indeed, in their zeal they went so far as to deny that their predecessors in the Junto had had any share in it.[92] By 1734, when the opposition moved the repeal of the Septennial Act, it had become current orthodoxy to assert that the Triennial Act was the work of the enemies of the Revolution.[93] The strongest argument put by the opponents of the Peerage Bill in 1719 was that it proposed to tamper with a constitution now regarded as unchangeable, and it was useless for John Toland to protest:

No reasons can be assigned why the legislature, in this or the last age, might not, as well as six or seven ages ago, make new laws, limitations and precedents, which will be the ancient constitution (if there be any charm in this expression) to our posterity, six or seven ages hence. In effect, to enact a law for posterity is no more than recommending a thing to their choice, since if they think there's a reason for it, they can no more be divested of the power to repeal any laws enacted by their ancestors, than we are of repealing such laws as have been enacted by ours.[94]

Any idea of a developing constitution was sacrificed in the interests of stability.

But stability seemed as far off as ever when the South Sea Bubble burst in 1720. Much has been written before on this celebrated scandal,[95] and it is now not so much a matter of setting the record straight as of rotating it through ninety degrees. First, to the public this was no real surprise; it came as the culmination of twenty years' suspicion that serious malpractices in government were being hidden or condoned. And the process was still going on. The convenient disappearance abroad of Knight, the South Sea Company's treasurer, the death of the Craggses, father and son, one of them almost certainly by his own hand, the amply pensioned retirement of John Aislabie, and even the sudden deaths of Stanhope in 1721 and Sunderland in 1722, were regarded by a sceptical public as part of the cover-up operation, and *Cato's Letters* (1724), by John Trenchard and Thomas Gordon, are only an outstanding example of the kind of criticism which the ministry now had to sustain from the Old Whigs.[96] Secondly, it is remarkable that the man who organised this cover-up, 'The Skreenmaster-General', was none other than Robert Walpole, who now hastened to abandon his 'patriotic' opposition, and rushed forward to defend men and measures he had only a few months before affected to despise. Looking back down the years, we see Walpole as a large figure; not great, perhaps, and certainly not good, but imposing in stature, commanding at least our grudging respect. His contemporaries, unfortunately, saw him as an avaricious, dishonest hypocrite – as late as 1742 his symbol in the satiric prints was a screen, just as the Pretender's was a windmill.[97] His emergence in 1722 as the leader of the

Whig party may have been a triumph in terms of political dexterity, but in many ways it was a moral disaster. Though a new generation of MPs emerging in the 1720s were to accept him at his own valuation, in the traditions of an older generation of Country Whigs he remained a moral leper.[98]

The end of the first septennial parliament, which had begun in such triumph in 1715, and with such high hopes, was ominous. As John Trenchard said,

As I am now upon the decline of a public life, I have had an opportunity of observing a great deal of the variety and inconstancy of public affairs, but I never yet knew so great a ferment, so prevailing a dissatisfaction, as at present we see throughout the whole kingdom. Parties have been preferred, discarded, restored, mixed, and the several friends of each have by turn complained of reciprocal violence and injury, mismanagement and corruption, but I don't know that any of them have ever persuaded the whole body of the people into their quarrel. No private little wrongs could have effected a discontent so universal. That administration must affect everyone, which everyone complains of. Indeed, when a nation is plundered and oppressed, they cannot but feel and resent it.[99]

Indeed, there were strong rumours that the paladins of Whiggism were not prepared to meet the electors, now or ever, and that the Septennial Act would be suspended.[100] Certainly they could not stomach a 'clean' election, or what the makers of the Bill of Rights would have called a 'free' election. Almost the last action of the Lords in this parliament was to reject a bill sent up by the Commons 'for better securing the freedom of elections', which was the first decisive step towards suppressing corruption. At the request of either candidate any voter could be put on oath to testify whether he had been bribed or not, with the prospect of being prosecuted for perjury if he lied, and those having the disposal of the public money were forbidden to spend it on elections under pain of heavy punishment. (Sunderland said the Act could not be implemented 'without exposing the most innocent persons to the guilt of perjury'.) In an excess of party spite a protest entered by twenty-six peers was expunged from the Journals.[101]

II

CONCLUSION

In retrospect it is clear that the Revolution of 1688 was as much an embarrassment to the Whigs as it was to the Tories. In theory the dogma of divine right and non-resistance still applied with all its old rigour, and the innate conservatism of the nation and the church was affirmed in such practices as the cult of Charles I. However, in terms of practical reality, after an anxious discussion in 1689 and 1690 most Tories settled down comfortably enough with the doctrine of *de facto* obedience to King William, a doctrine endorsed by such important luminaries as Archbishop Sharp and the Earl of Nottingham.

On their side the Whigs were convinced that the Revolution had involved in some sense the deposition of James II, but they were saddled with the unfortunate pretence of abdication, which had been adopted to enlist bipartisan support in 1689 and continued to be official government doctrine, though it is to be doubted if anyone at all sincerely believed it. Some of them fell back on a historicist view of the ancient constitution, tied to the idea of an Original Contract, itself a historical phenomenon, regularly re-appearing at the beginning of each reign; no one, including most Whigs, was ready for the idea of a notional or abstract contract of the kind adumbrated by Locke. Again, though it was easy to assume that the Revolution hinged on contract, it found no place in the Bill of Rights.

The Whig historicist view implied the exercise of popular will and the invocation of popular rights, but no one, including Locke, was very clear which section of the people enjoyed such rights. In a context of intellectual imprecision the propaganda of a small group of radicals and republicans confirmed the association in the popular mind between Whiggism and the exercise of sovereign power by the people at large, an imputation it proved difficult to evade. Meanwhile, by a process difficult to trace, the Whigs in the 1690s increasingly assumed sole responsibility for the Revolution, many Tories being ready enough to surrender their claims to participation, so that the Revolution itself was increasingly besmirched by the mud thrown at the Whigs. Towards the end of William's reign the High Church revival also brought with it a hardening of public opinion against the Dissenters, who were regarded as the Whigs' inseparable allies; indeed, to many the terms 'Whig' and 'Dissenter' were interchangeable.

The situation became critical once a majority of Tories threw over the *de facto* theory. The theory came under strain early in 1702, when the Abjuration Bill obliged men not just to acquiesce in the authority of William III but to deny the rights of the exiled Stuarts. The Tories were saved by the accession of Anne, a blood Stuart who enjoyed a hereditary as well as a parliamentary title, but they declined to acknowledge that this relief was only temporary; instead there was a marked increase in non-resistance preaching. The Tories' insistence that Anne's hereditary title was superior to her parliamentary title seemed to the Whigs implied Jacobitism, and at the same time the vogue for passive obedience was an indirect criticism of the Revolution itself. For since the argument that the Revolution had not involved resistance (as put by Sacheverell in his famous sermon) was untenable on the evidence, the implication was that the Revolution had involved resistance, and was therefore wrong.

It was difficult for the Whigs to make any convincing response to all this, except by demanding blind adherence to 'Revolution Principles', which were not really principles at all, it seemed, but paradigms for future action drawn from the circumstances of 1688. In any case, the Modern or Junto Whigs had by now emerged as an establishment or government party, with elitist attitudes borrowed from the pre-Revolution Tories. The Old or Country Whigs, with their embarrassing and even damaging concepts of 'freedom' and 'toleration', found themselves increasingly in opposition. The Junto were now committed to the idea of authoritative, centralised, even militarist government, and therefore found it difficult to counter the arguments for passive obedience put forward by their opponents, though they were uneasily aware that such ideas were better calculated at this juncture to serve the Pretender than the Hanoverians.

Sacheverell's trial was the turning point. Here at least two of the next generation of Whig leaders, Stanhope and Walpole, learned the futility, even the danger, of discussing the Revolution in depth. The result was that Whig doctrine emerged from the trial more conservative than when it went in; the Whigs were driven to endorse passive obedience as a general doctrine, with resistance permitted only in specific and narrowly defined instances. Sacheverell's trial and its aftermath also taught them the power of High Churchmanship, and the uselessness of continuing to defend the Dissenters, a bitterly unpopular group who now seemed politically inert. The end result was a new alliance between the political leadership and the powerful Whig element in the upper ranks of the clergy, epitomised in the persons of Robert Walpole and Edmund Gibson. Religious toleration was no longer an issue worth fighting for, and extreme clerics like Hoadly who showed signs of rocking the political boat found themselves out of favour. Stanhope's proposal to repeal the sacramental test in 1719 was a desperate attempt to rally support to a failing ministry.

The election of 1710 was another turning point. It strongly suggested that the Whigs had lost what ability they had to contest the polls on even terms, except in uncommon, once-a-generation crises such as that of 1715. Francis Hare wrote, 'The spirit of the gentry of the nation is Toryism, and...nothing but the influence of the court has made it otherwise in any parliament [since the Revolution].'[1] Whether this was true or not is beside the point; the trepidation with which the ministers approached the long-delayed election of 1722 is in itself significant.

This naturally damped down any radical or even independent ideas. Between 1689 and 1714, with the nation at war most of the time, and with the succession in dispute and after 1700 in serious doubt, it was only sensible for the Whigs to try to broaden the basis of their support, to represent themselves as a party of 'the people' (whoever they might be), and to champion popular rights, electoral freedom and religious liberty against a potential Catholic authoritarianism, which could easily have become an actuality with the support of a High Church movement brainwashed into unthinking passive obedience. But once France was defeated, the High Church movement blasted and the Protestant succession assured for several generations, the pressure was off, and the establishmentarian, elitist tendencies in whiggery (always evident in pre-Revolution noblemen like Shaftesbury and Devonshire) gained complete ascendency. The Whigs became oligarchic and mercenary, with no thought for reform, toleration or popular participation in government. Having consolidated their power by the Septennial Act, they viewed with complacency an increasing electoral corruption which worked in the interests of the governing class. After 1722 the frequency of contested elections begins to decline, and after 1734 this decline becomes precipitous. The broad and active electorate seen by J. H. Plumb as existing between 1689 and 1714 was being strangled at birth.[2]

The corruption and moral stagnation of eighteenth-century England were denounced by a succession of liberal nineteenth-century historians culminating in Basil Williams and Charles Grant Robertson. Modern cynicism applauds the skilful techniques employed, and justifies the means by reference to the end, which was constitutional parliamentary government unruffled by popular revolutions.

But this begs the question; had another choice been made, a better, or at least a different kind of government could have emerged much earlier. Had the Septennial Act not been passed, had a firm line been taken with electoral corruption, had the abuse of patronage been curbed, had a proper system of government accounting been instituted and all placemen barred from the House of Commons, the face of eighteenth-century England could not have been worse, and might well have been better.

Instead England subsided into what has been called 'stability' but was in fact stasis. There was precious little stability in a system in which savage and dangerous rioting was frequent, in which a Prime Minister could stand in danger of his life at the very door of the Commons, as Walpole did in 1733, or another Prime Minister could be forced by ill-informed public pressure from outside parliament to withdraw a modest measure of reform like the Jewish Naturalisation Act of 1753.[3] Of other reform was there none. So inviolate was the law that it took until 1732 to change the language of the courts from bastard French to English. The administration of justice if anything deteriorated, and the courts remained much as they had been under Henry VIII or even Henry IV; the administration of the fiscal system if anything declined in efficiency under the pressures of political patronage. Parliamentary elections grew increasingly corrupt (for we need not tie ourselves down by Namier's definition of 'corruption' as involving outright cash transactions), and at the same time the power of the House of Commons declined. For, despite the pretence of the Commons' overwhelming constitutional importance subscribed to by everyone from Walpole downwards, by 1750 it had become a machine which voted increasingly large sums of money for purposes over which it had diminishing control.[4] The Scotsman George Lockhart had it right when he said,

Though the English please themselves with the notion of liberty, it consists in nothing more than that they themselves are the instruments of their own slavery, being bubbled and imposed upon by those in authority over them more than any other nation in Europe...They value their constitution much, because no taxes can be raised but by consent of parliament, whilst at the same time greater taxes are imposed, and greater abuses committed in the application of them, than if the power was solely vested in the sovereign.[5]

Whiggism of principle gave way to what one historian has characterised as 'the Whiggery of office-holding, the political philosophy of Shaftesbury as transmuted by Wharton, regulated by Walpole, and distilled by Hardwicke and Newcastle'.[6] And though much of Walpole's and Pelham's ascendency over George I and George II depended on their ability to convince them that party differences did exist, and were important,[7] they increasingly behaved as if they were not.

Of course, the radical vein of whiggery exploited by writers like Molesworth, Trenchard and Gordon never died out, and recent American historians have shown that their writings were a potent influence in preparing the eighteenth-century colonists to reject the English political system.[8] In 1721 we find Hoadly trying to accommodate Whig tradition to the current political situation in the unusual context of a 30 January sermon to the House of Lords:

What is the liberty contended for by all men of honesty and understanding? Not licentiousness, not a right to overturn laws and constitution whenever passion or rage dictate and the favourable opportunity of power offers itself; much less a licence, under pretence of liberty, to destroy all freedom in parliament, to set up an arbitrary power and sustain it by force of arms. Nothing of all this, but everything contrary to it. It is the liberty which results from being governed by laws made by consent; the liberty which results from those laws being settled in such a manner that the innocent shall always know their own defence from injuries, and even the most guilty know beforehand upon what their guilt shall be founded; it is the secure enjoyment of property, and privileges granted by laws, free from everything that looks like violence.[9]

This was a tradition denied by the law courts themselves, which administered with increasing severity an increasingly savage penal code. Capital punishment in eighteenth-century England was not so much a way of government as a way of life, enforcing by fear an increasingly stratified class system.[10] The system was enforced, too, by the pressure of government and aristocracy on parliamentary elections, and the difficulty now of translating the public will into action. Walpole ruled as chief minister of the crown for nearly twenty years, yet he fought only three general elections, of which he won one, drew one and lost one. In 1734 he survived at the polls despite the fact that only twelve months before he had sustained the greatest defeat of his career and could fairly be described as the most unpopular man in England. The reconstruction of the ministry after his eventual fall in 1742 demonstrates the incompetence of the House of Commons itself to translate public opinion into political action.

It is clear that the Sacheverell Riots of 1710 and the Jacobite Riots of 1715 had given Walpole, at least, an unhealthy fear of the people. In the debate on the Septennial Act in 1734 he spoke of the need to restrain the popular will if the balanced constitution was to be preserved: 'In all the regulations we make with respect to the constitution', he said, 'we are to guard against running too much into that form of government which is properly called democratical', and later in the same speech he added, 'As for faction and sedition, I will grant that in monarchical and aristocratical governments it generally arises from violence and oppression; but in democratical governments it always arises from the people's having too great a share in the government.'[11] Indeed, he was prepared to go further. Amongst his papers is a draft pamphlet (written about 1735 in reply to Bolingbroke's *Dissertation upon Parties*) which states, 'It can never be conceived but that a gentleman of liberal fortune and tolerable education is fitter to serve his country in parliament than a man bred to a trade, and brought up in a shop.'[12]

Henry Pelham thoroughly agreed. He said in 1740, 'We know how giddy the populace are in every country; we know how apt the people are to be led away by the artful heads of faction'; and eleven years later William Murray, the future Lord Mansfield, declared that 'All limited governments are liable to faction, and the more they are limited the more they are liable to that political distemper.'[13] Edmund Burke went so far as to say, 'To govern according to the sense and agreeably to the interests of the people is a great and glorious object of government. [But] this object cannot be obtained but through the medium of popular election, and popular election is a mighty evil.'[14] There was in fact a steady tendency to diminish the role of the people, even 'the people' in the comparatively modest terms of the seventeenth century. In the words of John Brewer,

The role of the people was rather like that of the deity in a Newtonian universe. Just as the clockwinder was chiefly necessary only to start the cosmological chronometer, so the body of the people was needed to make the contract that established civil society, and set up the much praised institutions of the British Constitution; but thereafter the populace was largely banished from the political arena. The people's return was only permitted at times of crisis, and then with the proviso that expressions of public opinion be mediated and controlled by the leaders of political society.[15]

Therefore, though the Revolution of 1688 was still central to the Whig myth, it was a rather different revolution. The pamphleteers hired by Walpole to answer Bolingbroke's writings on English history simply reversed the views of their predecessors; they gladly allowed the full validity of the Norman Conquest, and declined to support their case on the theory of the ancient constitution. In fact, there was no such thing. The centuries from 1066 to 1688 had been a period of unrelieved autocracy, and the Revolution was not the restoration of something temporarily lost but a radical new departure, and one controlled, therefore, by its makers.[16] One of the most influential philosophers of the late eighteenth century, William Paley, rejected everything that was sacrosanct in the Whig tradition: not only did he dismiss the Norman Conquest (and therefore all the past history of England) as of no account – 'No subject of the British Empire conceives himself engaged to vindicate the justice of the Norman claim or conquest, or apprehends

that his duty in any manner depends upon that controversy' – he also dismissed Locke's social contract: 'It is to
suppose it possible to call savages out of caves and deserts
to deliberate and vote upon topics which the experience
and studies and refinements of civil life alone suggest.' To
him the only motive for obedience to the civil power was
'The will of God as collected from expediency.'[17]

In the melting-pot of the 1760s and 1770s, of course, a
man's views could change very rapidly, as we see in the case
of Edmund Burke. At one stage he deprecated any
research into the origins of politics: 'It is always to be
lamented', he said, 'when men are driven to search into
the foundation of the commonwealth.' Faced by George
III's encroachments, he took another look at the Revolution, and he devoted most of one pamphlet, *An Appeal from
the New to the Old Whigs* (1791), to Sacheverell's trial. Even
now, however, his view of events was essentially conservative, sufficiently so to form the ideological basis of Toryism
in the next generation. 'What we did [in 1689]', he said,
'was in truth and substance, and in a constitutional light,
a revolution not made but prevented. We took solid
securities; we settled doubtful questions; we corrected
anomalies in our law. In the stable, fundamental parts of
our constitution we made no revolution, no, nor any
alteration at all.'[18]

APPENDIX A

Vox Populi Vox Dei

The author of *Vox Populi Vox Dei* is unknown. Some nineteenth-century bibliographers gave the honour to Somers, others to Defoe, but neither attribution is very plausible. It seems unlikely that the veteran Lord President ventured into party polemics again at this stage of his career, and contemporaries do not seem to have attributed the pamphlet to him as they did *Anguis in Herba* (1701) or *Jura Populi Anglicani* (1701). Defoe is a more plausible possibility, but no more than that; *VPVD* is not really extreme enough for him, when we consider what he was writing between 1706 and 1709,[1] and the style is not his.

An exact attribution is made more difficult by the fact that the pamphlet swelled from edition to edition, until the third edition of 1710, under the title *The Judgment of Whole Kingdoms. . .* was nearly twice the length of the original. But these later editions do purport to offer some clues to the author's identity. Thus the title-page of the first edition of the pamphlet under its new name identifies him as 'a true lover of the queen and country, who wrote in the year 1690. . .in a challenge to Sir R. L'Estrange, Dr Sherlock and eleven other divines'.[2] Obviously, this refers to *Political Aphorisms; or The True Maxims of Government* (1690),[3] which had as a subtitle 'By way of challenge to Dr William Sherlock, and ten other new Protestant Dissenters'. Moreover, 'the third edition corrected' (also 1710)[4] added that the author also 'wrote in 1689 in vindication of the Revolution, in a challenge to all Jacobites, which was answered, and printed with a reply annexed to it'. This points to *A Brief Justification of the Prince of Orange's Descent into England. . .*(1689).[5]

These two works bear very little relation to each other, but it is obvious, even on a cursory reading, that each has made a contribution to *VPVD*, in ideas and even phraseology, though *VPVD* is far from being a mere conflation of the two. The trouble is, what little evidence we have suggests that the two pamphlets had different authors. *A Brief Justification* was written before the Convention had decided the question of the crown, and it is the work of a strong Whig, and probably one who had sailed with William. This much is clear from internal evidence. It was signed 'R. F.', and there seems no reason to challenge the accepted attribution to Robert Ferguson. But long before 1709 Ferguson had turned Jacobite, and it is unlikely that he turned back. As for *Political Aphorisms*, this was signed 'T. H.', and Professor Maurice Goldsmith's suggestion[6] that this was Thomas Harrison the publisher, who brought out *VPVD* as well as *Political Aphorisms*, is plausible enough. Unfortunately we know little about him, and there seems no reason why he should want to claim *A Brief Justification*, unless to excuse his own plagiarism or to cover his tracks.

But the issue is further complicated by the fact that there are strong resemblances between parts of *VPVD* and certain published work by Gilbert Burnet. Indeed, more than resemblance is involved. For instance, the statement 'In all disputes between power and liberty, power must always be proved, but liberty proves itself, the one being founded upon positive law, the other upon the law of nature' is transcribed, word for word, from Burnet's *An Enquiry into the Measures of Submission to the Supreme Authority* (1689).[7] Even more remarkably, the passionate and idiosyncratic passage in praise of past revolutionaries, which forms one of the climaxes of *VPVD*,[8] beginning 'The greatest and wisest of nations and the best of men of all ages' and ending 'will be held in veneration by all posterity', is a direct transcript from *The Revolution Vindicated* (1698), also ascribed to Burnet.[9]

Plagiarism it could be, of course, but if so it is a concealed plagiarism alongside admitted plagiarism from two other pamphlets. It is equally possible that the cautious Burnet, in the fraught conditions of 1709, chose to use Harrison as a cover. More informed speculation must await an exact collation of all the available editions of this pamphlet, and their comparison with a wide range of Burnet's work. This is a task for which I have not yet been able to find time.

ABBREVIATIONS

These abbreviations are used throughout the notes which follow. All books are published in London unless otherwise stated.

Boyer, *Annals*	Abel Boyer, *The History of the Reign of Queen Anne Digested into Annals*, 11 vols. (1703–15)
Burnet, *History*	Gilbert Burnet, *History of My Own Time*, ed. M. J. Routh, 2nd edn, 6 vols. (Oxford 1833)
CJ	*Journals of the House of Commons*
DNB	*Dictionary of National Biography*
EHR	*English Historical Review*
Grey, *Debates*	Anchitel Grey, *Debates of the House of Commons...* [*1667–94*], 10 vols. (1763)
Hearne, *Collections*	*The Remarks and Collections of Thomas Hearne*, 6 vols. (Oxford 1884–1902)
HJ	*Historical Journal*
HLQ	*Huntington Library Quarterly*
HMC	*Reports of the Historical MSS. Commission*
LJ	*Journals of the House of Lords*
Lords Papers	*Manuscripts of the House of Lords 1678–1714*, 15 vols. (1887–1962)
Luttrell, *Brief Relation*	Narcissus Luttrell, *A Brief Historical Relation of State Affairs*, 10 vols. (1857)
Parl. Debates	*A Collection of Parliamentary Debates in England from the Year 1688 to the Present Time*, 21 vols. (1741–2)
Parl. Hist.	*The Parliamentary History of England*, ed. William Cobbett, 36 vols. (1806–20)
Somers Tracts	*A Collection of Scarce and Valuable Tracts...of the Late Lord Somers*, ed. Sir Walter Scott, 13 vols. (1809–15)
State Tracts	*A Collection of State Tracts Published on Occasion of the Late Revolution in 1688 and during the Reign of King William III*, 3 vols. (1705–7)
State Trials	*State Trials*, ed. William Cobbett and T. C. Howell, 34 vols. (1809–28)

NOTES

CHAPTER 1. INTRODUCTION

1 For instance, see J. H. Plumb, *The Growth of Political Stability in England 1675–1725* (1967), Geoffrey Holmes, *British Politics in the Age of Anne* (1967), and W. A. Speck, *Tory and Whig: The Struggle in the Constituencies 1701–15* (1970), to mention only the most significant.
2 With a few notable exceptions, such as Quentin Skinner, 'History and Ideology in the English Revolution', *HJ*, VII (1965), 151–78.
3 Lord Somers, *Jura Populi Anglicani* (1701), in *Parl. Hist.*, V, app., pp. clxxxviii–ccxxx, and *State Tracts*, III, 257–89. For Locke and Somers, see William L. Sachse, *Lord Somers: A Political Portrait* (Madison, Wisc. and Manchester 1975), pp. 105–6, 116–17, and Peter Laslett (ed.), John Locke, *Two Treatises of Government* (1960), pp. 37–44.
4 Burnet, *History*, IV, 289n.
5 For instance, as early as 1628 Sir Robert Phelips told the Commons, 'It is well known the people of this state are under no other subjection than what they did voluntarily assent to by their Original Contract between king and people', qu. S. R. Gardiner, *History of England 1603–42*, 10 vols. (1883–4), VI, 237n.
6 James L. Axtell (ed.), *The Educational Writings of John Locke* (1968), pp. 400–1.
7 Plumb, *Growth of Political Stability*, p. 151; Holmes, *British Politics*, p. 248; Speck, *Tory and Whig*, pp. 5, 65; *Britain after the Glorious Revolution, 1689–1714*, ed. Geoffrey Holmes (1969), p. 216.
8 Holmes, *British Politics*, p. 246.

CHAPTER 2. BY FORCE OR BY MIRACLE

1 *State Trials*, XV, 91.
2 Declaration of 4/14 October, in *State Tracts: Being A Farther Collection of Several Choice Treatises relating to the Government from the Year 1660 to 1689* (1692), pp. 424, 426.
3 This was at Plymouth; see *Correspondentie van Willem III*, ed. N. Japikse, 2nd ser. III (The Hague 1937), 69. For Norwich, King's Lynn and Derby, see *State Tracts 1660 to 1689* (1692), pp. 427, 438.

4 15 November 1688, in *State Tracts 1660 to 1689* (1692), p. 435.
5 In *State Tracts 1660 to 1689* (1692), p. 436 (italics in original).
6 Grey, *Debates*, IX, 12, 20.
7 Philip Yorke Earl of Hardwicke (ed.), *Miscellaneous State Papers*, 2 vols. (1778), II, 404, 417.
8 Ibid. p. 406; Roger Morrice: 'Entering Book', MS., 3 vols. (1677–91), II, 444 (Dr Williams's Library, London).
9 Hardwicke, *State Papers*, II, 403–4; Grey, *Debates*, IX, 21–3. Sawyer made another attempt on 19 February, supported by Sir Thomas Clarges; see Grey, *Debates*, IX, 85–6, 100–1, 105–6.
10 *Some Remarks upon Government...in Two Letters Written by and to a Member of the Great Convention...* (1689), pp. 23–8 (also in *State Tracts*, I, 149–63).
11 *Reasons Humbly Offered...* in *An Eighth Collection of Papers relating to the Present Juncture of Affairs in England* (1689), p. 17 (also in *Cal. S.P. Dom. James II*, III, no. 2136). See also *Some Short Considerations relating to the Settling of the Government...* in *Somers Tracts*, X, 273 (and see n. 35); *Reasons for Crowning the Prince and Princess...* in *The Harleian Miscellany*, ed. T. Park, 10 vols. (1810–13), VI, 606; and *Four Questions Debated...* in *State Tracts*, I, 163–6.
12 *Now Is the Time* and *Good Advice before It Be Too Late*, in *Somers Tracts*, X, 197ff.
13 T. B. Macaulay, *The History of England from the Accession of James II* (Everyman edn 1906), II, 598.
14 George Roberts, *The Life, Progresses, and Rebellion of James Duke of Monmouth* (1844), I, 235.
15 Morrice, 'Entering Book', II, 444.
16 Ibid.
17 Grey, *Debates*, IX, 12–15. Cf. IX, 116, and Hardwicke, *State Papers*, II, 404.
18 See particularly the analysis of the resolution given in *The Revolution Vindicated*, cited on p. 44 above; see also *Cursory Remarks on the Late Disloyal Proceedings* (1699), in *Somers Tracts*, XI, 172–4.
19 See the speeches of Somers, Holt and Treby on 5 February, *Parl. Debates*, II, 191–7, 211–13. They really had no answer to the Bishop of Ely's criticisms (ibid. pp. 203–4).
20 Andrew Browning (ed.), *English Historical Documents 1660–1714*, (1953), pp. 635–6. Cf. *A Vindication of the Proceedings of the Convention of the Estates in Scotland*, in *State Tracts*, III, 441. In later years the Scots example was viewed with envious approval by many Whigs. See, for instance, Johnson's remarks, p. 39 above, and *The False Steps of the Ministry after the Revolution* (1714), in *Somers Tracts*, XIII, 565.
21 Morrice, 'Entering Book', II, 444.
22 *Lords Papers 1689–90*, p. 15.
23 Ibid. pp. 16–17.
24 *The Debate at Large between the House of Lords and House of Commons ...1688* (1695), p. 61 (photo reprint, Dublin, Irish University Press, 1972).

25 Browning, *Historical Documents*, pp. 122–3.
26 See Betty Behrens, 'The Whig Theory of the Constitution in the Reign of Charles II', *Camb. Hist. Jnl*, VII (1941), 42–71, and Carolyn Andervont Edie, 'Succession and Monarchy: The Controversy of 1679–81', *Amer. Hist. Review*, LXX (1964–5), 350–70.
27 This was King Sigismund, in 1607. See also *A Protestant Precedent Offered to the Bishops . . . in An Eighth Collection*, p. 11.
28 H. C. Foxcroft, *A Life of Gilbert Burnet* (Cambridge 1907), p. 538.
29 Gilbert Burnet, *A Collection of Eighteen Papers* (1689), pp. 120–4.
30 *An Enquiry into the Present State of Affairs*, pp. 14–15.
31 In *State Tracts*, I, 135–6, 139.
32 *An Essay*, p. 9.
33 In *State Tracts*, I, 227.
34 In *State Tracts*, I, 163–6.
35 *Proposals Humbly Offered to the Lords and Commons in the Present Convention*, in *An Eighth Collection*, pp. 1–6. (The same pamphlet, under the title *Some Short Considerations relating to the Settling of the Government*, is in *Somers Tracts*, X, 273ff.)
36 In *State Tracts*, I, 218.
37 In *An Eighth Collection*, pp. 19ff.
38 *Lords Papers 1689–90*, pp. 15–16.
39 *The Debate at Large*, p. 61.
40 *Parl. Debates*, II, 202–3, 248–9 (Conference of 5 February).
41 *Some Remarks upon Government . . . in Two Letters Written by and to a Member of the Great Convention* (1689), p. 8.
42 [Pierre Allix], *An Examination of the Scruples of Those Who Refuse to Take the Oath of Allegiance*, in *State Tracts*, I, 302.
43 John Dunn, *The Political Thought of John Locke* (1969), p. 8. See also *John Locke: Perspectives and Problems*, ed. John Yolton (1969), pp. 56–7.
44 Martyn P. Thompson, 'Ideas of Contract in English Political Thought 1688–1704', unpublished Ph.D. dissertation, University of London (1974), pp. 244ff.
45 John Locke, *Two Treatises of Government*, ed. Peter Laslett (1960), p. 429.
46 Atwood, *The Fundamental Constitution of the English Government* (1690), p. 101.
47 Ibid. p. 4 (cf. p. 102).
48 *Bibliotheca Politica* (1694), pp. 72–4, 81–3, 88–9, 100, 155–6. For a more detailed discussion of Tyrrell, see pp. 36ff above.
49 Charles Bastide, *John Locke* (Paris 1907), pp. 286–7.
50 See p. 63 above.
51 Thompson, 'Ideas of Contract', pp. 251–2.
52 Ibid. p. 244. (At a late stage in the preparation of this book I received a copy of Dr Thompson's article 'The Reception of Locke's *Two Treatises of Government* 1690–1705', *Political Studies*, XXIV (1976), 184–91, which sets out most of the points from his dissertation which I have cited in this chapter.)

CHAPTER 3. THE MEASURES OF SUBMISSION

1 See p. 33 above.
2 In fact, constitutionally Mary's death was a non-event, though some Jacobites and non-jurors did assert that her title died with her, including the renegade Whig Robert Ferguson, in *Whether the Parliament Be Not Dissolved on the Death of the Princess of Orange* (1695). Up to 1694 some non-jurors prayed for 'the king and the two queens' (James II, Mary Beatrice and Mary II), but all this attitudinising seems to have had little political impact.
3 In *State Tracts*, I, 598–614 passim. See also Robert Todd Carroll, *The Commonsense Philosophy of Religion of Bishop Edward Stillingfleet* (The Hague 1975), pp. 32–6.
4 Linda Cook, 'Richard Cumberland', unpublished Ph.D. dissertation, University of London (1976), p. 184.
5 *The Unreasonableness of a New Separation*, in *State Tracts*, I, 599.
6 *Reflections upon the Opinions of Some Modern Divines. . .* in *State Tracts*, I, 466–514, esp. 512–13. For Allix's career, see *DNB*.
7 See pp. 140–1 above.
8 *A Resolution of Certain Queries concerning Submission to the Present Government. . .by a Divine of the Church of England*, in *State Tracts*, I, 443. For Long, see *DNB*.
9 In *State Tracts*, I, 298.
10 Amongst others, *A Brief Vindication of the Parliamentary Proceedings against the Late King James II* (1689), pp. 40–6; Pierre Allix, loc. cit.; *A Letter of a Bishop concerning the Present Settlement*, in *Somers Tracts*, IX, 374; *The Advantages of the Present Settlement*, in *State Tracts*, I, 273; *An Essay upon the Original and Design of Magistracy*, p. 9.
11 See the Claim of Right, in Andrew Browning (ed.), *English Historical Documents 1660–1714* (1953), p. 636, and *An Account of the Proceedings of the. . .Estates in Scotland* (1689), Scottish Historical Society Publications, 3rd ser. XV–XVII (Edinburgh 1954–5). On the day of William's death Anne summoned a meeting of the Scots Privy Council to St James's, and formally took the oath (Boyer, *Annals*, I, 3).
12 *Some Considerations touching Succession and Allegiance*, in *State Tracts*, I, 336.
13 Sermon to the House of Commons, 31 January 1688/9, p. 3 (cf. p. 34); Sermon before King George I, 31 October 1714.
14 Sermon to House of Lords, 30 January 1703. For other examples see Gerald M. Straka, *Anglican Reaction to the Revolution of 1688* (Madison, Wisc. 1962), ch. 6.
15 In *An Eighth Collection of Papers relating to the present Juncture of Affairs in England. . .* (1689), p. 6.
16 'The Final Phase of Divine Right Theory in England 1688–1702', *EHR*, LXXVII (1962), 638–58 (p. 655).
17 *The History of the Desertion* (1689), in *State Tracts*, I, 99.
18 *The Speech of Mr Johnston. . .June 6, 1690*, in *State Tracts*, III, 677. The

new service for 5 November was promulgated in a royal letter to the Archbishop of Canterbury, 18 October 1690.

19 Johnson, *An Argument Proving That the Abrogation of the Late King James... Was According to the Constitution* (1693), p. 39 (for fuller title see ch. 4 n. 23); *A Vindication of the Proceedings of the Convention of the Estates in Scotland*, in *State Tracts*, III, 463.

20 *Reflections upon the Opinions of Some Modern Divines*, p. 15.

21 *Bishop Overall's Convocation Book MDCVI concerning the Government of God's Catholick Church and the Kingdom of the Whole World* (1689), p. 59.

22 The controversy is summarised by Charles F. Mullett in 'A Case of Allegiance: William Sherlock and the Revolution of 1688', *HLQ*, x (1946–7), 83–103.

23 Patrick Riley, 'An Unpublished MS. of Leibniz on the Allegiance Due to Sovereign Powers', *Jnl Hist. Philosophy*, XI (1972), 319–26; Nicholas Jolley, 'Leibniz on Hobbes, Locke's *Two Treatises* and Sherlock's *Case of Allegiance*', *HJ*, XVIII (1975), 21–36. Leibniz made a distinction between 'ordinary Providence', which may be said to govern all men's affairs, and 'signal Providence' ('la providence spéciale'), the result of God's personal intervention. Clearly he was not convinced that the English Revolution came into this last category, and preferred a theory of conquest, which was unacceptable to the Whigs and to most Tories.

24 *Case of Allegiance*, pp. 18, 22, 50.

25 See Samuel Johnson, qu. Mullett, 'A Case of Allegiance', p. 90.

26 *Proteus Ecclesiasticus, or Observations on Dr Sherlock's Late Case of Allegiance* (1691), pp. 8, 10.

27 MS. notes, qu. John Dunn, *The Political Thought of John Locke* (1969), p. 145, n. 5.

28 *Case of Allegiance*, p. 3.

29 Kettlewell, *The Duty of Allegiance Settled upon Its True Grounds* (1691).

30 E.g., *A Friendly Conference concerning the New Oath of Allegiance* (1689), p. 5; *The Doctrine of Non-Resistance... No Way Concerned...* (1689), in *State Tracts*, I, 350–1, 360–1, 363.

31 *Political Aphorisms; or The True Maxims of Government* (1690), p. 29, in *State Tracts*, I, 401; Johnson, *An Argument*, pp. 15–16.

32 Lloyd, *A Discourse*, pp. 19–24.

33 Ibid. pp. 28–9, 49.

34 Ibid. pp. 50–1.

35 Ibid. pp. 55–6.

36 *Case of Allegiance*, p. 49.

37 Quentin Skinner, 'History and Ideology in the English Revolution', *HJ*, VII (1965), 151–78; J. G. A. Pocock, *The Ancient Constitution and the Feudal Law* (1957), passim.

38 In *State Tracts*, I, 291.

39 What follows is based on Mark Goldie, 'Edmund Bohun and *Jus Gentium* in the Revolution Debate 1689–93', *HJ*, XX (1977). I am very

grateful to Mr Goldie for allowing me to read this important article in advance of publication.

40 *Parl. Debates*, II, 359–60; *Parl. Hist.*, v, 756; *The Parliamentary Diary of Narcissus Luttrell*, ed. Henry Horwitz (1972), pp. 376–87 passim; Grey, *Debates*, x, 297–8.

41 *An Enquiry into the Nature and Obligation of Legal Rights with respect to the Popular Pleas of the Late King James's Remaining Right to the Crown* (1693), pp. 28–40. Tyrrell also introduced the concept of the 'just war' into the eleventh dialogue of *Bibliotheca Politica*, published in 1694 (pp. 776, 783, 799 of the complete edn of 1694), citing Bohun and Puffendorf.

42 See p. 29 above.

43 Roger Morrice, 'Entering Book', MS., 3 vols. (1677–91), III, 138 (Dr Williams's Library, London).

44 *Parl. Hist.*, v, 598–9 (24 April 1690).

45 Carmarthen's own position was ambiguous. He finally voted to make William and Mary king and queen in February 1689, 'yet no man', he said, 'could affirm they were rightfully so by the constitution' (Andrew Browning, *Thomas Osborne Earl of Danby*, 3 vols. (Glasgow 1944–51), I, 432).

46 Henry Horwitz, *Revolution Politicks: The Career of Daniel Finch Second Earl of Nottingham* (1968), passim.

47 Morrice, 'Entering Book', II, 460 (6 February 1689).

48 See debate of 30 November 1692, and Wharton's remarks on 20 December: *Luttrell Diary*, pp. 274–5, 330.

49 Ibid. pp. 314–19.

50 *Lords Papers 1695–7*, p. 208; *Parl. Hist.*, v, 992.

51 *Parl. Hist.*, v, 992.

52 J. E. Thorold Rogers, *A Complete Collection of the Protests of the Lords*, 3 vols. (Oxford 1875), I, 161–3. He was supported by eight other peers, but the House later ordered the above clause to be expunged.

53 Finch MSS., qu. Geoffrey Holmes, *British Politics in the Age of Anne* (1967), p. 88.

54 Loc. cit.

55 See p. 88 above.

56 Thomas Sharp, *The Life of John Sharp* (1825), I, 263–4. (This was 'when he first went down to his diocese', i.e., in 1694.)

CHAPTER 4. THIS SKEIN OF TANGLED PRINCIPLES

1 *Fundamental Constitution*, pp. 3–4, 101.

2 Ibid. p. 92.

3 See p. 18 above.

4 *Fundamental Constitution*, pp. 101–2.

5 Ibid. pp. 28–84 passim.

6 In *State Tracts*, I, 575–97.

7 J. G. A. Pocock, *The Ancient Constitution and the Feudal Law* (1957), ch. 8; D. C. Douglas, *English Scholars 1660–1730* (2nd edn 1951), ch. 6.

8 Internal evidence suggests that the dialogues were published ser-
iatim, but it is strange that the British Library does not have any of the
individual dialogues, and the two listed by Wing are bibliographically
eccentric. Wing T.3581 is 'Bibliotheca Politica, a Discourse', published 1691/2, and T.3582 is the first dialogue, but published 1694,
not 1692. (The collected edition of 1694, used here, is continuously
paginated.)

9 Tyrrell is a neglected figure. Apart from the *DNB* article, there is
only a brief and unsympathetic summary in Caroline Robbins's *The
Eighteenth-Century Commonwealthman* (Cambridge, Mass. 1959), pp.
73-5. The British Library has many of his own copies of his works,
with MS. revisions and annotations.

10 *Bibliotheca Politica* (1694), pp. 373-614.

11 Ibid. pp. 707ff.

12 Ibid. pp. 704, 712.

13 Ibid. pp. 813-14.

14 Hearne, *Collections*, IV, 232. (*Bibliotheca Politica* was reprinted in 1717.)

15 *A View of the English Constitution with respect to the Sovereign Authority
of the Prince and the Allegiance of the Subject...* (1709).

16 *Parl. Hist.*, V, 425, 628.

17 *Some Short Considerations concerning the State of the Nation* (1693), in
Parl. Hist., V, app., p. lxxii.

18 Collier, *The Desertion Discussed* (1689), in *State Tracts*, I, 115; 'Nonsense
Authenticated and Vindicated by a Vow of Our Late English Convention', Regenstein Library (University of Chicago), MS. F559, p. 23.

19 *A Free Discourse Wherein the Doctrines That Make for Tyranny Are
Displayed* (1697), pp. 36-40.

20 In *State Tracts*, III, 733.

21 He also mentioned William's 'election of the people': *A Brief Vindication of the Parliamentary Proceedings against the Late King James II*
(1689), preface (n.p.) and p. 9.

22 Grey, *Debates*, IX, 64.

23 *An Argument Proving That the Abrogation of the Late King James... Was
according to the Constitution of the English Government... in Opposition
to All the False and Treacherous Hypotheses of Usurpation, Conquest,
Desertion, and of Taking Powers that be upon Content* (5th edn 1693), pp.
11, 41; *A Confutation of a Late Pamphlet Entitled A Letter Balancing the
Necessity of Keeping a Land Force...* (1698), pp. 5, 31. For Charles I's
Answer to the Nineteen Propositions, see J. P. Kenyon, *The Stuart
Constitution* (Cambridge 1966), pp. 21-3.

24 *A Short History of Standing Armies* (1698), in *State Tracts*, II, 653.

25 *Some Short Considerations*, loc. cit.

26 Strangely enough, this point does not seem to be well established,
even now. But a scrutiny of William's short speech in response to a
reading of the Declaration of Right shows that he entered upon no
commitment whatsoever, except to view reform legislation sympathetically (*Twelfth Collection of Papers* (1689), pp. 20-1). The House
of Lords at once ordered the speech to be printed, thus ending the

matter. For William's marked distaste for constitutional reform, see Robert J. Frankle, 'The Formulation of the Declaration of Rights', *HJ*, xxvii (1974), 265–79 (pp. 278–9), and Henry Horwitz, 'Parliament and the Glorious Revolution', *Bull. Inst. Hist. Research*, xlvii (1974), 36–52 (pp. 48–9).

27 *The Charge of the Rt Hon. Henry Earl of Warrington...on the 25th day of April, 1693*, in *State Tracts*, ii, 346.

28 *A Free Discourse Wherein the Doctrines That Make for Tyranny Are Displayed* (1697), p. 32. This pamphlet has been attributed, though not very confidently, to Defoe. The Harvard University Houghton Library copy (EC65.A100, 697f) has a contemporary annotation ascribing it to Sir Robert Howard, which is far from impossible.

29 Grey, *Debates*, x, 45, 75 (9, 26 April 1690). (This was no relative of the earls of Bristol, but an Irish Tory peer, the sixth Lord Digby of Geasehill.)

30 Robert Walcott, *English Politics in the Early Eighteenth Century* (1956), p. 86n.; J. A. Downie, 'The Commission of Public Accounts', *EHR*, xci (1976), 33–51; J. P. Kenyon, 'The Earl of Sunderland and the King's Administration 1693–95', *EHR*, lxxi (1956), 576–602.

31 Qu. John Carswell, *The Old Cause* (1954), p. 8n.

32 *The Parliamentary Diary of Narcissus Luttrell*, ed. Henry Horwitz (1972), pp. 390–416 passim. For Montague and Somers see pp. 406, 407.

33 Grey, *Debates*, x, 370; Luttrell, *Brief Relation*, iii, 11. Cf. Grey, *Debates*, x, 329–31; William L. Sachse, *Lord Somers: A Political Portrait* (Madison, Wisc. and Manchester 1975), pp. 55–6.

34 J. P. Kenyon, *Robert Spencer Earl of Sunderland* (1958), pp. 270–5.

35 See p. 183 above.

36 *The Debate at Large between the House of Lords and House of Commons ...1688...* The circumstances of its publication are obscure, but it cannot be supposed that such confidential material could be printed without the connivance of the government, or at least the House of Lords. The publisher, John Wickens, had published whiggish material under Charles II, but too much importance should not be attached to this.

37 *The Revolution Vindicated in an Answer to the Two Memorials and the Protestation against the Peace Treated at Ryswick and Other Papers Published by the Late King...* Supposed to have been drawn up by Burnet, and corrected by various unnamed ministers of state (H. C. Foxcroft, *A Life of Gilbert Burnet* (Cambridge 1907), p. 545). First published in *State Tracts*, iii, 694ff.

38 *State Tracts*, iii, 716.

39 *A Memorial Drawn by King William's Special Direction, Intended to Be Given In at the Treaty of Ryswick Justifying the Revolution and the Course of His Government*. Foxcroft, *Burnet*, p. 545, suggests that this was also written by Burnet, as an alternative version of the preceding item. It was first published, in pamphlet form, in 1705, and reprinted in *Somers Tracts*, xi, 103ff.

40 *Somers Tracts*, XI, 107, 109–10.
41 Ibid. pp. 109, 110, 111–12.
42 *Jura Populi Anglicani* (1701), in *Parl. Hist.*, v, app., p. cxciii.
43 *A Dialogue betwixt Whig and Tory* (1692), in *State Tracts*, II, 389. This also contains (p. 391) a most unflattering picture of the Whigs' general conduct in the Commons.
44 Burnet, *History*, IV, 6n. (Dartmouth).
45 Lord Halifax, *Complete Works*, ed. J. P. Kenyon (Harmondsworth 1969), p. 184.
46 Drake, *History of the Last Parliament* (1702), preface (n.p.).
47 See p. 14 above.
48 Sermon to the House of Commons, 30 January 1692, pp. 18, 22.
49 Tyrrell, *Bibliotheca Politica* (1694), pp. 163–5.
50 Ibid. pp. 178, 181–2.
51 It is not clear whether this advertisement was always part of the dialogue it precedes, or whether it was inserted in the collected edition.
52 Ibid. pp. 698, 699, 702–3.
53 Ibid. p. 773.
54 Ibid. pp. 778, 781.
55 *General History of England*, I (1696), p. xciv.
56 Robbins, *Eighteenth-Century Commonwealthman*, p. 75.
57 Burnet, *History*, IV, 398.
58 Leslie Stephen, *English Thought in the Eighteenth Century* (1902), I, 93–119; Paul Hazard, *The European Mind* (1953), pp. 148–52.
59 See p. 68 above.
60 *Oceana*, 1737 edn, p. vii. In a little-known pamphlet of 1711 Toland revealed that Harley had encouraged him to republish *Oceana*, and to publish his *The Memorial of the State of England* in 1706. See *Another Memorial for the Most Honourable the Earl of Oxford* (1711), in *A Collection of Several Pieces* (1726), II, 227–8.
61 Dr Blair Worden has discovered a substantial fragment of Ludlow's lost MS., which shows that the edition of 1698 was not only abridged but considerably distorted. He considers Toland the culprit, and it is also reasonable to associate Toland with the publication of Sidney's *Discourses*.
62 Martyn P. Thompson, 'Ideas of Contract in English Political Thought 1688–1704', unpublished Ph.D. dissertation, University of London (1974), pp. 244ff; Caroline Robbins, 'Algernon Sidney's *Discourses Concerning Government*: Textbook of Revolution', *William and Mary Qtly*, IV (1947), 267–96.
63 *Discourses*, 2 vols. (Edinburgh 1750), I, 131–2 (sect. II. 5).
64 Ibid. I, 142 (II. 5); II, 300 (III. 36).
65 Ibid. I, 208ff (II. 13), 239 (II. 17).
66 Halifax, *Complete Works*, p. 63; J. P. Kenyon, *The Stuart Constitution* (Cambridge 1966), p. 17.
67 In *State Tracts*, II, 645.
68 In *State Tracts*, III, 1–21.

69 *The Art of Governing by Parties*, pp. 47–8.
70 Ibid. p. 112.
71 Ibid. pp. 32–3, 149–50.
72 Ibid. pp. 164ff; *Some Reasons for an Annual Parliament...* (1702), in *State Tracts*, III, 289; *Considerations upon Corrupt Elections of Members to Serve in Parliament* (1701).
73 J. G. A. Pocock, *The Machiavellian Moment* (Princeton 1975), pp. 364–5. See also ch. 13 (pp. 423–61), where Pocock argues that the attack on corruption mounted by men like Charles Davenant was part of a campaign to establish the state on a basis of money and credit. (I regret that this important book came to hand too late for most of its conclusions to be incorporated or even discussed here.)
74 Caroline Robbins, *Two English Republican Tracts* (1969), pp. 30–1, and *The Eighteenth-Century Commonwealthman*, ch. 4.
75 *An Account Shewing That a Standing Army Is Inconsistent with a Free Government*, in *State Tracts*, II, 565.
76 *Contests and Dissensions*, ed. Frank H. Ellis (Oxford 1967), p. 83.
77 Burnet, *History*, IV, 552–3; Sir Richard Cocks's diary, 10 February 1702, Bodleian Library MS. Eng.Hist.b.209.
78 *The Dangers of Europe from the Growing Power of France* (November 1701), in *State Tracts*, III, 351. The 'addresses' were for the dissolution or continuance of the 1701 parliament; the 'Company' was of course the East India Company.
79 Burnet, *History*, IV, 454–5.
80 In *State Tracts*, III, 312ff. Sachse (*Somers*, p. 206, n. 13) attributes this to Henry Maxwell, but the important thing is that at the time it was thought to be by Somers.
81 Examples are legion. Particularly interesting is *Corrupt Ministers the Cause of Public Calamities* (1700). See also the better-known *Dangers of Mercenary Parliaments* (1698), in *State Tracts*, II, 638–44.
82 *A Letter to King William III* (1698), pp. 10–11; *The Militia Reformed* (1698), in *State Tracts*, II, 595. Cf. Toland, *The Art of Governing by Parties*, pp. 47–51, and third Earl of Shaftesbury, in *Original Letters of Locke, Algernon Sidney and Lord Shaftesbury*, ed. T. Forster (1830), pp. 109–11 (5 November 1700).
83 *British Politics in the Age of Anne* (1967), pp. 108–9 (cf. p. 63).
84 In *Parl. Hist.*, V, app., pp. cxci, cxcvi.
85 See John Robert Moore, *Daniel Defoe: Citizen of the Modern World* (Chicago 1958), ch. 10, and 'Daniel Defoe, King William's Pamphleteer', *HLQ*, XXXIV (1970–1), 251–60. Moore assumes that Defoe was in direct correspondence with the king, which is unlikely, if not impossible.
86 *A New Test of the Church of England's Loyalty* (1700), in *Somers Tracts*, IX, 577.
87 Lines 802–19, in *Poems on Affairs of State*, VI, ed. Frank H. Ellis (New Haven and London 1970), 292–3.
88 *Later Stuart Tracts*, ed. George A. Aitken (1903), pp. 184–5.

89 *The Original Power*, pp. 5, 8, 17. (Dated 1700, but obviously written the previous year.)
90 *The Dangers of Europe from the Growing Power of France*, in *State Tracts*, III, 351 (my italics).

CHAPTER 5. KING CHARLES'S HEAD

1 Richard Harvey, 'The Problem of Socio-Political Obligation for the Church of England in the Seventeenth Century', *Church History*, XL (1971), 159–69.
2 Filmer, *Patriarcha*, ed. Peter Laslett (Oxford 1949), p. 41. For Bentham see Gordon J. Schochet, *Patriarchalism in Political Thought* (Oxford 1975), p. 280.
3 John Dunn, *The Political Thought of John Locke* (1969), p. 156.
4 *The Tryal of Dr Henry Sacheverell* (1710), p. 285.
5 12 Car. II c. 30, *Statutes of the Realm*, V, 288.
6 The ninth dialogue (1694 complete edn, pp. 615–89) is devoted to this and the non-resistance oath.
7 J. P. Kenyon, *The Stuart Constitution* (Cambridge 1966), pp. 167–8.
8 Ibid. p. 471.
9 *An Entire Confutation of Mr Hoadly's Book of the Original of Government, Taken from the London Gazette...* (1710).
10 J. G. Muddiman, *The Trial of King Charles I* (1928), p. 78.
11 J. P. Kenyon, *Robert Spencer Earl of Sunderland* (1958), pp. 112, 181, and *The Stuarts* (Fontana edn 1970), p. 148.
12 Church Statutes Bill, *Statutes of the Realm*, VIII, 840, and *CJ*, XV, 601. For Wharton, see Andrew Browning, *Thomas Osborne Earl of Danby* (Glasgow 1944–51), I, 427n.
13 George Sensebaugh, *That Grand Whig Milton* (Stanford, Calif. 1952), ch. 4, and Francis Madan, *A New Bibliography of the Eikon Basiliké* (Oxford 1950); also the introduction to the latest edition of the *Eikon*, ed. Philip A. Knachel (Ithaca, N.Y. 1966).
14 Madan, *A New Bibliography*, pp. 139–46.
15 The British Library Catalogue under a name like 'Ludlow, Edmund' or 'Milton, John' gives a good idea of the field.
16 Hunterian Library, University of Glasgow, MS. 73, no. 72 (7 September 1698).
17 *Life of Milton*, pp. 92–3.
18 See p. 27 above.
19 *Some Observations upon the Keeping the Thirtieth of January* (1694), in *Somers Tracts*, IX, 481. Helen W. Randall provides a good general survey in 'The Rise and Fall of a Martyrology', *HLQ*, X (1946–7), 135–67. Byron S. Stewart's 'The Cult of the Royal Martyr', *Church History*, XXXVIII (1969), 175–87, is more superficial.
20 This did not deter Henry Brydges from venturing a similar comparison in a sermon before the queen on 30 January 1709. He argued that the Crucifixion had been a blessing to mankind, and therefore fell short of the horror of 1649.

21 *LJ*, XVII, 132 (16 May 1702).

22 *Animadversions*, in *State Tracts*, III, 297–8.

23 White Kennett, for instance, was accused of softening down his celebrated *Compassionate Enquiry into the Causes of the Civil War* of 1704 (*White against Kennett* (1704), pp. viii–ix). For a contrary example, of a young Oxford don amending an anti-Hoadly sermon, see Hearne, *Collections*, II, 339–40, 345.

24 *Diary*, ed. E. S. de Beer (1955), V, 165–6.

25 Ibid. p. 271.

26 Luttrell, *Brief Relation*, VI, 164, 177. Alexander Cunningham (*History of Great Britain*... [*1688–1714*], 2 vols. (1787), II, 275) seems to regard Higgins as mad, or very near it.

27 *Observator*, VIII, no. 3 (5 February 1709). This was perhaps a Mr Agate, whose 30 January sermon the following year brought forth a lengthy reply from John Withers, *The History of Resistance as Practised by the Church of England*, in *Somers Tracts*, XII, 249.

28 Sermon before the House of Commons, 30 January 1697, pp. 26–7, 29.

29 Sermon before the House of Commons, 31 January 1704, p. 12.

30 See for instance p. 88 above.

31 See pp. 133–4 above.

32 Sermon before the House of Commons, 30 January 1700, pp. 9, 11, 27.

33 *Reflections upon Mr Stephens' Sermon*... (1700), p. 4.

34 *CJ*, XVI, 287–8.

35 Which was in fact delivered by William Delaune, President of St John's, Oxford, and Vice-Chancellor of the University.

36 Norman Sykes, in *The Social and Political Ideas of Some English Thinkers of the Augustan Age*, ed. F. J. C. Hearnshaw (1928), pp. 132–3.

37 Sermon before the House of Lords, 30 January 1712, preface (n.p.); Jonathan Swift, *Journal to Stella*, ed. Harold Williams, 2 vols. (Oxford 1948), II, 476. The *Lords Journals* are silent.

38 Sermon, 30 January 1712, pp. 21–2.

39 In fact he did preach to the Lords on 30 January 1699 (*LJ*, XVI, 371), but the sermon was never published, and one of his critics in 1710 laments that 'the world should be bereaved of a piece of so extra-ordinary doctrine, and timely loyalty' (*A Vindication of the Bishop of Salisbury and Passive Obedience*, p. 7). He was probably deterred by the pointed republication in 1689 of *The Royal Martyr and the Dutiful Subject*, two sermons of his from the 1670s, when there had been no stronger advocate of passive obedience than he.

40 Sacheverell's counsel cited passages from Lloyd of St Asaph's sermon to the Lord Mayor in 1699, Nicholson of Carlisle's to the Lords in 1702, White Kennett's to the Commons in 1705, Robert Eyre's to the Commons in 1707 and Wake of Lincoln's to the Lords in 1708; see *The Tryal of Dr Henry Sacheverell* (1710), pp. 182–5 passim.

41 *A Layman's Lamentation*, p. 12.

42 Roger Morrice, 'Entering Book', MS. 3 vols. (1677–9¹), II, 449 (Dr Williams's Library, London).

43 Sermon before the queen, 30 January 1709, p. 21.

44 Sermon at St Ethelburga's, 30 January 1708, p. 16.

45 The BL Catalogue lists a variety of editions, including two sixth editions, one for 1705, another for 1707. Some of them are ascribed to 'B. Bridgewater', but they are all, in fact, by Ward. See *DNB*, which succinctly characterises him as 'a humorist, of low extraction'.

46 *A Letter to the Authors of an Answer to the Case of the Allegiance Due to Sovereign Powers* (1691), p. 5. In this context the name 'Trimmer' denotes a Low Churchman.

47 Defoe, *Reflections on the Late Great Revolution* (1689), p. 65.

48 Astell, *An Impartial Enquiry into the Causes of Rebellion and Civil War...* (1704), p. 16. 'Sherlock' is Thomas Sherlock, who had preached a whiggish sermon before the queen on 31 January (see p. 97 above). 'Dr Binks' can hardly be William Binckes, who was a rabid High-Flyer (see p. 70 above), but I have been unable to identify him.

49 G. V. Bennett, *White Kennett* (1957), pp. 91–3.

50 *Compassionate Enquiry*, pp. 21, 27.

51 Sermon before the House of Commons, 30 January 1706, pp. 24–5.

52 Ibid. p. 7.

53 *A New Test of the Church of England's Loyalty: or Whiggish Loyalty and Church Loyalty Compared* (1702), p. 13 (italics as in original).

54 However, he made the transition to the Hanoverians easily enough. In 1715 he chose the rather ambiguous title 'The Danger of Changes in Church and State, or The Fatal Doom of Such as Love Them', but in 1716 he preached on 'The Christian Subject's Duty to His Lawful Prince'. Rather typically, Milbourne was the son of a Dissenting minister, but one who deplored Charles I's execution, and kept the anniversary as a personal fast all his life. (See *DNB*.)

55 Thomas Sherlock's sermon before the queen, 31 January 1704, drew heavily on Clarendon; so, less obviously, did Kennett's *Compassionate Enquiry* of the same date.

56 *Memoirs of the Press* (1742), pp. 35–6 (cf. pp. 37, 39).

57 Hunterian Library, University of Glasgow, MS. 73, no. 86 (from J. Topham, 18 September 1698).

58 Lord Clarendon, *History of the Rebellion and Civil Wars in England*, ed. W. D. Macray (Oxford 1888), I, p. xxvi.

59 David Green, *Queen Anne* (1970), p. 120. It is indeed strange that the first volume was not dedicated to Anne, who was, after all, a granddaughter of Clarendon and of Charles I. It is equally strange that her permission was not sought for the dedication of the second volume.

60 Clarendon, *History*, I, pp. xlvii, liii.

CHAPTER 6. THE BLOODY FLAG

1 G. V. Bennett, in *Britain after the Glorious Revolution, 1689–1714*, ed. Geoffrey Holmes (1969), pp. 162–3, and *The Tory Crisis in Church and State 1688–1730: The Career of Francis Atterbury* (Oxford 1975), ch. 1.

2 *Plain English: or An Inquiry concerning the Real and Pretended Friends to the English Monarchy*, in *State Tracts*, II, 79.

3 *Plain English: or An Inquiry into the Causes That Have Frustrated Our Expectations from the Late Happy Revolution*, in *State Tracts*, II, 184.

4 *A Modest Enquiry into the Causes of the Present Disasters* (1690), in *State Tracts*, II, 96.

5 *A New Test of the Church of England's Loyalty: or Whiggish Loyalty and Church Loyalty Compared* (1702), pp. 13, 20.

6 *Some Necessary Considerations relating to All Future Elections* (1702), in *Somers Tracts*, XII, 199–200.

7 Burnet, *History*, IV, 387.

8 *State Trials*, XV, 97.

9 *Cursory Remarks upon Some Late Disloyal Proceedings* (1699), in *Somers Tracts*, XI, 151–2.

10 *A Just Defence of the Royal Martyr King Charles I from the Many False and Malicious Aspersions in Ludlow's Memoirs and Some Other Virulent Libels of That Kind* (1699), preface (n.p.).

11 Of course, the identification between these three is neither complete nor exclusive. Davenant was a virulent critic of the Whigs, but he was also a financial materialist, and his thought had distinct republican undertones. See J. G. A. Pocock, *The Machiavellian Moment* (Princeton 1975), pp. 437–46.

12 The following is based on G. V. Bennett, *The Tory Crisis*, ch. 3, and White Kennett (1957), chs. 2–3; also Norman Sykes, *William Wake* (1957), I, ch. 2.

13 Sykes, op. cit. p. 131.

14 *Sermons Preached on Several Occasions* (1729), II, 45–6, 48–9.

15 Ibid. pp. 51–2, 54, 55–7.

16 Ibid. pp. 59–62.

17 David Green, *Queen Anne* (1970), pp. 86–7.

18 See pp. 33–4 above.

19 Burnet, *History*, V, 12.

20 *Sermons*, II, 108.

21 Henry Horwitz, *Revolution Politicks: The Career of Daniel Finch Second Earl of Nottingham* (1968), p. 183.

22 Burnet, *History*, V, 434. The best analysis is, of course, by Geoffrey Holmes, in *The Trial of Doctor Sacheverell* (1973).

23 William Bissett, *The Modern Fanatick* (1710), p. 1.

24 See Defoe, 'Hymn to the Pillory' (1703), in *Later Stuart Tracts*, ed. George A. Aitken (1903), p. 209; *Observator*, I, no. 35 (19 August 1702), II, no. 57 (20 October 1703), IV, no. 22 (13 June 1705).

25 This imprimatur was rendered unnecessary in the lapse of the Licensing Act in 1695. It may have been a precautionary measure; in the

previous session the House of Lords had started a campaign to suppress anti-Whig pamphlets by James Drake and Charles Davenant (*LJ*, xvii, 114–25 passim; Boyer, *Annals*, i, 33–9).

26 *The Political Union*, p. 9.
27 Ibid. pp. 18–19, 22–4.
28 Ibid. p. 17.
29 Ibid. p. 45.
30 Ibid. pp. 50–1, 53, 59.
31 Ibid. pp. 61–2.
32 *The Character of a Low Churchman*, p. 9.
33 *The Danger of Priestcraft*, pp. 6, 20, 21.
34 *Observator*, i, no. 35 (19 August 1702). 'Old Towser' was Sir Roger L'Estrange.
35 See the Lords' arguments against the first bill, and Burnet's speech against the second (*Parl. Hist.*, vi, 70–2, 76–91, 157–65); also Geoffrey Holmes, *British Politics in the Age of Anne* (1967), pp. 101–3.
36 *The Nature and Mischief of Prejudice and Partiality*, p. 31.
37 Ibid. p. 54.
38 *State Trials*, xiv, 1095ff; *Observator*, i, no. 23 (8 July 1702).
39 G. V. Bennett, in *Britain after the Glorious Revolution*, p. 167.
40 Sermon before the queen, 31 January 1704, pp. 3, 4, 5, 7.
41 Ibid. pp. 9–11, 16. Sherlock succeeded his father as Master of the Temple in November 1704.
42 Holmes, *British Politics*, p. 103.
43 *The Memorial of the Church of England Humbly Offered to All True Lovers of Our Church and Constitution*, p. 6.
44 Boyer, *Annals*, iv, 172–7.
45 *CJ*, xv, 7 (1 November 1705); Boyer, iv, 185.
46 *Parl. Hist.*, vi, 479–506; *CJ*, xv, 65.
47 At the same time a reward was offered for the author of the *Memorial*, but the embarrassing discovery that at least one MP had been associated with its publication caused the matter to be dropped (Luttrell, *Brief Relation*, v, 627, vi, 7, 10; Boyer, *Annals*, iv, 218). For Drake, see pp. 102–4 above.
48 Qu. Bennett, *Kennett*, p. 67.
49 Dennis Rubini, *Court and Country 1688–1702* (1967), passim.
50 J. P. Kenyon, *Robert Spencer Earl of Sunderland* (1958), ch. 8.
51 Burnet, *History*, iv, 5n.

CHAPTER 7. REVOLUTION PRINCIPLES

1 Angus McInnes, 'The Political Ideas of Robert Harley', *History*, l (1965), 309–22, and *Robert Harley: Puritan Politician* (1970), pp. 102–4, 108–9, 161–2; Geoffrey Holmes, *British Politics in the Age of Anne* (1967), pp. 369–76.
2 *Mercurius Politicus*, no. 28 (11 September 1705).
3 Ibid. no. 29 (15 September 1705).
4 *English Reports*, vol. 90, 1092, 1093. See also ibid. vol. 88, 905, 911, 919;

Luttrell, *Brief Relation*, v, 602, vi, 16, 43, 54, 121; and *DNB* under 'Drake'. The case was dismissed on a technicality; the Attorney General sued out a writ of error, but Drake died before he could be brought to trial again, in 1707. It is surprising to find Hawles amongst the Commons managers against Sacheverell, and his speech on that occasion certainly caused disquiet amongst the Whigs. See p. 136 above.

5 *A Letter from a Foreign Minister in England to Monsr Pettecum* (1710), in *Somers Tracts*, xiii, 67.

6 R. Geikie and I. A. Montgomery, *The Dutch Barrier 1705–1719* (1930), passim (for the treaty of 1709, see p. 378).

7 *An Argument Shewing That the Prince of Wales, Tho' a Protestant, Has No Just Pretensions to the Crown of England* (1701), esp. pp. 12–13.

8 See James Drake's *History of the Last Parliament* (1702), and the Lords' investigation of the matter, *LJ*, xvii, 114–25 passim, and Boyer, *Annals*, i, 33–9. The only hard evidence is from Dartmouth, who says he was approached by the Dukes of Bolton and Newcastle; Burnet, *History*, iv, 553n.

9 Current doubts were ventilated in the Commons debate on the Regency Bill. See 'An Anonymous Parliamentary Diary for 1705–6', ed. W. A. Speck, *Camden Society*, 4th ser. vii (1969), 39–81 passim.

10 *Advice to All Parties*, p. 6.

11 *Observator*, iv, no. 79 (29 December 1705).

12 *Cal. S.P. Dom. 1702–3*, p. 580; *Cal. S.P. Dom. 1703–4*, pp. 169, 175, 196.

13 *Observator*, ii, no. 47 (15 September 1703).

14 Ibid. i, preface, pp. 1–2.

15 Ibid. i, no. 99 (31 March 1703).

16 Ibid. ii, no. 54 (9 October 1703).

17 Ibid. i, nos. 17, 18, 99 (17, 20 June 1702, 31 March 1703).

18 Ibid. i, no. 15 (10 June 1702), ii, no. 15 (26 May 1703).

19 *A Vindication of Magna Charta As the Summary of English Rights and Liberties, in Which . . . the Excellency of the Old English Constitution as the Noblest Commonwealth in the World Is Clearly Demonstrated* (1702), p. 63. Cf. *Observator*, ii, no. 49 (22 September 1703). It is interesting that this book was written principally to combat the views of Samuel Daniel, whose *Collection of the History of England* had been published as long ago as 1617, and last reprinted in 1685. Daniel's work was republished in 1706 as part of a *Complete History of England*, a project with which several Whig divines were closely associated.

20 *Observator*, ii, no. 69 (1 December 1703).

21 James Tyrrell, *General History of England*, ii, (1700), 984, 1032ff, iii (1704), 1.

22 *Observator*, iii, nos. 9–14 (19 April–10 May 1704).

23 Ibid. iii, nos. 19–21, 23, 29 (24, 27, 31 May, 7, 28 June).

24 P. 96 above.

25 Boyer, *Annals*, ii, 210–11; *CJ*, xiv, 270, 336; Luttrell, *Brief Relation*, v, 317–593 passim; *English Reports*, vol. 87, 1014, vol. 90, 929; *Observator*, iii, no. 59 (11 October 1704).

26 *The Wolf Stripped of His Shepherd's Clothing* (1704), p. 59.
27 *Cassandra (But I Hope Not) Telling What Will Come of It, No. 1* (1705), pp. 1–2, 8, 25–6, 41.
28 In June 1704 he fell into the dialogue mode, between 'Observator' and 'Countryman', with unfortunate results. 'Countryman' started out as an alert, intelligent freeholder, but soon degenerated into a straw-chewing yokel, addressing his companion as 'Master'.
29 *Observator*, III, no. 31 (5 July 1704).
30 *Memorial of the State of England*, p. 76.
31 *The Rights of the Church of England Asserted and Proved* (1705), pp. 5–6. (Edward Perkes was credited with joint authorship.)
32 *An Address to the Clergy of England* (1705), pp. 5, 9–12.
33 This pamphlet, which was in fact a thanksgiving sermon for the battle of Ramillies, is discussed by Gerald Straka in 'Revolutionary Ideology in Stuart England', in *Studies in Change and Revolution*, ed. Paul J. Korshin (Menston, Yorks. 1972), pp. 13–14.
34 He was fined 100 marks and sentenced to the pillory. The second part of the sentence was remitted out of respect for his cloth, but only at the last moment. (Boyer, *Annals*, v, 487–8.)
35 For example, *Review*, II, 170 (12 June 1705), 307–8 (30 August).
36 David H. Stevens, *Party Politics and English Journalism 1702–42* (Chicago 1916), pp. 8, 47–51; John Robert Moore, *Daniel Defoe: Citizen of the Modern World* (Chicago 1958), ch. 16.
37 *Review*, III, 289 (18 June 1706), 333–4 (13 July).
38 Ibid. III, 334 (13 July 1706). These ideas are further developed in III, 429 (10 September).
39 *Jure Divino: A Satyr in Twelve Books* (1706), book I, pp. 2, 10.
40 Ibid. book I, p. 2, book IX, pp. 205, 213, book X, p. 219.
41 Ibid. preface, pp. ix–x, xii.
42 Ibid. book X, p. 223; *Review*, IV, 489 (25 November 1707), VI, 83 (21 May 1709).
43 Sermon, 25 July 1706, pp. 20, 22.
44 *Sermons and Discourses on Several Occasions*, 4th edn, 2 vols. (1735), II, 107.
45 Ibid. pp. 131–2. Halifax was accused of homosexuality, Somers of adultery and Cowper of bigamy; Wharton was never allowed to forget that once, on a drunken spree, he had defecated in a church pulpit.
46 The only modern account is by Norman Sykes, in *The Social and Political Ideas of Some English Thinkers of the Augustan Age*, ed. F. J. C. Hearnshaw (1928), pp. 112–56.
47 Qu. C. J. Abbey and J. H. Overton, *The English Church in the Eighteenth Century*, 2 vols. (1878), I, 34.
48 Benjamin Hoadly, *Works*, 3 vols. (1773), II, 18ff.
49 Ibid. p. 22.
50 Boyer, *Annals*, IV, 205–6.
51 Burnet, *History*, v, 438.

52 E. Cardwell, *Synodalia* (Oxford 1842), II, 723.
53 *Some Proceedings in the Convocation A.D. 1705[–6] Faithfully Represented*... (not in fact published until 1708).
54 Hoadly, *Works*, II, 123.
55 Sermon, 8 March 1705, pp. 7–10.
56 *An Essay upon Government Wherein the Republican Schemes Revived by Mr Locke, Dr Blackall, etc., Are Fairly Represented and Refuted* (1705), pp. 68–9.
57 *A Sermon Preached before the London Clergy at St Alphage, May the 17th, 1709... Translated from the Latin* (1710), pp. 23, 25. This was, in fact, the same sermon as he had delivered to the Lord Mayor and Aldermen the previous September, which they had asked him not to publish (G. V. Bennett, *The Tory Crisis in Church and State 1688–1730: The Career of Francis Atterbury* (Oxford 1975), pp. 107–8).
58 Notwithstanding the fact that in this case the offender was St Paul himself. The pamphlet was *A Vindication of the Rt Rev. the Lord Bishop of Exeter, Occasioned by Mr Benjamin Hoadly's Reflections on His Lordship's Two Sermons of Government*... (1709).
59 Sermon preached at St Paul's, 6 December 1709, p. 15; reprinted in *Sermons and Discourses*, II, 282–3.
60 *A View of the English Constitution with respect to the Sovereign Authority of the Prince and the Allegiance of the Subject*... (1709), pp. 97–9. See p. 37 above.
61 *The Constitution, Laws and Government of England Vindicated* (1709), p. 2.
62 *Observator*, VII, nos. 37, 42 (19 June, 7 July 1708); Luttrell, *Brief Relation*, VI, 440.
63 *Review*, VI, 82 (21 May 1709).
64 See app. A.
65 *Vox Populi Vox Dei* (1709 edn), pp. 4, 6.
66 Ibid. pp. 13, 20.
67 Ibid. p. 26.
68 Leslie, *A Letter to a Noble Lord about His Dispersing Abroad Mr Hoadly's Remarks upon the Bishop of Exeter's Sermon*... (1709), p. 7; Atterbury, *The Voice of the People* (1709), p. 24.
69 Hearne, *Collections*, II, 101 (11 April 1708).
70 Henry L. Snyder, 'Queen Anne versus the Junto: The Effort to Place Orford at the Head of the Admiralty', *HLQ*, XXXV (1972), 323–42.
71 G. V. Bennett, 'Robert Harley, the Godolphin Ministry and the Bishoprics Crisis of 1707', *EHR*, LXXXII (1967), 726–46.
72 This measure too rebounded on the Whigs, because it flooded the English employment market with thousands of destitute refugees, but this was not immediately apparent. See W. A. Speck, 'The Poor Palatines and the Parties', *EHR*, LXXXII (1967), 464–85.
73 Bennett, *Tory Crisis*, pp. 101–2.
74 *Review*, VI, 422 (8 December 1709).
75 Qu. G. V. Bennett, *White Kennett* (1957), p. 103.
76 Hoadly, *Works*, II, 177–8.

CHAPTER 8. BLACK AND ODIOUS COLOURS

1 Geoffrey Holmes, *The Trial of Doctor Sacheverell* (1973), p. 20. My general debt to Professor Holmes's work will be obvious in the pages that follow.
2 One of the managers at the trial admitted that 'had it been preached in some obscure county town 'twould have hardly been taken notice of' (*The Tryal of Dr Henry Sacheverell* (1710), p. 69).
3 Holmes, relying on W. A. Speck, says it sold 100,000 copies (see his preface to the ROTA reprint of the sermon, 1974).
4 Atterbury's sermon is in his *Sermons and Discourses on Several Occasions*, 4th edn, 2 vols. (1735), II, 311–45. He reached the Revolution on p. 343, and dropped it on p. 344. Beveridge reached 1688 on p. 24, then left it on p. 25 for a general summing-up.
5 *The Perils of False Brethren, Both in Church and State* (qto edn 1710), pp. 20–1.
6 Ibid. pp. 19–20.
7 Ibid. p. 34.
8 *The Thirteenth Chapter to the Romans Vindicated* (1710), p. 1.
9 *Perils of False Brethren*, p. 29.
10 *Review*, VI, 446 (22 December); see also the issues for 8, 10 December.
11 Holmes, *Trial*, pp. 78–9.
12 *The Proceedings of the Lords and Commons in the Year 1628 against Roger Manwaring (the Sacheverell of Those Days) for Two Seditious High-Flying Sermons...* (1709). Cf. *Observator*, VIII, no. 91 (10 December 1709).
13 *An Appeal from the Old to the New Whigs* (1791), in *Works* (World's Classics edn 1906), V, 52.
14 *CJ*, XVI, 242; *State Trials*, XV, 16.
15 *Review*, VI, 464, 473, 542 (7, 10 January, 18 February 1710); *Observator*, VIII, no. 96 (28 December 1709), IX, no. 8 (8 February 1710); *The Managers Pro and Con* (1710), pp. 35–6, 77–8.
16 Luttrell, *Brief Relation*, VI, 529.
17 *State Trials*, XV, 16; Holmes, *Trial*, p. 95; Sarah Duchess of Marlborough, *Private Correspondence*, 2 vols. (1838), II, 16, 54.
18 Hearne, *Collections*, II, 351; *Observator*, IX, no. 8 (8 February 1710). Cf. *High Church Politicks: or The Abuse of the 30th of January Considered, with Remarks on Mr Luke Milbourne's Railing Sermons* (1710).
19 *Sermon Preached before the...Commons...January 30th 1709* [1710], pp. 7, 22, 25, 27. The patriotic theme was, however, taken up by Lechmere in his closing speech for the prosecution (*Tryal*, p. 125).
20 See p. 73 above.
21 *CJ*, XVI, 297–8. I am grateful to Professor Geoffrey Holmes for enlightening me on the implications of this incident.
22 Among Walpole's papers is a draft of a speech to Article II, but it was not delivered (Cholmondeley (Houghton) MSS., 67/4–2, in Cambridge University Library).
23 *Tryal*, pp. 51, 261.

24 Ibid. pp. 22–3. It is worth reading *Thoughts of a Country Gentleman upon Reading Dr Sacheverell's Trial* (1710) for a biassed but devastating analysis of the prosecution's case. It has been suggested that Lechmere's view of the Original Contract was exclusive to him (see, for instance, H. T. Dickinson, 'The Eighteenth-Century Debate on the Glorious Revolution', *History*, LXI (1976), 28–45, p. 35). But the supporting counsel on both sides were expected to supplement rather than repeat their leader's views, and arguments *ab silentio* must be used with caution. (As it is, Jekyll did return to the contract theme in his closing speech; *Tryal*, p. 285.)

25 *Tryal*, p. 285.

26 Ibid. pp. 57, 121.

27 Ibid. pp. 74–5.

28 Ibid. p. 126. See p. 88 above.

29 Ibid. p. 151.

30 'An Account of the Trial of Dr Sacheverell', Osborn MSS. (Yale University) box 21, no. 22, pp. 4, 5; *Tryal*, pp. 63–71.

31 *Tryal*, p. 104.

32 Ibid. pp. 111, 113.

33 Ibid. p. 127.

34 Ibid. p. 147.

35 Ibid. p. 140.

36 Ibid. p. 248. (Atterbury is generally supposed to have written the speech.)

37 Ibid. p. 259.

38 *Parl. Hist.*, VI, 847; *The Lockhart Papers*, ed. Anthony Aufrere, 2 vols. (1817), I, 312; Boyer, *Annals*, VIII, 316–17. 'The Duke of Leeds gave a very long [?sight] of the Revolution and the very great interest more than any man he had in it, but said that [he] was sure no lord would offer to call it lawful if [it] was contrary to law and beside law, which was [?surely] rebellion, and he himself was a rebel in it, at which the House laughed very much' (PRO Shaftesbury MSS. 30/24/21).

39 *Parl. Hist.*, VI, 846–7; Henry Horwitz, *Revolution Politicks: The Career of Daniel Finch Second Earl of Nottingham* (1968), p. 219.

40 *Parl. Hist.*, VI, 834–6.

41 Boyer, *Annals*, VIII, 316. There is a brief abstract of Cowper's speech on PRO Shaftesbury MSS. 30/24/21.

42 *Parl. Hist.*, VI, 831.

43 *State Trials*, XV, 479.

44 *Tryal*, app., pp. 2–6. For North and Grey, see PRO Shaftesbury MSS. 30/24/21.

45 PRO Shaftesbury MSS. 30/24/21.

46 *State Trials*, XV, 476.

47 Boyer, *Annals*, VIII, 333–5; *CJ*, XVI, 383; *LJ*, XIX, 122.

48 *Tryal*, pp. 21–2.

49 Ibid. p. 48.

50 Ibid. p. 61.

51 Ibid. p. 59.

52 The full title runs to over 200 words.
53 *An Explanation of Some Hard Terms Now in Use*, in *Somers Tracts*, XII, 661.
54 *An Old Story Everyone Knows*... (1712), pp. 9–10.
55 Ibid. pp. 25–6.
56 *Resistance and Non-Resistance Stated and Decided* (1710), p. 15. The Houghton Library catalogue attributes this to Richard Steele.
57 *The True Genuine Tory Address*... (1710), p. 3.
58 Edward Ward, 'Vulgus Britannicus', in *Poems on Affairs of State*, VII, ed. Frank H. Ellis (New Haven and London 1975), p. 403; John Oldmixon, *Memoirs of the Press* (1742), p. 6.
59 *A Vindication of the Reverend Dr Henry Sacheverell*... (1711), p. 9.
60 Hearne, *Collections*, II, 355.
61 Duchess of Marlborough, *Private Correspondence*, II, 3–5.
62 *A Caveat against the Whigs in a Short Historical View of Their Transactions, Part I* (1710), p. 105 (see p. 159 above).

CHAPTER 9. THE FOUR LAST YEARS

1 See p. 130 above.
2 *The Tryal of Dr Henry Sacheverell* (1710), pp. 68, 69.
3 Ibid. p. 147.
4 See p. 140 above.
5 David Green, *Queen Anne* (1970), pp. 104–5.
6 Sermon, 29 May 1710, pp. 9–10. Cf. *History*, III, 388, and *An Enquiry into the Present State of Affairs* (1688), pp. 12–13.
7 Robert Molesworth, *The Principles of a Real Whig* (1711), p. 20 (1775 edn).
8 E.g., *Thoughts of a Country Gentleman upon Reading Dr Sacheverell's Trial* (1710), pp. 53–4, and 'Four Letters to Four Ministers of State in South Britain', BL Harley MS. 6233, fols. 30–1. See the remarks of Francis Hare to Sarah Duchess of Marlborough, November 1710, in her *Private Correspondence*, 2 vols. (1838), II, 20–2.
9 14 November 1710, qu. Lord John Campbell, *Lives of the Lord Chancellors*... 8 vols. (1884–9), IV, 210–11.
10 Green, *Queen Anne*, p. 219. See Charles Hornsby, *A Caveat against the Whigs in a Short Historical View of Their Transactions, Part IV* (1712), p. 99. She told Sir David Hamilton that Sacheverell deserved a mild punishment, but the impeachment 'had been better left alone'; *The Diary of Sir David Hamilton*, ed. Philip Roberts (1975), p. 6.
11 *The Correspondence of Sir James Clavering*, ed. H. T. Dickinson, Surtees Society, CLXXVIII (1967), p. 71.
12 Boyer, *Annals*, IX, 406; Luttrell, *Brief Relation*, VI, 602; William Bissett, *The Modern Fanatick* (1710), p. 9.
13 Geoffrey Holmes, *The Trial of Doctor Sacheverell* (1973), pp. 210–11.
14 *Tryal*, p. 138; Boyer, *Annals*, VIII, 316–17; Hearne, *Collections*, II, 364–5, III, 35–6; *Four Letters to a Friend in North Britain* (1710), p. 11 (and see n. 34 below).

15 *Hamilton Diary*, p. 7.
16 G. M. Trevelyan, *England under Queen Anne*, 3 vols. (1930–4), III, ch. 4.
17 *The High Church Address to Dr Henry Sacheverell...* (1710), pp. 7–8. Cf. *Chuse Which You Please: or Dr Sacheverell and Mr Hoadly Drawn to the Life* (1710), p. 3.
18 'Hudibras Imitated', qu. C. J. Abbey and J. H. Overton, *The English Church in the Eighteenth Century*, 2 vols. (1878), II, 376n.
19 In *Somers Tracts*, XII, 678–707. Cf. *The Declaration of an Honest Churchman...* (1710) and similar tracts.
20 *HMC Portland*, IV, 537.
21 Holmes, *Trial*, ch. 10.
22 Boyer, *Annals*, IX, 185.
23 *LJ*, XIX, 145.
24 Boyer, *Annals*, IX, 159–60.
25 Ibid. 161–4.
26 Ibid. 166–9.
27 Ibid. 177–80.
28 Ibid. 180–2.
29 *Collections*, III, 44. See *High Church Miracles: or Modern Inconsistencies* (1710); and *A Letter concerning Allegiance...* (1710), in *Somers Tracts*, XII, 320–7.
30 Grey, *Debates*, X, 378.
31 *HMC Portland*, V, 196.
32 Hearne, *Collections*, II, 352–3.
33 *The True Genuine Tory Address*, in *Somers Tracts*, XII, 654–8, differs from the one just cited, and is actually Tory.
34 This pamphlet was attributed first to Walpole, then to Defoe. Pat Rogers, *Bull. Inst. Hist. Research*, XLIV (1971), 229, and Henry L. Snyder, *HLQ*, XXIII (1970), 133, agree, however, that it was by Arthur Maynwaring.
35 'Four Letters to Four Ministers of State'. It breaks off at the beginning of the second letter.
36 W. A. Speck, *Tory and Whig: The Struggle in the Constituencies 1701–15* (1970), p. 113. Trevelyan, *Queen Anne*, III, 73, gives it as 170, or 130 overall.
37 See the suggestive essay by Speck in *Britain after the Glorious Revolution, 1689–1714*, ed. Geoffrey Holmes (1969), pp. 135ff.
38 *Advice to the Gentlemen Freeholders, Citizens and Burgesses...* (1710), pp. 2–9, 11–12, 14.
39 *The Harleian Miscellany*, ed. T. Park, 10 vols. (1810–13), VI, 315.
40 Swift, *Prose Works*, ed. Herbert Davis, 13 vols. (1939–59), III, 6–7, VI, 53. For an interesting comment on the failure of the Commission see *The Lockhart Papers*, ed. Anthony Aufrere, 2 vols. (1817), I, 349.
41 *The Examiner*, 5 April 1711. (Misquoted in *Prose Works*, III, 130.)
42 *Prose Works*, III, 162–7, VI, 78, VII, 3. His attitude is epitomised in the title of his pamphlet *Some Reasons to Prove that No Person Is Obliged*

by His Principles as a Whig to Oppose Her Majesty or Her Present Ministry (1712).

43 See, for instance, *The Declaration of an Honest Churchman* and *The Character of a Moderate Churchman* (both 1710).

44 Toland, *Another Memorial for the Most Honourable the Earl of Oxford* (1711), in *A Collection of Several Pieces* (1726), II, 226–7. Cf. *Review*, VIII, 149, 365 (19 June, 23 October 1711).

45 Alexander Cunningham, *The History of Great Britain*... [1688–1714], 2 vols. (1787), I, 455–9, 462.

46 *The Principles of a Real Whig* (1775 edn), pp. 6–7, 12–14, 16–17, 20, 21.

47 *The History of Resistance as Practised by the Church of England* (1710), in *Somers Tracts*, XII, 265.

48 Fleetwood, *The Thirteenth Chapter to the Romans Vindicated* (1710), p. 13.

49 Qu. Abbey and Overton, *The English Church*, I, 71. Cf. Hearne, *Collections*, III, 36.

50 See *DNB* under 'Bedford'.

51 See, in general, David H. Stevens, *Party Politics and English Journalism 1702–42* (Chicago 1916), ch. V, and *Poems on Affairs of State*, VII, ed. Frank H. Ellis (New Haven and London 1975), 570–1.

52 *Caveat, Part II* (3rd edn 1713), pp. 79–80, 81–2.

53 *Part III* (2nd edn 1712), p. 2.

54 *Part IV* (2nd edn 1712), pp. 123–4.

55 *Part I* (1710), p. 2.

56 Trapp, *Character and Principles*, pp. 5, 7, 23.

57 E.g., *Revolution Principles Represented and Defended* (1712) and *Whiggism Vindicated* (dated 1715, but from internal evidence clearly written before Anne's death).

58 *A Brief Justification of the Principles of a Reputed Whig* (1714).

59 Wake MSS, qu. Norman Sykes, in 'Queen Anne and the Episcopate', *EHR*, I (1935), 463.

60 *Parl. Hist.*, VI, 1155, 1156–7nn. The preface is printed in Swift, *Prose Works*, VI, 192–5.

61 *Histrio-Theologicus* (1715), p. 13. (I owe this reference to Dr Alan Bower.)

62 Sermon in Salisbury Cathedral, 5 November 1710, p. 12.

63 Burnet, *History*, VI, 78. Cf. *Hamilton Diary*, p. 31 (28 November 1711).

64 *Discourse*, pp. 5, 13–14, 21–2.

65 George Sewell, *Speculum Sarisburianum* (1714), p. 4.

66 *Introduction* (1714) [published separately], pp. 27, 47, 61.

67 [George Sewell], *The Clergy and Present Ministry Defended* (1713), p. 22. This was actually in reply to the *Pastoral Care*, but Sewell also answered Burnet's other publications as they appeared, in *The Oxford Scholar's Answer*... (1713) and *Speculum Sarisburianum* (1714). Swift also entered the controversy with *A Preface to the Bishop of Sarum's Introduction* (1713), but his main purpose was to defend the integrity of the English clergy. See I. Ehrenpreis, *Dr Swift* (1967), pp. 692–6.

68 *A Second Letter to the Bishop of Salisbury*... (1713), pp. 6–7.
69 Speck, *Tory and Whig*, p. 113, and 'The General Election of 1715', *EHR*, XC (1975), 508–9.
70 *Memoirs of the Press* (1742), p. 21.
71 *The Englishman*, ed. Rae Blanchard (Oxford 1955), no. 20 (19 November 1713), p. 81. See also pp. 23, 25, 58, 74, 93.
72 Ibid. pp. 103ff.
73 Ibid. pp. 113–15.
74 Ibid. p. 116.
75 Ibid. pp. 128, 184 (17 December 1713, 19 January 1714). Later Steele referred to Anne as 'the Mother of all her People' (ibid. p. 230).
76 Steele, *Tracts and Pamphlets*, ed. Rae Blanchard (Baltimore 1944), pp. 169–70, 176–9; *The Englishman*, p. 231.
77 *The Grand Mystery Laid Open* (1714), pp. 6, 13; *Lockhart Papers*, I, 462–3; Trevelyan, *Queen Anne*, III, 301.
78 Sermon before the king, St James's, 31 October 1714. (He died on 17 March 1715.)

CHAPTER 10. THAT TRIUMPHANT APPELLATION

1 'We are the only true Whigs. Carnal men have assumed that triumphant appellation, following him whose kingdom is of this world' (Balfour of Burleigh, in Sir Walter Scott's *Old Mortality*, ch. 1).
2 See, for instance, *A Rebuke to the High Church Priests for Turning the 30th of January into a Madding Day*... (1717), and Thomas Gordon, *A Political Dissertation upon Bull Baiting and Evening Lectures with Occasional Meditations on the 30th of January* (1718).
3 W. A. Speck points out that though the Whigs were publicly optimistic on the eve of the poll there were really no rational grounds for this; see 'The General Election of 1715', *EHR*, XC (1975), 507–9.
4 Sarah Duchess of Marlborough, *Private Correspondence*, 2 vols. (1838), I, 401–2, II, 6, 11, 14.
5 See the acute analysis by Bertrand A. Goldgar, *The Curse of Party: Swift's Relations with Addison and Steele* (Lincoln, Nebraska 1961), pp. 64–7.
6 *The Englishman*, ed. Rae Blanchard (Oxford 1955), p. 74.
7 Ibid. pp. 231–2.
8 *Correspondence*, ed. G. Sherburn (1956), I, 245 (27 August 1714). Cf. David H. Stevens, *Party Politics and English Journalism 1702–42* (Chicago 1916), p. 23.
9 John, Lord Campbell, *Lives of the Lord Chancellors*...8 vols. (1884–9), IV, 429.
10 H. T. Dickinson, 'The Eighteenth-Century Debate on the Glorious Revolution', *History*, LXI (1976), 28–45 (p. 36).
11 *The Secret History of One Year*, in *Somers Tracts*, XIII, 575.
12 Campbell, op. cit. IV, 423.
13 Steele still thought it worth while to ridicule patriarchalist theories

and summarise William Higden's arguments for taking the oaths in 1709; see *The Englishman*, pp. 347–9, 353–7 (30 September, 7 October 1715).

14 *The Englishman*, p. 357 (10 October 1715).

15 *The Freeholder*, no. 12 (30 January 1716), no. 16 (13 February), no. 28 (26 March), no. 29 (30 March), in *Works* (Bohn edn 1856), IV, 443, 444, 457, 499, 503.

16 *A Letter to Sir William Wyndham* (1753), p. 19 (written, of course, in 1717).

17 *Parl. Hist.*, VII, 228.

18 *CJ*, XVIII, 332.

19 *Parl. Hist.*, VII, 297–8 (13 February 1716); *Diary of Mary Countess Cowper* (1865), pp. 73–4. Peers who wished to were invited to sign this declaration before the end of the session, but none did (MS Journals, House of Lords Record Office, LXXXVII, p. 183).

20 J. H. Plumb, *Sir Robert Walpole*, I (1956), 73, 292; William Coxe, *Memoirs of...Sir Robert Walpole*, 3 vols. (1798), II, 75–6; *Diary of Mary Countess Cowper*, pp. 119–20; *Parl. Hist.*, VII, 73.

21 Cunningham, *The History of Great Britain...* [1688–1714], 2 vols. (1787), I, 455–9, 462.

22 Ibid. I, 397; *Parl. Hist.*, VI, 1045.

23 *Review*, VIII, 491 (3 January 1712), 493 (5 January). See also Edward Harley's comments, *HMC Portland*, V, 661.

24 Burnet, *History*, VI, 86; Boyer, *Annals*, IX, 296.

25 Cunningham, *History*, I, 397. Cf. Henry Horwitz, *Revolution Politicks: The Career of Daniel Finch Second Earl of Nottingham* (1968), pp. 230ff.

26 Burnet, *History*, VI, 85n.

27 Swift, *The Four Last Years of the Queen*, in *Prose Works*, ed. Herbert Davis, 13 vols. (Oxford 1939–59), VII, 21.

28 Defoe said in 1712, 'This has ruined the interest of the Whigs in almost all the corporations in England, and put them into such a posture as never, but by a miracle, to recover it', *Review*, VIII, preface (n.p.).

29 Campbell, *Lord Chancellors*, IV, 215–17; Onslow's note to Burnet, *History*, VI, 159–61. Cf. Geoffrey Holmes, *British Politics in the Age of Anne* (1967), p. 113. But Holmes misses the point when he argues in extenuation that any dissolution bill would have contained safeguards for the succession. The Union of 1707 was not just a device to peg Scotland to the Hanoverian succession, but a great act of constructive statesmanship to which the Junto had been committed by their hero William III. (For further details see *Parl. Hist.*, VI, 1216–20, and *The Lockhart Papers*, ed. Anthony Aufrere, 2 vols. (1817), I, 432–7.)

30 Atterbury, *English Advice to the Freeholders of England* (1714), in *Somers Tracts*, XIII, 524, 538–9.

31 See p. 41 above.

32 *The Principles of a Real Whig* (1711), p. 12 (1775 edn). He himself was a High Whig, of course.

33 The only modern study is by Owen C. Lease, 'The Septennial Act of 1716', *Jnl Mod. Hist.*, XXII (1950), 42–7. This is brief, and necessarily superficial, but it makes some useful points.
34 See Campbell, *Lord Chancellors*, IV, 220, 372; Coxe, *Walpole*, I, 75–6; Henry Hallam, *Constitutional History of England* (Everyman edn 1912), III, 207–8.
35 Wolfgang Michael, *England under George I*, 2 vols. (1936–9), I, 262.
36 *Works*, IV, 488–91.
37 Coxe, *Walpole*, I, 76–7, II, 62.
38 For Leeds, see Andrew Browning, *Thomas Osborne Earl of Danby*, 3 vols. (Glasgow 1944–51), II, 253.
39 It was also mentioned in *Arguments about the Alteration of Triennial Elections of Parliament in a Letter to a Friend in the Country* (1716), pp. 2–3.
40 Loc. cit.
41 *An Epistle to a Whig Member of Parliament*, qu. Lease, op. cit. p. 42.
42 *Parl. Hist.*, VII, 299.
43 Ibid. 296–7, 303–4.
44 Ibid. 307.
45 As Peterborough said in the Lords, 'If this parliament continued beyond the time for which they were chosen, he knew not how to express the manner of their existence, unless, begging leave of that venerable bench [of bishops], they had recourse to the distinction used in the Athanasian Creed, for they would be neither made, nor created, but proceeding, etc.', ibid. 303.
46 Ibid. 312–21.
47 Coxe, *Walpole*, II, 62–4; *Parl. Hist.*, VII, 339ff.
48 *Parl. Hist.*, VII, 325–6; an argument put in pamphlets like *A Letter to a Friend upon Occasion of the House of Commons Passing...* (1716), p. 9, and *The Suspension of the Triennial Bill the Properest Means...* (1716), p. 6. It is significant that apologias continued to appear after the Bill had been passed.
49 *CJ*, XVIII, 432; *Parl. Hist.*, VII, 312–16; Coxe, *Walpole*, II, 62–4; *HMC Stuart*, II, 144–5.
50 Holmes, *British Politics*, p. 219.
51 *Parl. Hist.*, VII, 303. For Defoe, see his *Some Considerations on a Law for Triennial Parliaments* (1716).
52 *Several Speeches against the Bill...* (1716), qu. Lease, op. cit. p. 42. Cf. *Parl. Hist.*, VII, 316 (Shippen), and *The Triennial Act Impartially Stated* (1716), p. 28.
53 Betty Kemp, *King and Commons 1660–1832* (1957), ch. 6.
54 *The Alteration in the Triennial Act Considered* (1716), pp. 7–8.
55 *Lords Papers 1706–8*, pp. 563–5.
56 See his letter to Bernstorff, 19 May 1716, Coxe, *Walpole*, II, 51–4; also his interview with the dying Somers, p. 183 above.
57 Basil Williams, *Stanhope* (1932), pp. 209ff.
58 G. V. Bennett, 'Jacobitism and Walpole', in *Historical Perspectives*, ed. Neil McKendrick (1974), p. 70.

59 George Hilton Jones, *The Mainstream of Jacobitism* (Cambridge, Mass. 1954), pp. 113–24; Romney Sedgewick (ed.), *The House of Commons 1715–54* (1970), I, 109.

60 Frederick S. Allen, *The Supreme Command in England 1640–1780* (New York 1966), pp. 44–5, 48–9.

61 Plumb, *Walpole*, I, 243–4.

62 *Parl. Hist.*, VII, 452. See in general Plumb, *Walpole*, I, ch. 7, and Williams, *Stanhope*, ch. 14.

63 Plumb, *Walpole*, I, 249. Coxe was also shocked (*Walpole*, I, 109–11), though it is typical that his sternest rebuke is to be found in the table of contents: 'Remarks on the baneful spirit of a systematic opposition to all the measures of government – Walpole not exempted from that censure' (p. vii).

64 *The Defection Considered: And Those Who Divided the Friends of the Government Set in a True Light* (1717), pp. 9–10.

65 Ibid. pp. 4–5, 11, 20, 23.

66 Ibid. p. 21.

67 *The Old and Modern Whig Revived in the Present Divisions at Court* (1717), p. 32; *The History...of Count Hotspur and Colonel Headstrong* (1717), p. 74.

68 *The Defection Considered*, p. 27 (also pp. 34–7); *An Answer to the Character and Conduct of R— W—, Esq....* (1717), esp. pp. 19–20, 22–3, 27, 40.

69 *Some Persons Vindicated against the Author of the Defection Considered* (1718), p. 33. See also *The Conduct of Robert Walpole, Esq.* (1717), which is entirely silent on this vital point.

70 *The Resigners Vindicated: Part I* (1718), pp. 14–17; *Part II* (1718), pp. 38–41.

71 *Parl. Hist.*, VII, 478.

72 *An Answer to the Character...* p. 27.

73 See in general E. R. Turner, 'The Peerage Bill of 1719', *EHR*, XXVIII (1913), 243–59; A. S. Turberville, *The House of Lords in the Eighteenth Century* (Oxford 1927), pp. 169ff; Williams, *Stanhope*, pp. 403ff; Plumb, *Walpole*, I, 271ff; John F. Naylor (ed.), *The British Aristocracy and the Peerage Bill* (New York 1968).

74 In fact, the voting habits and party loyalties of individual peers often changed from generation to generation. See the appendix on divisions in the House of Lords 1701–16 in Holmes, *British Politics*, pp. 421–35. By making the Scots peers non-elective, the government may even be said to have relaxed its control.

75 I have found twenty-eight pamphlets, and my search has been far from exhaustive. There was also a fourth periodical, *The Moderator*, but it seems to have lapsed after the second issue, or perhaps even the first.

76 *Considerations concerning the Nature of the Bill..* (1719), pp. 15–17, 20–2, 25–6.

77 *Thoughts of a Member*, pp. 6, 9, 18–19.

78 Ibid. pp. 16–18; Steele, *Letter to the E—l of O—d*, in *Tracts and*

Pamphlets, ed. Rae Blanchard (Baltimore 1944), pp. 35–7; *A Discourse upon Honour and Peerage...from an Elector Peer of Scotland* (1719); *Lord Bellhaven's Speeches...[in] November 1706* (1719).

79 Williams, *Stanhope*, pp. 410ff, 459–63. Williams points out that to repeal the Septennial Act would simply have been to reinstate the Triennial Act, though Stanhope intended no such thing, of course.

80 Plumb, *Walpole*, I, 280; *Parl. Hist.*, VII, 618–23.

81 See p. 177 above.

82 Norman Sykes, *Edmund Gibson* (1926), pp. 72–4. John Toland admitted that they had considerable lay support in the party, in *The Second Part of the State Anatomy of Great Britain...* (1717), p. 24.

83 J. E. Thorold Rogers, *A Complete Collection of the Protests of the Lords*, 3 vols. (Oxford 1875), I, 218–22.

84 Toland, *The State Anatomy of Great Britain...* (1717), pp. 73–6. For Atterbury, see the pamphlet cited p. 236, n. 30 above.

85 The bill is printed in Williams, *Stanhope*, app. D.

86 Hoadly, *Works*, 3 vols. (1773), II, 404, qu. Sykes, in *The Social and Political Ideas of Some English Thinkers of the Augustan Age*, ed. F. J. C. Hearnshaw (1928), p. 143.

87 Williams, *Stanhope*, pp. 391–4, 399–403, 456–8; Plumb, *Walpole*, I, 269–70.

88 *Parl. Hist.*, VII, 452.

89 Dickinson, 'The Eighteenth-Century Debate on the Glorious Revolution'.

90 This theme is explored by Gerald Straka in '1688 as the Year One', in *Studies in Eighteenth-Century Culture*, ed. Louis T. Milc (Cleveland, Ohio 1971), p. 143.

91 *Parl. Hist.*, V, 1335.

92 *Parl. Hist.*, VII, 346–7.

93 *Parl. Hist.*, IX, 433, 457.

94 *The State Anatomy of Great Britain*, p. 10.

95 See P. G. M. Dickson, *The Financial Revolution in England* (1967), chs. 5–6; John Carswell, *The South Sea Bubble* (1961); and Plumb, *Walpole*, I, chs. 8–9.

96 See also Thomas Gordon, *A Complete History of the Septennial Parliament* (1722).

97 British Library, *Catalogue of...Political and Personal Satires*, III, part i, nos. 2539–40.

98 See Edward Wortley Montagu's scathing denunciation of Walpole, 'On the State of Affairs When the King Entered', apparently written as early as 1716, and printed in *Letters of Lady Mary Wortley Montagu* (Bohn edn 1887), I, 15–21. This is partisan stuff, of course, but it reflects a contemporary view of Walpole now largely ignored.

99 *The Sense of the People concerning the Present State of Affairs*, in *A Collection of Tracts by the Late John Trenchard* (1751), II, 6.

100 Coxe, *Walpole*, II, 217.

101 *Parl. Hist.*, VII, 966–70. The bill itself is in the Lords Record Office. A much weaker measure had been passed in 1696 (7 & 8 Wm III c. 4).

CHAPTER 11. CONCLUSION

1 Sarah Duchess of Marlborough, *Private Correspondence*, 2 vols. (1838), I, 399.
2 J. H. Plumb, *The Growth of Political Stability in England 1675–1725* (1967), p. 47, and 'The Growth of the Electorate 1660–1715', *Past & Present*, no. 45 (1969), 90–116. See the table of contested elections in John Cannon, *Parliamentary Reform 1640–1832* (1973), app. 3.
3 Thomas W. Perry, *Public Opinion, Propaganda and Politics in Eighteenth-Century England* (Cambridge, Mass. 1962); George Rudé, *The Crowd in History 1730–1848* (New York 1964), chs. 2–4, *Paris and London in the Eighteenth Century* (1970), passim, and *Hanoverian London* (1971), chs. 10–11. Paul Langford has shown how public opinion was manipulated in favour of William Pitt in 1757: 'William Pitt and Public Opinion in 1757', *EHR*, LXXXVIII (1973), 54–80.
4 See the comments of Henry Roseveare in *The Treasury* (1969), pp. 85–6, 88–91.
5 *The Lockhart Papers*, ed. Anthony Aufrere, 2 vols. (1817), I, 350.
6 Reed Browning, *The Duke of Newcastle* (New Haven 1975), p. 135.
7 John Brewer, *Party Ideology and Popular Politics at the Accession of George III* (1976), p. 14.
8 Bernard Bailyn, *The Intellectual Origins of the American Revolution* (Cambridge, Mass. 1967); also Caroline Robbins, *The Eighteenth-Century Commonwealthman* (Cambridge, Mass. 1959).
9 Sermon before the House of Lords, 30 January 1721, pp. 19–20.
10 See Douglas Hay, 'Property, Authority and the Criminal Law', in *Albion's Fatal Tree*, ed. Hay *et al.* (1975), pp. 17–63.
11 *Parl. Hist.*, IX, 473, 474. In the same speech he specifically mentioned the Sacheverell Riots, and their effect on the election of 1710 (ibid. 477).
12 'A Letter to the Advocates for Modern Patriotism', MS. draft, Cholmondeley (Houghton) MSS. 73/49 (Cambridge University Library). Certain references to events in Anne's reign suggest that this could have been written by Walpole himself, or at least one of his generation.
13 *Parl. Hist.*, XI, 349, XIV, 1036.
14 'Speech on a Bill for Shortening the Duration of Parliaments', in *Works* (World's Classics edn 1906), III, 339.
15 Brewer, op. cit. p. 236.
16 Isaac Kramnick, *Bolingbroke and His Circle* (Cambridge, Mass. 1968), pp. 117, 127ff.
17 *Moral and Political Philosophy* (1785), book VI, ch. 3, in *Works* (1839), pp. 102–5.

18 'Speech on a Bill for Shortening the Duration of Parliaments', in *Works*, III, 338; 'Speech on the Army Estimates' (1790), in *Works*, III, 284. For *An Appeal* see *Works*, V, 1–136 passim.

APPENDIX A

1 See pp. 113–15 above.
2 Houghton Library, Harvard University, EC7 D3623 A709sb.
3 In *State Tracts*, I, 386. (*VPVD* had as its subtitle 'True Maxims of Government'.)
4 Harvard Law School Library [no class mark available].
5 In *State Tracts*, I, 134ff.
6 In a private letter to the author. I am grateful to Professor Goldsmith for other illuminating comments.
7 In *A Collection of Eighteen Papers* (1689), p. 122; *VPVD*, p. 13.
8 P. 26.
9 In *State Tracts*, III, 695. See pp. 43, 124 above.

ADDENDUM

The following publications, which would have been of considerable assistance to me in writing this book, appeared after it had gone to press.

H. T. Dickinson, 'The Eighteenth-Century Debate on the Sovereignty of Parliament', *Transactions of the Royal Historical Society*, 5th ser. XXVI (1976), 189–210.

J. A. Downie, 'Robert Harley and the Press', unpublished Ph.D. dissertation, University of Newcastle (1976).

D. W. L. Earl, 'Procrustean Feudalism: An Interpretative Dilemma in English Historical Narration 1700–1725', *HJ*, XIX (1976), 33–52.

J. W. Gough, 'James Tyrrell: Whig Historian and Friend of John Locke', *HJ*, XIX (1976), 581–610.

B. W. Hill, *The Growth of Parliamentary Parties 1689–1742* (1976).

Geoffrey Holmes, 'The Sacheverell Riots', *Past & Present*, no. 72 (1976), 55–85.

M. C. Jacob, *The Newtonians and the English Revolution 1689–1720* (1976).

Lois G. Schwoerer, 'A Jornall [sic] of the Convention at Westminster begun the 22 of January 1688/9', *Bull. Inst. Hist. Research*, XLIX (1976), 242–63.

INDEX

243

Cambridge Studies in
the History and Theory of Politics

Editors: MAURICE COWLING, G. R. ELTON, E. KEDOURIE,
J. G. A. POCOCK, J. R. POLE *and* WALTER ULLMANN

A series in two parts, studies and original texts. The studies
are original works on political history and political philosophy
while the texts are modern, critical editions of major texts in
political thought. The titles include:

TEXTS

LIBERTY, EQUALITY, FRATERNITY, by James Fitzjames
Stephen. Edited with an introduction and notes by R. J. White

VLADIMIR AKIMOV ON THE DILEMMAS OF RUSSIAN MARXISM
1895–1903. An English edition of 'A Short History of the Social
Democratic Movement in Russia' and 'The Second Congress of
the Russian Social Democratic Labour Party', with an introduction and notes by Jonathan Frankel

TWO ENGLISH REPUBLICAN TRACTS: PLATO REDIVIVUS OR,
A DIALOGUE CONCERNING GOVERNMENT (C. 1681), by Henry
Neville and AN ESSAY UPON THE CONSTITUTION OF THE
ROMAN GOVERNMENT (C. 1699), by Walter Moyle. Edited by
Caroline Robbins

J. G. HERDER ON SOCIAL AND POLITICAL CULTURE, translated, edited and with an introduction by F. M. Barnard

THE LIMITS OF STATE ACTION, by Wilhelm von Humboldt.
Edited with an introduction and notes by J. W. Burrow

KANT'S POLITICAL WRITINGS, edited with an introduction and
notes by Hans Reiss; translated by H. B. Nisbet

KARL MARX'S CRITIQUE OF HEGEL'S 'PHILOSOPHY OF
RIGHT', edited with an introduction and notes by Joseph
O'Malley; translated by Annette Jolin and Joseph O'Malley